Families and Aging

Patricia Drentea

University of Alabama at Birmingham

ROWMAN & LITTLEFIELD
Lanham • Boulder • New York • London

Executive Editor: Nancy Roberts
Assistant Editor: Megan Manzano
Senior Marketing Manager: Amy Whitaker
Interior Designer: Ilze Lemesis

Credits and acknowledgments for material borrowed from other sources, and reproduced with permission, appear on the appropriate page within the text.

Published by Rowman & Littlefield
An imprint of The Rowman & Littlefield Publishing Group, Inc.
4501 Forbes Boulevard, Suite 200, Lanham, Maryland 20706
www.rowman.com

6 Tinworth Street, London SE11 5AL, United Kingdom

British Library Cataloguing in Publication Information Available

Library of Congress Cataloging-in-Publication Data Available

ISBN 978-1-5381-0433-0 (cloth : alk. paper)
ISBN 978-1-5381-0434-7 (pbk. : alk. paper)
ISBN 978-1-5381-0435-4 (electronic)

♾™ The paper used in this publication meets the minimum requirements of American National Standard for Information Sciences—Permanence of Paper for Printed Library Materials, ANSI/NISO Z39.48-1992.

Printed in the United States of America

Contents

Preface

iStock/JohnnyGreig

The experiences of families and aging are both changing in today's society. Many people are staying healthier and living longer. Because an unprecedented number of Americans will be over sixty-five years old in the twenty-first century, the aging experience now permeates family life and society. The aging family is influenced by social trends. Ending one's work life and replacing work with other activities is also a process that affects most Americans. Health is an important topic as it is a factor in most family circumstances and influences choices in later life.

This book serves as an overview on the topic of families and aging. It touches on the many different considerations of work, activities, parenting, and health, and examines how demographic and social trends will affect families in later life. This preface presents some of the major issues discussed in detail in this book, provides an explanation of how data was used, and ends with a chapter outline. All of the ideas introduced below will be presented with scholarly evidence throughout the following chapters.

iStock/photoschmidt

Many changes have occurred in the past century with regard to families. The aging family has more intergenerational linkages because people are living longer and because more generations of people are alive at any given time. A longer life expectancy also means that we are engaged in our families for a longer period of time. For instance, grandparenting can become a second career for some. In addition, extended stepfamilies are a major part of our social landscape; these will continue to grow in number as those who divorced between the 1970s and the 2020s form more complicated family connections in their lifetimes. Those in developed nations, including the United States, generally have smaller families, and more reconstituted families of myriad forms with stepparents, stepchildren, half-brothers, and half-sisters, all of whom negotiate their familial ties with one another with varying degrees of obligation and love. With fewer children, there are fewer obligations over time. Additionally, more of us are staying single throughout our lifetimes. Later in life, we may find that we have fewer individuals who are "obliged" to us—perhaps at a time when many of us need assistance. This book discusses these trends and how a burgeoning aging population will affect families and family life.

Families exist in a multitude of configurations. Diversifications in family structure—such as single parenthood, divorce, cohabitation, remarriage, and lifetime singlehood—all extend their unique circumstances into later life. Thus, how families live and function is examined. Gender roles have also changed throughout history. There has been a gradual loosening of expected gender behavior, and we predict this will be even more visible in the coming generations. Some family structures and processes are well known and studied, such as the traditional tract of a two-parent family launching children and then experiencing an empty nest. However, many other arrangements are becoming more commonplace, such as gay or lesbian parents raising children, parents sharing joint custody of children, grandparents raising grandchildren, boomerang children returning home, and so on. All of these unique family processes will affect families' experiences in later life.

Work and retirement must be also considered. How and when family members decide to stop working and how these transitions occur is examined. Economic insecurity, savings, pensions, health, family, and the economy are all factors which influence a family's choices and decisions.

Additionally, activities are changing for older adults. After retirement, older adults, who are often healthy, may have many more years to pursue hobbies and to take care of grandchildren. Individuals should think about how they want to live out their final years, which could be upward of thirty or more. Technology and globalization are changing the ways, and with whom, we communicate. Families keep in touch via mobile phones, emails, Facebook and text messaging, and other forms of social media—creating real-time conversations. Thus technology is changing how we experience aging, and we are more likely to communicate across generations and age cohorts. This may help older individuals to stay more connected to their children and grandchildren.

Older adults are healthier than ever before, and the implications of this longer, active, healthy life suggest that there will be not only an increased need for leisure and activity but also eventually for help as we enter our last years. With an extended life-span comes the possibility of an extended time dealing with chronic illness and other health issues. Caregiving is thus discussed in detail in this book. Another major change in families is that, with scientific advances, a woman's potential childbearing age has been extended into her later thirties, and even through her forties, using assisted reproductive technologies. Delayed childbearing leads to a later active parenthood going into one's sixties and seventies. This family situation creates new challenges and rewards. Older parents are typically more mature and financially stable. Often they very much want children and, in fact, work to have them via infertility treatments involving a lot of money and time. But at the same time, they are older and have fewer years to give to their children. Their children may find that they need to care for aging parents, possibly while they themselves are starting their own families. Opportunities for children of older parents to call upon them for help with their own offspring may be lessened if these grandparents are already in their eighties. Thus, we dedicate a section of the book to parenting in later life.

The concluding chapter of this book seeks to sum up many of its major themes. Globalization is affecting family life by augmenting the possibilities for social interaction worldwide, increasingly calling upon technology to bridge geographic and cultural distances. As our world shrinks socially, it is more commonplace for young people in particular to intermarry, disregarding boundaries once imposed by race, country of origin, or religion. This expanded heterogeneity presents potential challenges for both older and younger generations.

Throughout the book, an eye will be kept on the increasing diversity of our society and the dramatic changes within our aging population. While we are aging from the moment we are born, this book concentrates on the experiences of those aged 65 and older. The one exception to this is the chapter devoted to a discussion of the use of assisted reproductive technologies by people in their late thirties and even forties, and the resultant group of parents who are raising children into their sixties. The experiences of these families differ from those in which children are born to younger parents.

Aging theories have not undergone a renaissance. Many of the reviews of the theoretical literature point to a lack of theory (Alley, Putney, Rice, and Bengtson 2010). Part of the problem is that aging is a wide-ranging and interdisciplinary topic. Finding a theory that encompasses the social, psychological, physical, and economic aspects of people embedded in their cultures is too broad in scope. Such macro-theory is also difficult to test in actual research projects (for example, feminist theory or the life course paradigm). Indeed, the life course paradigm is the most mentioned in aging articles (Alley, Putney, Rice, and Bengtson 2010). And note, it is a paradigm—a way of looking at the social world—rather than a theory. Nevertheless, I introduce a theory in each chapter in order to help readers situate the topic, and also to help us remember to consider social life through a theoretical lens.

Data and Methods

Both qualitative and quantitative data are used for this book. For the qualitative data, each chapter opens with a vignette that reflects the issues of the chapter. The vignettes may come from previously published works, historical documents, oral histories, or interviews. The vignettes set the tone for the chapter.

Institutional review board (IRB) approval was established for all interviews. Most of the vignettes are derived from face-to-face interviews conducted by the author. In order to find willing interview participants, convenience and snowball sampling was used. Occasionally, agencies and social groups were contacted to assist in finding participants. Effort was made to vary social backgrounds, race and ethnicities, and gender of those interviewed. Prior to meeting with an individual, the author sent an informed consent document to their home and requested that the interview subject read it carefully. Upon meeting with the participant, before the interview, we reviewed the informed consent document and then the author obtained the necessary signatures. All screened participants agreed to participate in the study. Interviews usually took place in a public place, such as a local coffee shop, and generally lasted about an hour. A semi-structured interview guide was used. This type of interview confirms that certain questions are asked of participants but also allows them to talk about whatever they think is important. The author took notes throughout the interviews. After each interview, additional notes were made about the interview and impressions were also noted in the left-hand column. The vignette was then written within the next day or two. All names and locations of participants have been changed for confidentiality. Very specific details about family life and dates were eliminated or changed as well. Not only are vignettes used at the beginning of chapters but occasionally they are used in other places in the book to add context to social patterns.

For the quantitative results, this book reports current statistics from several sources that all use U.S. Census data. Each chapter provides information about current trends using tables, figures, and/or current statistics. When possible, I use secondary data analysis with one-year point estimates of the American Community Survey (ACS) (2012) to report the sociodemographic trends in each chapter. The American Fact Finder allows complicated (multivariable) queries of the data as well. For these queries, data were drawn from the following website using the guided search feature: http://factfinder2.census.gov/, sometimes utilizing the five-year estimates. Finally, I used a graphing utility to create customizable graphs to look at trends in U.S. Census data provided by the Stanford Center on Poverty and Inequality along with the Russell Sage Foundation (http://web.stanford.edu/group/recessiontrends/cgi-bin/web/), part of the Harvard Dataverse Network, which pulls from four decades of trend data in various large, nationally representative data sets such as the U.S. Census, National Center for Health Statistics, the World Bank, and so on.

The ACS is sponsored by the U.S. Census Bureau, and is part of the 2010 Decennial Census Program. The American Community Survey sample was interviewed from January 1, 2012, through December 31, 2012. It is selected from all counties and county-equivalents in the United States. These data include people in group quarters such as military barracks and nursing homes (American Community Survey 2014). The universe for the ACS consists of all valid, residential housing unit addresses in all county and county-equivalents in the fifty states, including the District of Columbia. The Master Address File (MAF) is a database maintained and updated by the U.S. Census Bureau containing a listing of residential and commercial addresses in the United States and Puerto Rico (American Community Survey 2014).

Not all information from the ACS can be compiled from American Fact Finder, thus I also downloaded original data from the Integrated Public Use Microdata Series (IPUMS) to create some of the charts and figures. IPUMS is a project housed at

A couple completes the Census questionnaire at home.
United States Census Bureau

Minnesota Population Center at the University of Minnesota that is dedicated to facilitating the use of census data (IPUMS USA 2014; Ruggles et al. 2010). Using the IPUMS allows original data analysis on the data set. When this is the case, data were analyzed using Stata 12. Much of these analyses involve selecting a population, possibly over several years if the same question is available over time, and then reporting frequencies for each group. For instance, the sample may be limited to all people over sixty who are currently taking care of grandchildren in their home, and show the results by race. Results are reported in table and figure formats for these secondary data analyses as well. In addition, statistics may be reported in the text.

For the 2012 ACS survey American Community Survey 2010 sample, I use the 1 percent sample. These data are a 1-in-100 national random sample of the population. It is a weighted sample, and the smallest identifiable geographic unit is the PUMA, containing at least 100,000 persons. PUMAs do not cross state boundaries. The housing unit response rate for the 2010 American Community Survey was 97.5 percent (https://www.census.gov/acs/www/methodology/sample-size-and-data-quality/response-rates/). There were initially 2,899,676 addresses selected, but only 1,917,799 final interviews were conducted (https://www.census.gov/acs/www/methodology/sample-size-and-data-quality/sample-size/). The response rate for the 2012 sample is 97.3 percent.

Finally, some data are gathered from the U.S. Census website and put into a table or figure. In these instances, the data come from U.S. Census Population Projections and are labeled as such. These data come from the summary tables available at the U.S. Census Population Projections and typically charts and figures were made in Microsoft Word (https://www.census.gov/population/projections/data/national/2012/summarytables.html).

In summary, while all original data analysis comes from the U.S. Census, some were produced from American Fact Finder, some were analyzed using the data set from IPUMS, some were generated from the chart utility in recessiontrends.org, and some were taken from population projection tables. Each analysis specifies where the data come from, and if needed, how they are analyzed.

Structure of the Chapters

Each chapter begins with objectives, and then a vignette, to introduce the reader to the topic. From the second chapter forward, a theory is introduced that can be used to examine the main points of the chapter, thus framing the discussion. Occasionally more than one theory is examined to help provide the reader with an understanding of the topic's history. A review of current ideas is then discussed and supported by data from the American Community Survey. Each chapter also includes key terms that are defined in the glossary. Chapters end with critical thinking questions.

Organization of the Book

Chapter 1 gives readers a sense of some of the major social forces that shape the aging family experience. It discusses major demographic, health, and social trends that affect families and aging with predictions for the future. These themes are explored in detail in the chapters that follow. As an overview, it does not have a theory introduced at the beginning.

Chapter 2 discusses major changes in American family dynamics including divorce, remarriage, singlehood, childfree living, and cohabiting, and also addresses the increase in the number of lesbian, gay, bisexual, transgender, and queer (LGBTQ) individuals and families. In this chapter and throughout the book, the diversification of American families in society—and how they vary by race, ethnicity, and family forms—is discussed in more detail. The reader should note that the term LGBTQ was chosen, but other terms may be used if a specific study, for instance, only discusses LGB. Similarly, the terms African American and Native American were chosen, but at times Black or American Indian are used if the Census table or research used these terms.

Chapter 3 shows how changing gender roles affect families and aging. It examines how an unprecedented number of women in the labor force (including those with small children) as well as an unprecedented number of women in the breadwinner role impact gender relations in families. It also examines the changing role of fathers, who now take on more active parenting duties than ever before. The chapter ends with a discussion of the less-traditional roles for men and women overall and how more gender-neutral roles may affect society.

Chapter 4 examines parenthood later in life. Changes in fertility, including delayed age of first birth and the optimal time to have a baby (later than you might expect), are discussed. The explosion of assisted reproductive technology (ART) and the implications of older first-time mothers and families are considered here. Other issues of older parents are discussed, including boomerang children and intergenerational links such as the sandwich generation. Also discussed is the increase in twin births in the United States. Finally, the negotiation of different types of transfer flows, such as money and resources, among generations is examined.

Chapter 5 centers on work and retirement. It begins with a discussion of estimated work life and career cycles, as well as the now-extended length of retirement. It then discusses the dependency ratio. The chapter shifts to work and family issues surrounding work in later life and work cessation. Financial issues are discussed, as well as the Great Recession, unemployment, and debt. Last, it covers the increased need to start saving for retirement earlier in life.

In chapter 6, activities in later life—including grandparenting, shopping, moving, and using technology—are discussed. It considers new pastimes in the United States, suggesting that America's favorite hobby may be shopping, and how the transformation of consumerism and consumption is changing from one of meeting needs to one of self-expression. Grandparenting is taking on new meaning, time, and energy as older grandparents live longer and either voluntarily or involuntarily become more active caretakers of their children's (or stepchildren's) children. This chapter also discusses the effects of divorce and reconstituted families on grandparents, including the often painful loss of contact grandparents experience, for example, when their son divorces and loses contact with his children through remarriage.

Chapter 7 examines the improved levels of health overall, and the new interest in vitality and aging well. The debate of expansion versus compression is introduced. Caregiving and the need for social support are explored here as well. The chapter also focuses on Alzheimer's disease and assistive technologies. It discusses products American families will need in the future—with an emphasis on ergonomically appropriate homes or home remodels.

Chapter 8 concludes the book with an examination of major societal trends and points to research needed in the future. Changing demographics—including smaller families, more distance between family members, varied living arrangements, and the need to develop more social roles—are reviewed. The effects of increasing globalization and technology are also tied into the experiences of families and aging, as the chapter is written with an eye on future issues. Finally, issues of elder mistreatment are addressed in this chapter.

As you read this book, it is my hope that you will come to understand not only how aging affects and impacts individuals and families but also how it weaves in and out of every aspect of our society as a whole.

Acknowledgments

This book would not have been possible without the help of many. I thank the University of Alabama at Birmingham. In the Department of Sociology, I thank fellow professors and colleagues Drs. William Cockerham, Ferris Ritchey, and Mark LaGory, all of whom supported the project and coached me on aspects of how to get a book published. Early in the project, editor Peter Wissoker guided me in my writing and helped me flesh out my "journal" prose into book language. I thank the University of Alabama at Birmingham Comprehensive Center for Healthy Aging for financial support. I am indebted to those who read and edited early chapters of the book, including Gabriela Oates, Julie Brannon, and Jennifer Moren Cross.

Many graduate students contributed to this project. I wish to thank the many graduate research assistants who helped me over the years on this book. These great students include: Mercie Mwaria, Libby Yost, Tim Hale, Sarah Ballard, Philip Gibson, Deborah Ejem, Lingfei Guo, Zachary Simoni, Kristi Stringer, Jay Irwin, Gabriela Oates, Hayley Medved Kendrick, Jessica Valles, and Stephanie Kirkland. Most of these students have gone on to become sociologists and work as PhDs in research centers and academia.

Finally, I thank my husband, Paul, who encouraged me and helped me find time to write. I also thank my two daughters, who provide meaning to everything I do. My parents and Paul's parents also asked for updates and were supportive. I thank Rowman & Littlefield and editor Nancy Roberts for having faith in the project.

Introduction

CHAPTER OBJECTIVES

1. Appreciate the growing number of older adults in the United States.
2. Understand how life expectancy is increasing.
3. Have a general sense about how families are changing, and what the future holds.
4. Familiarize yourself with how socioeconomic status (SES), race, and ethnicity are related to aging families.
5. Be able to describe how health will affect aging families.

Eleanor is in her midnineties. She lives in her home with near round-the-clock assistance. Her days are quite scheduled. Each morning, her caretaker Lynn arrives. Together they get ready and she eats breakfast. Eleanor then settles in for some reading, usually the Bible, a devotional book, or a large-print novel someone picked up for her at the library. Sometimes they go to the beauty parlor, for a doctor's appointment, or on a special shopping trip. Around 11:30 AM she has her lunch, rests, watches television, takes her medicines, and works on personal matters such as bills, balancing her checkbook, and shopping lists for her caretakers. At 2:00 PM, Lynn returns to her own house and cooks supper for her two children, husband, and Eleanor. She drives back and delivers the dinner to Eleanor. They visit for a little while, and sometimes Eleanor has friends stop by. Lynn cleans up and then goes home to her own family. Around 7:00 PM, Lynn's mother comes for the night shift. She helps Eleanor with anything she needs, and then stays up while Eleanor sleeps through the night—just in case Eleanor needs any help. However, that is rare, as Eleanor can sleep straight through the night once she "finds her spot." In the morning, it all starts over again. It doesn't vary much over weekends, other than that the caretakers are different week-end crews. The major outing is each Sunday. Eleanor dresses up, in a blue suit with a matching hat, and goes to church. Her caregiver drives her in

Eleanor's own car. That way her car is used weekly, even though Eleanor doesn't drive anymore. Eleanor reports being happy. She continues to live in her home, she likes having company, her needs are taken care of, and she has time to read the Bible and pray—two things that she says are very important to her.

Of course, it wasn't always like this. Up until five years ago, Eleanor drove herself, taking short shopping trips to the Piggly Wiggly. Her husband died about eight years ago at 101 years of age, but for the last ten years of his life, *she* was the caretaker. He was blind and she helped him, though it seems he didn't need much. Eleanor says he still went out to his wood shop in the backyard each day and made furniture, feeling his way through it.

In her early thirties, Eleanor had married a widower whose wife had died in childbirth. She raised a stepson (with whom she was never close), and she never had children of her own. Eleanor worked for the Navy in the 1940s and 1950s as a decoder and then for an insurance company until she retired, about thirty years ago. She receives a reliable pension, as well as Social Security. It is likely that she will outlive her seventy-year-old stepson, as he has been fighting lung cancer. She has outlived four sisters and one brother and their spouses. She has some nieces and nephews who are geographically scattered across the United States, and they occasionally check in on her.

Is this a typical story? Yes and no. Eleanor's situation—with one stepson, a long work career, and an extended lifespan—is typical of what *will* be the case for many women in the future. It will also be more common that men and women never have children and, as such, cannot depend on sons and daughters. What is not typical is that Eleanor was born almost one hundred years ago, a time when most women had larger families, did not have long careers or their own pensions, and had a much shorter life expectancy.

This book examines several of the themes exemplified by Eleanor's life, such as extended lifetime, caretaking, and smaller immediate families. Eleanor's example is used to touch upon some of the main issues and common threads to be considered with regard to families and aging, including parenthood, work, activities in later life, and health. This chapter begins with an overview of the general demographic changes in today's aging population.

Increase of Older Adult Population

A tremendous increase in the older adult population has been occurring and is expected to grow in the early twenty-first century. In 1900, there were only about 3 million people aged 65 or older. This number has grown considerably in the past one hundred years. In the year 2000, there were about 35 million people who were 65 or older in the United States—about 13 percent of the 2000 U.S. population (AoA 2014). Clearly, what was once relatively rare is now commonplace, as a little more than one in ten persons are over the age of sixty-five. It is projected that this number will more than double to 72 million by the year 2030 (AoA 2014). A substantial percentage of the population growing older affects many aspects of society, including labor force needs, health care, and Social Security.

Interestingly, the population of those aged 85 and over is the fastest growing segment of the older population (FIFARS 2016). Often defined as the oldest-old, this group numbered 6.2 million people in 2014. It is projected that it could grow to almost 20 million by 2060 (FIFARS 2016). The over-80 population is feminized, as many men die before their eightieth year. These women are often widows, many of whom have health care needs and limited financial resources. When a substantial percentage of a population is over eighty-five, it impacts society. Older adults with leisure time may affect the social climate. One might expect them to be more readily available to help their families, perhaps offering wisdom and conversation as well as providing childcare for grandchildren, as this cohort seeks meaningful activity in their later years. Volunteer opportunities may also be pursued in schools and other organizations.

There are numerous health issues for this group. Of older adults over sixty-five, 22 percent reported at least one physical impairment (for instance trouble seeing, hearing, or with mobility) to which they must adapt (FIFARS 2016), and for those over eighty-five years old, 10 percent reported trouble with tasks such as bathing, dressing, eating, walking, getting in and out of chairs or bed, and using the toilet (AoA 2011). The percentage per each category varies widely, with only about 10 percent having trouble eating but almost 50 percent having trouble walking (AoA 2011). Older adults also report difficulty in climbing stairs, an inability to drive, needing help with grocery shopping, and difficulty caring for themselves. These impairments, when magnified by the number of older people in society experiencing such problems, become a societal issue as government agencies, the health care system, and religious institutions attempt to create programs to support those in need. Assisted living facilities are also trying to help older individuals. It becomes a family issue as well since most families want to take care of their aging loved ones, and many of these older adults will be unable to live alone without help.

The Baby Boomers

Currently, there are about 76 million **Baby Boomers** (those born between 1946 and 1964). Beginning in 2011, the first of the Baby Boomers turned sixty-five (FIFARS 2016). Baby Boomers have set the tone and societal needs for the country for some time. As they age, they will continue to affect many aspects of our society in terms of Social Security, health service utilization, housing, consumer demand, and so on. While the sudden increase in older people currently places stress on our government planning, the United States has time to catch up with this rapid change in aging (Uhlenberg 2013). In addition, the growth rate of the older population will slow after 2030, when the last Baby Boomers turn sixty-five years old (FIFARS 2016).

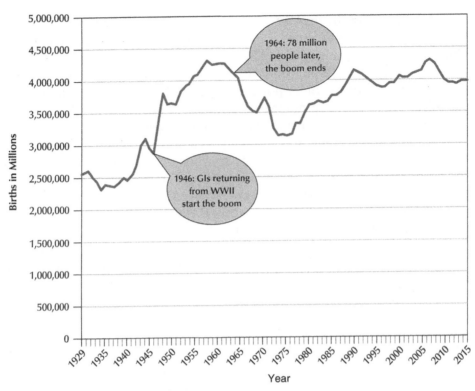

FIGURE 1.1 Baby Boomers by Age Range

Life Expectancy in the United States
The Past, Present, and Future

In order to predict the future, the past must be understood. Table 1.1 shows life expectancy from birth for those born in 1900 and 2010. There has been a dramatic rise in life expectancy since 1900 when the average age at death was in the midforties for whites and in the early thirties for nonwhites. Naturally, there were "outliers"—people who lived into their sixties and

TABLE 1.1   Life Expectancy from Birth for Those Born in 1900 and 2010

	All Races		White		Nonwhite	
Year	Men	Women	Men	Women	Men	Women
1900	46.3	48.3	46.6	48.7	32.5	33.5
2010	76.2	81.0	76.5	81.3	71.8	78.0

Source: Adapted from National Center for Health Statistics. Health, United States, 2013. Hyattsville, MD. 2014. Table 18. Retrieved April 16, 2015, from http://www.cdc.gov/nchs/data/hus/hus13.pdf#indextotrendtablesand.

seventies—and this table's averages also include those who died as infants and children. Even given these considerations, life expectancy has been on the rise for decades (Oeppen and Vaupel 2002). By 2010, average life expectancy had reached the seventies and eighties.

The ramifications of a shorter life span meant that many people were widowed early. Some did not remarry, and many children lost a parent early in life. Many parents experienced the death of a child due to an infectious disease. Grandparents were often not present because they passed away earlier in a grandchild's life. Fewer people experienced older age, with its concerns of disability and infirmity. Because life spans were shorter, it also meant that one died not of chronic ailments such as cardiovascular disease or cancer but rather from causes such as infectious diseases (frequently due to sanitation problems) or due to accidents.

In the year 2015, life expectancy at birth was between seventy-two and eighty-three years, depending on race and sex (see figure 1.2). Living into our seventies and eighties allows many of us to experience a fuller life spanning childhood, schooling, jobs, families, divorce, launching children, extended work lives, and, for some, retirement and leisure. Additionally, health issues take up more time in later life. However, the experience of the life cycle is not the same for all. Women generally still live longer than men, and there are great disparities in longevity between races and ethnicities. Below is a figure examining the racial and gender gap in mortality. For each racial or ethnic category, women live longer than men. Women's greater longevity means women today must be even savvier in planning for their later years. They must garner social support and save more money. However, for a variety of reasons to be discussed in this book, this is particularly difficult due to interrupted work histories, lower levels of pay, single parenthood, and other work and family situations that affect women's later years. All women can expect to live into their eighties except for Black (African American) women, who are projected to live to 78.7 years old. The racial and ethnic gaps in mortality are still wide, with the greatest disparity between Black (African American) men and Hispanic women (projected to live 72.7 and 83.9 years, respectively) (see figure 1.2). Interestingly, Hispanic women have the highest life expectancy at 83.9 years, followed by White women, Asian women, American Indian (Native American) women, and finally Black (African American) women. Among men, only Hispanic men (at a projected 79.1 years) have a higher life expectancy than Black (African American) women (78.7). Otherwise, all men are projected to live shorter lives, with Black (African American) men having the lowest life expectancy at 72.7 years.

In a little more than one hundred years, average life expectancy has increased by about thirty-five years depending on one's race and sex. Whereas before 1950, most of the gain in life expectancy was the result of more children living longer, in the second half of the twentieth century gains were due to people living beyond sixty-five years of age (Oeppen and Vaupel 2002). These extra years allow some a third phase in life in which earlier social roles, such as parent and worker, may have ended or abated. However, new roles, such as being a single person (by separation, divorce,

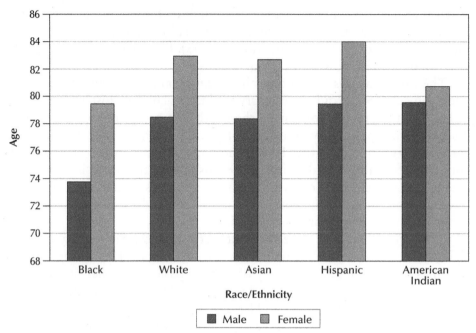

FIGURE 1.2 Projected Life Expectancy at Birth by Race, Ethnicity, and Sex for Year 2020
Source: Adapted from U.S. Census Bureau, Population Division. Projected Life Expectancy at Birth by Sex, Race, and Hispanic Origin for the United States: 2015 to 2060 (NP2012-T-10). Table 10.

or death of partner) may be added to one's role repertoire. Other new roles may include being a grandparent, a caregiver, or, as often occurs in late life, a patient. Today one can be retired for upward of thirty years and some may find they are seeking new activities in their free time as a retiree.

Do we expect another major increase in the next one hundred years? Will most of us live to be over one hundred years old? Experts disagree. Many say no. Most researchers believe that there is a biological limit to the human life span, estimating its upper end to be about 120 years. Some think that life expectancy will climb to 83 years (for men) and 93 years (for women) by 2050, if biomedical progress continues (Olshansky et al. 2009). Still others claim, based on current trends, that estimates of women in the United States living from 92.5 to 101.5 years on average by 2070 are plausible (Oeppen and Vaupel 2002). We certainly anticipate the greatest number of centenarians ever living in the future.

A countervailing prediction is that of a potential decline in life expectancy. The epidemic of obesity coupled with a sedentary lifestyle may shorten our lives (Mirowsky 2010; Mirowsky and Ross 2015; Olshansky et al. 2005). Mirowsky and Ross (2015) discuss these trends, explaining how the current "default American lifestyle"—in which we no longer prepare our own food regularly, rely too much on our cars, and use too many over-the-counter and prescription drugs (Mirowsky 2010; Mirowsky and Ross 2015)—is harming us. This lifestyle of infrequent exercise, high fat/high calorie diets, and a buildup of medicine in our bodies has ramifications

How to Become a Centenarian

There are about 50,000 centenarians currently, which is almost three times that in 1980 (Perls, Silver, and Lauerman 2000). What are the factors that play into living to 100? The largest study of centenarians has taken place by Thomas Perls and associates at Boston University. Through interviews with centenarians, they found that those living to 100 are more likely to have the following: genetic predisposition (such as having a parent who lived to 100), an ability to handle stress better than most, an optimistic attitude, learning new things, avoiding smoking, and keeping body weight in check (Perls, Silver, and Lauerman 2000; Perls 2006). Perls and his associates encourage us to adopt life-extending behaviors. For a personal evaluation, you can find out your own life expectancy using the "Living to 100" calculator (https://www.livingto100.com).

for American society which could include more sickness, earlier death, and cognitive decline (Mirowsky 2010; Mirowsky and Ross 2015), thus diminishing average life expectancy.

Similarly, Dan Buettner (2009) wrote the book *The Blue Zones: Lessons for Living Longer from the People Who've Lived the Longest*. He and his team of medical researchers, demographers, anthropologists, and epidemiologists identified four areas of the world that he names Blue Zones. These geographic regions have the greatest concentrations of the world's healthiest and longest-living inhabitants. Rather than biological or genetic factors, inhabitants of these areas share common social or environmental traits that promote longevity. The four Blue Zones are:

1. Barbagia region of Sardinia
2. Nicoya Peninsula, Costa Rica
3. Seventh-Day Adventists (highest concentration in Loma Linda, California)
4. Okinawa, Japan

The researchers found nine commonalities among people living in the four regions, shown in table 1.2.

Of these commonalities, clearly diet and exercise matter, but so does being with people and having shared experiences and social support. Taking downtime to relax and be mindful is also important. By practicing these behaviors, Buettner (2009) says we can all hope to live longer. See https://www.bluezones.com/ to see what your longevity looks like.

Changes in World Population

Estimates of Future World Population

Consistent with the pattern of increased population and life expectancy in the United States is the fact that more people than ever before live on this planet. Historically, demographers are successful in predicting at most only

TABLE 1.2   Nine Commonalities of Blue Zones

moving naturally rather than regimented exercise	having a sense of purpose	finding time to de-stress
eating smaller meals at night	eating more beans/less meat	drinking 1–2 glasses of wine/day (except Adventists)
belonging to a faith-based community	putting loved ones first	being in social circles conducive to healthy behavior

Source: Adapted by author from Dan Buettner (2009), *The Blue Zones: Lessons for Living Longer from the People Who've Lived the Longest.*

about one hundred years into the future. Our planet currently has over 7 billion people, more than double the population since 1950 (UN 2015). The International Data Base, a computerized data source operated by the U.S. Census, is currently estimating over 9 billion people in the year 2050 (International Data Base 2014). As the world population increases, virtually every society will experience an increase in its older population.

Demographic models predicting world population are estimated depending upon whether one assumes high, medium, or low fertility. A

iStock/JohnnyGreig

World Population in the Next *Millennium*

Below is an estimate of the world population in the next *millennium* based on the estimates of one-half billion per decade (the current trend). Following this pattern of increase, the population will be 56 billion by the year 3000. Of course, no demographer would be willing to project this far; many different factors affect the growth rate of the world. What are some of the pros and cons of an earth with 56 billion people? Do you think it will happen? Why or why not? What social factors might affect the current increase?

medium-fertility model estimates that the population by the year 2100 will be 11 billion (UN 2015), which is based on a global fertility rate of 2.5 children per woman, falling to a global rate of 2.0 from 2095 to 2100. The most reliable estimate is the medium-level fertility model, which takes into account countries that have two or fewer children per couple (such as in most of Europe) to higher-fertility countries that have more than two children per couple. However, these are all *estimates*; no one knows what will happen in the future.

As with any circumstance in which we attempt to look into the future, we are unable to consider aspects of science, technology, or natural events that have yet to occur—including changes in fertility and mortality. For instance, the implications of future gene therapy or changing the genetic blueprint of our species—both of which may extend life—are unknown at present (Olshansky, Carnes, and Grahn 1998). We cannot predict the effect of a possible reemergence of infectious or parasitic diseases we once thought eradicated (Olshansky, Carnes, and Grahn 1998) nor the implications of the epidemic of obesity (Mirowsky and Ross 2015; Olshansky et al. 2005). The emerging patterns of political and social unrest remain unclear as well. Nonetheless, these shifts in demographics in an aging society have lasting implications for all our main institutions, including family.

Facts about Families

Diverse Family Forms

Multiple family forms have emerged, become more commonplace, and will continue to proliferate. In the early twentieth century, women had more children and extended family was more reliant upon one another, both for financial and basic survival needs (Coontz 2016; Dobriansky, Suzman, and Hodes 2007). While it is true that a nuclear-family-based society really never existed (Coontz 2016), it is also true that the freedoms and varied ways of living that families experience today were not as prevalent (Garrison and Scott 2012; Silverstein and Giarrusso 2010). The many constellations of families, with myriad family structures, will continue to change any preconceived notion of what is the norm. Moreover, the number of options Americans have for creating families is much broader than in most societies and these changes will continue in the future.

What Is a Family?

Before discussing families, a definition of family must be adopted for the purpose of this book. There are many ways to define family. Some definitions are highly structured and limiting. For instance, the U.S. Census Bureau must define a family narrowly and consistently in order to make clear the statistics they address. According to the U.S. Census, family is "a group of two or more people who reside together and who are related by birth, marriage or adoption" (https://www.askcensus.gov 2006). A rigid definition such as this is useful to the census when it tries to examine families and make some statements about the state of families today. However, the census definition leaves out cohabitors, who may raise children and live most of their lifetimes together, and it also leaves out gays and lesbians. Extended family such as grandparents, aunts, uncles, and cousins are also excluded

when they don't live in the same household. This is too narrow a definition for a book discussing families and aging. This book takes into consideration the legal and genetic linkages families have, but also the relational linkages that are stated by the people in the families themselves. It also includes multigenerational families.

In this book, *family* is considered any group of people who create an intimate/financial/emotional, and/or legal union. Its members (ideally) love and care for one another, share resources, and sometimes have legal connections. This includes extended family, same-sex couples, cohabiting couples, and **fictive kin**, that is, those who are not considered traditional family but who serve the function of family by supplying one another with social/emotional and/or instrumental support.

Major societal changes in the past one hundred years—including the Women's Rights Movement, access to birth control, and increased opportunities for women in general—have affected families dramatically. Women's roles continue to change as overall fertility is decreasing and later marrying, cyclical marrying, and single-parent mothering are on the rise. Women are in the workforce en masse, with most women with children under six years of age in the workforce (64.7 percent of women with children under six and 76 percent of women with children aged 6–17 are in the workforce) (BLS 2014). Men too are experiencing significant role changes, some based on societal structures, such as an overall decline in earnings, and others based on expectations of and desires for increased parenting responsibilities. These days, many men want closer relationships with their children than their fathers had with them.

More Options

There is an increasing diversity in family structures, family households, and living arrangements in raising families (Silverstein and Giarrusso 2010). Some are new, some are not so new, but certainly they are more visible than in the past (Coontz 2016). Additionally, there is more cultural acceptance for family types beyond the two-parent heterosexual married couple (that is, the nuclear family). For instance, while not entirely new, one family form that is becoming commonplace is legally married gay or lesbian parents raising children. It is no longer considered unusual for fathers to be raising their children alone nor for a father to be the stay-at-home parent while the mother goes to work. As men become more active in childrearing, more complex joint-custody arrangements will be common. As these children grow up, their fathers (and grandfathers) will have more active roles in their lives than ever before.

Cohabiting has also steadily increased, as has remaining single. An unprecedented number of people will remain single for their entire lives. Singlehood can be classified as a diverse family form as it has implications for health and well-being in the later years. Since those who are single won't have spouses or partners to help them, and they may be less likely to have adult children, concerns may arise regarding social isolation, social support mechanisms, and provision of assistance if it is needed. Additionally, divorce and remarriage are still very common in U.S. society. All these trends are explored in depth throughout this book.

The growing racial and ethnic diversity of the United States increases the heterogeneity of the population. The future will bring us more interracial and interethnic unions. Already by 2010, about 15 percent of all new marriages were considered interracial (Wang 2012). Different racial and ethnic backgrounds are accompanied by different family belief systems and traditions. These intermarriages will change how families relate to one another in old age.

iStock/photoschmidt

Trends in the Aging Family

Longer Life Span

A few major trends in the aging family should be noted. As referenced above, Americans are simply going to live longer, and there will be more of us. A society with a greater proportion of older adults will change the social landscape. We will live together (or apart) for a longer period of time, through unions, divorces, and reconstituted families. More Americans will experience the full life cycle, from birth to old age, which will also bring more intergenerational linkages. More families will continue to have children later in life. Thus the many forty-year-olds beginning their families in the 2000s will be raising and launching their children when they are well into their sixties. This trend will be discussed later.

More Needs for Caregiving

Regarding the aging family, another main trend is caregiving for an older adult. Never has our society had such a need to provide care for others over such a long span of time. Contrary to sometimes popular belief, we are a nation that takes care of our older adult relatives, primarily via family care. One study estimated that we saved the economy $470 billion by caregiving in the home (Reinhard, Feinberg, Choula, and Houser 2015). All this caregiving has created several new issues, including caregiver burden, caregiver fatigue, and the need for respite care. The **sandwich generation** refers to those parents, usually women, who find themselves in the situation of taking care of both children and older adults (usually their own parents) at the same time. The workplace has to respond both on a structural level with policies for temporary leaves but also on an individual level as coworkers need to adjust their schedules to accommodate employees who must take time off to care for their loved ones.

Changes in Diversity—Race and Ethnicity

Current Versus Future Population of the United States

The twenty-first century will be marked by the increased diversity of the United States. Currently, per categories designated in the U.S. Census, 77.5 percent of the U.S. population self-reports as White, 13.2 percent as Black (African American), 5.4 percent Asian, and 17.4 percent Hispanic. In addition, 1.4 percent is considered American Indian, Alaska Native, and Native Hawaiian or Other Pacific Islander (AIAN/NHPI) (Colby and Ortman 2014). Which races are projected to increase in proportion? The answer is that Hispanics, Asians, and those of two or more races are expected to increase considerably. Hispanics, on the other hand, are predicted to comprise over one-quarter (28.6%) of the U.S. population by 2060 (Colby and Ortman 2014). Multiple races, ethnicities, and cultures bring different family experiences into society (Boswell 2015). Changing demographics bring more families who are Hispanic, Asian, Middle

Eastern, and African American. Each group experiences families, family life, and family structure differently. Increased intermarriage will further meld together family experiences. Clearly, as is already the case in many places in the South and Southwest, Spanish will be a key second language in the United States. Being able to speak Spanish fluently will allow us to better care for and converse with an increasing population of older adults and their families.

The Changing Landscape of the Population

The older adult population is also expected to become increasingly diverse. Figure 1.3 shows the population aged 65 and older, by race and Hispanic origin, projected for 2015 and 2060. While currently about 62 percent of the U.S. population is non-Hispanic white, this is projected to drop to 43 percent by 2060. All other projections show an increase over time. Each group will bring its nexus of social and cultural ways of life to the process of aging and caretaking. They will bring their work histories into later life, and we will examine subsequent outcomes of income and wealth among groups. In addition, families will be much more likely to have multiracial and multiethnic customs that they bring together as they age together. These themes will be explored throughout the text.

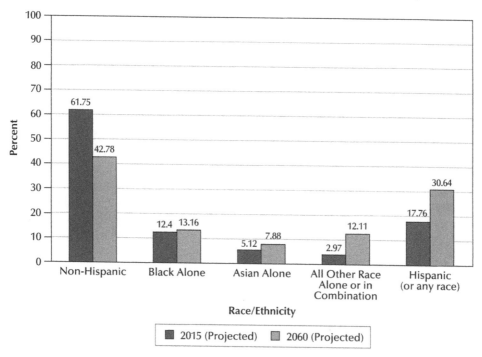

FIGURE 1.3   Population Aged 65 and Over, by Race and Hispanic Origin, 2015 and Projected 2060

Source: Based on data at U.S. Census Bureau, Population Division. Percent of the Projected Population by Race and Hispanic Origin for the United States: 2015 to 2060 (NP2012-T-6). Table 6.

Changes in Socioeconomic Status

Increased Standard of Living for Most

The older adult of today has more income and wealth than any other older adult cohort before it. In the late 1950s to 1960s, the poverty rate for those aged 65 years and over fell from 35 percent to 25 percent by 1968, but in 2015 only 8.8 percent of this same group were living in poverty (U.S. Census Bureau 2016a). Older adults today also have the highest levels of education ever. In 1965, only 24 percent of those over age 65 had a high school diploma; in 2015, 84 percent had a high school diploma (FIFARS 2016). By 2015, 27 percent of the population had a college degree or more. Thus while currently many older adults have only a high school education, the older adults of the future will be much better educated than previous generations. Higher levels of education are associated with better adult mental and physical health (Mirowsky and Ross 2003a; 2003b; 2008; Quesnel-Vallée and Taylor 2012), and are protective against the onset of disability (Taylor 2010).

More informed older adults may potentially desire more services and more leisure activities. They may have a more confident demeanor when dealing with professionals; in particular, they may have a greater rapport with their physicians. As such, they may question more rather than simply accept their doctors' advice. A more-educated cohort overall will have dramatic effects on older adults' well-being.

Families are now wealthier than they have ever been (Nazareth 2007; Schor 2004). More surplus income will lead to more consumer goods and services. Never before have Americans had so many things: homes, cars, electronic gadgets, computers, televisions, and other items now considered necessities (Ekerdt 2009). Families seemingly have an increasing need for more and more things, many of which are luxury items (Danziger 2011; Schor 2004). Americans often compare their standard of living to that of families who are much wealthier, including those seen on television, and they want to mimic them (Schor 2004). The desire for goods has created an enormous amount of things that accumulate in our homes by the time we reach old age (Ekerdt 2009). All these things must eventually be transferred or given away when an estate closes down. Such transfers and inheritances will be discussed. Homes too have become larger over the decades, as a place for storage, even though our families are smaller. More than ever before, consumerism and collecting are pastimes for aging Americans. With these trends, we may predict an increase in the standard of living of most over the next one hundred years.

Continued Inequality

While most of the older U.S. population will experience a higher standard of living, poverty is still prevalent, especially for women and minorities (Ozawa and Yoon 2008). The United States has also experienced an increasing divide between the rich and poor since the 1970s (Van Arnum and Naples 2013). Wealth continues to be concentrated among those in the upper class, and the average middle-class American has seen a downturn in their ability to balance their budget and make ends meet (Porter 2012).

Some of the major dividing lines fall between groups, affecting people differently based on variables like racial or ethnic background, immigrant status, and whether they live in urban or rural areas. Older women are more likely to experience a **double or triple jeopardy.** Double jeopardy is when one experiences two lower-level statuses at a time (for instance, being female and poor), while triple jeopardy involves the crisscrossing nexus of three statuses (such as being female, Hispanic, and older). For instance, in our study examining late-life wishes, a sixty-three-year old woman says:

> I just want to go to the grocery store and buy me some groceries with no dollar limit. I want to go through the produce and just pick up avocados and plums and stuff like that. I want to feed my family with fresh fruits of the earth. If I could, I'd leave them with enough to never have to sleep with no food in their stomachs or eat that bad-tasting poor man's food. But it ain't going to happen. Just look at me and what do you see? I'm like that old lady in the shoe with nothing to keep in her cupboard. (63-year-old Black female) (Williams, Woodby, and Drentea 2010)

There are racial and ethnic disparities in socioeconomic status that will carry into older age. For instance, higher education among those over twenty-five years of age in 2016 (bachelor's or advanced degree) was as follows: 54 percent of Asians, 33 percent of whites, 23 percent of African Americans, and only 16 percent of Hispanics (any race) (Ryan and Bauman 2016). Since levels of education do not change much beyond age 25, these educational differences carry into later life and may affect life trajectory and outcomes such as jobs, coping, health, and well-being in general. Similar patterns exist among income levels as well. The median income in 2015 for Asians was $34,360; for whites, it was $30,999; for African Americans, it was $23,951; and it was $23,629 for Hispanics (U.S. Census Bureau 2015). For both education level and income, we see the general pattern of Asians, whites, African Americans, and then Hispanics with the lowest socioeconomic status.

Wealth versus poverty disparities are also pronounced among different races and ethnicities. For instance, Hispanics and African Americans possess less than ten cents per a white person's one dollar in wealth (such as retirement income, vehicles, property, and so on) (Kochhar 2004). While in 2015, 8.8 percent of the population among those aged 65 and older was living in poverty, the breakdown by race and ethnicity was 7.5 percent for whites, 18.4 percent for African Americans, 11.8 percent for Asians, and 17.5 percent for Hispanics (of any race) (U.S. Census Bureau 2016a). These tremendous differences will translate into wealth disparities in later life.

Underrepresented minorities are not able to weather the financial storm of a job loss or serious illness in the family as well as their wealthier white and Asian counterparts. Moreover, African Americans and Hispanics typically have more children on average, and thus a picture of additional financial stress for these groups emerges. In later life, however, having more adult children could translate into more "obligatory" help should economic stress and the need for help arise, in part due to group norms and a culture of taking care of family (Dilworth-Anderson and Cohen 2009; Dilworth-Anderson and Hilliard 2013; Lehman 2012). Thus it is likely that there will be more financial hardship as these under-represented minority groups age. The more life expectancy increases, the longer families need to plan their finances to live out more years, and hardship will disproportionately fall onto minority groups. While one's dream may be to pass on property and inheritance to children, those who experience poverty have very little to give after their deaths (Williams, Woodby, and Drentea 2010).

Recently, the stock market crash and downturn of the U.S. economy, coupled with the housing crisis of the mid-to-late 2000s, have caused many older people to rethink their retirement. The Great Recession of 2007–2009 affected jobs, pensions, and stocks. Some lost part of their expected earnings. Many have gone back to work or are delaying retirement. Yet others became more frugal as their savings diminished. Still, at least among the older population, there does not seem to be as significant delay in retirements or a significant decrease in wealth (Gustman, Steinmeir, and Tabatabai 2011). Thus recovery appears to have occurred nearly ten years after the Great Recession.

Changes in Health

Healthier Than Before

Overall, people are healthier than previous cohorts of older adults. The last century has seen a tremendous transition in disease prevalence. The beginning of the twentieth century had not yet fully experienced the epidemiological transition of disease, that is, a shift from communicable diseases (influenza, tuberculosis, pneumonia, etc.) to chronic diseases (heart disease, cancer, etc.). In 1900 the leading causes of death were respiratory diseases (including pneumonia and influenza), tuberculosis, gastrointestinal diseases (including gastroenteritis and other diseases resulting in severe diarrhea), heart disease, and cerebral hemorrhages (including acute symptoms related to the blood supply of the brain, such as strokes, etc.) (CDC 2006). In 2013,

TABLE 1.3   Top Five Causes of Death in 1900 and 2013

1900	2013
Respiratory Disease (Pneumonia and Flu)	Heart Disease
Tuberculosis	Cancer
Gastrointestinal Disease	Respiratory Diseases
Heart Disease	Accidents
Cerebral Hemorrhages	Cerebrovascular Disease (Stroke)

Source: Centers for Disease Control (CDC 2006 and 2013). Table created by author.

most of the top five causes of death were chronic conditions: heart disease, cancer, chronic lower respiratory disease, and cerebrovascular disease (that is, strokes) (CDC 2013). Only accidents are not chronic.

Chronic Illness

In the future, chronic health problems are still likely to be a focus issue among older adults (Hoeymans et al. 2012). Other major chronic health problems experienced by many Americans include obesity and its related problems, such as wear and tear on joints, high blood pressure, and Type 2 diabetes. Cases of Alzheimer's disease are growing as the population ages. Individuals may spend the last ten to twenty years of life with difficulty performing some basic activities—such as climbing stairs. The implications of chronic illness for mental health, caregiving, health care utilization, and finances in the future are considered in future chapters.

Communicable Diseases

We may also see a resurgence of transmittable illness and a reemergence of parasitic and infectious disease. Some diseases such as tuberculosis are experiencing a comeback. Other new threats include viruses, such as the influenza virus that disproportionately affects older adults. These new strains of viruses experience quick proliferation in the population. Some bacteria, such as the more drug-resistant strains of staph, have increased resistance to antibiotics. HIV/AIDS has become a chronic disease for most of the Western world; however, the spread of the disease is still disproportionately growing among minority populations in the United States. All of these health concerns may affect our health care system and aging families.

Health Disparities

Health disparities are the differences in health outcomes of different subsets of the population. Most often disparities are due to racial bias, geographical limitation, or socioeconomic status. One key point about disparities is that they are preventable. That is, there is something about group disadvantage (or advantage) that causes the health disparity. Thus, while overall the U.S. population is getting healthier, great disparities still exist among different populations. Major government initiatives have pushed to find the sources of inequality, educate the public, and try to eliminate the disparity. For instance, Healthy People 2000, 2010, and now 2020 are all part of a governmental project aimed at increasing quality and years of healthy life. A major goal is to eliminate the health disparities that exist in the United States currently (https://www.healthypeople.gov). So far, this goal has not been met. For instance, African Americans have more chronic disease and illness such as hypertension, diabetes, and stroke, when compared to whites (Office of Minority Health 2016). Cultural and ethnic differences exist between groups. For instance, liver disease is a top ten cause of death for Native Americans over the age of sixty-five, and yet it does not show up in the top ten for whites, African Americans, Asians, or Hispanics in this age cohort (https://www.healthypeople.gov). Many of these health inequalities are due to different socioeconomic statuses among groups. As families age, those less advantaged—often African American, Hispanic, or Native American—are disproportionately affected by illness and disease. Additionally, they do not have the same level of resources available to them in terms of wealth, health education, quality health care, pensions, and so on. Often, however, these families do have strong networks of extended family and friends who can take care of one another (Drentea and Goldner 2006). In studying aging families, we will continue to monitor how the inequality of society affects the experience of aging.

Summary

At the beginning of this chapter, a woman named Eleanor was introduced who embodies some of the lifestyle concerns we have for those in their nineties. Most women born in the first half of the twentieth century lived very differently than she and did not survive beyond seventy years old. Eleanor is unusual. At ninety-six years of age, she is financially independent and still able to live in her home. She is a good example of what we expect to see more of in the future.

We are currently experiencing the highest life expectancies to date. Moreover, due to the Baby Boomers, the largest group of individuals is growing old together. The increase of older adults in the general population is affecting family life. Families include multiple generations alive at the same time, though there are fewer individuals in each generation than in the past. There is a new profound openness to the diverse family forms now visible in society. A growing multiculturalism is occurring as our population changes with increased diversity and immigration. This chapter reviewed some of the socioeconomic and economic issues for older adults, and also introduced the importance of health in studying family. These patterns have changed family ties and life expectations. This book examines how the changes in aging will affect the changes in families. Many of the themes in this chapter will be revisited throughout the book.

Critical Thinking Questions

1. Envision how longer life expectancies will affect your family in the future. Consider your parents, yourself, and existing or future children of yours. What will the constellation of family ties look like, in terms of family, aging, and health?

2. As the country becomes more racially balanced, what changes do you foresee in average life expectancy? Can you apply Buettner's Blue Zone characteristics for different geographic and cultural regions of the country?

3. Since the population of older adults is larger than ever before, list three to five businesses that could profit from this. Explain why.

4. What are some ways the United States can adapt to a large number of older adults staying active longer?

Chapter 2

Diversity in American Society

CHAPTER OBJECTIVES

1. Consider the myriad diverse family forms and how they will affect the aging experience.

2. Have a basic understanding of postmodern theory.

3. Be able to describe how divorce and remarriage can affect grandparents.

4. List the aging family repercussions of 18 percent of females remaining childfree.

Cathy married in the late 1970s, along with many of her friends who were doing the same. She became a teacher; her husband became a professor. They had two boys and one girl. By the time the youngest child was nine, Cathy realized she was living a lie. She had always been attracted to women. After almost twenty years, she decided to end the marriage. Cathy and her husband parted amicably. They talked to the children together and told them that while the information about their mother was not a secret, it was a responsibility. Not everyone would handle the news as well as their own family did. Cathy and her ex-husband shared custody of their children while they were raising them. The children decided to continue to go to the church they were raised in because it was known for its acceptance and support of diversity—especially of same-sex couples. A couple of years later, when her ten-year-old was baptized, Cathy met Julie. After a year of dating, they wanted to move forward and went through premarital counseling. In the year 2000, they were married by an Episcopalian priest in an open ceremony. The priest said that she could perform the ceremony as long as the congregation could read responsively. In that way, the congregation married them rather than the priest officially marrying the couple, which was not legally allowed at the time. Cathy's children attended and read responsively in the beautiful ceremony. Today, Cathy and Julie state that they are happy empty-nesters. They are worried about many of the same things as others their age: Will the children find good jobs after college? Because of the economy, will Cathy and Julie have to work much longer to retire? Will they have pensions? Will good health allow them to go on mission trips together in retirement? Julie says she is worried about who will take care of her when she is older (she is almost a decade younger than Cathy), and points out that she never shared custody of the children. The grown children consider her family, but it is unclear if they would actually take care of her in old age, and she's not sure if she would want that anyway. Rather, she brings up a group of lesbian, earthy, older women who are aging together outside Denver, but then both she and Cathy laugh that off as being too weird for them. . . . Julie and Cathy say they identify themselves more as a couple with kids than as a gay couple. When asked what they want for the future:

> We just hope for good jobs and relationships for the kids, as well as mar-
> riages and benefits for people such as ourselves . . . and we are ready for
> grandchildren!

Chapter 2 is about the diversity of American families. The term families is used (instead of family) to express the view that there are many types of families in our ever-changing world. It focuses on the families of today and examines how interactions and circumstances within families change as people age. Diversity reflects the changing landscape of American families and how the many family forms will continue to grow in number and become more commonplace. It is also about the broader acceptance and visibility of many nontraditional family forms. Postmodern theory will be used in an attempt to show the existence of multiple realities in such a diverse array of familial possibilities. This chapter seeks to explain the changes we have undergone and will undergo in the future, and ultimately how these changes will affect the aging family.

Theory of Postmodern Complex Life

The term postmodern theory dates to the late nineteenth century, with many of this worldview's writings and theoretical developments stretching over the course of the twentieth century. Postmodern theory began as a social commentary on the fast societal and technical changes happening, as an alternative way of seeing social life. As Best and Kellner (1991) so eloquently wrote in their overview of postmodern theory:

> Dramatic changes in society and culture are often experienced as an in-
> tense crisis for those attached to the established ways of life and modes
> of thought. The breaking up of once stable social orders and patterns of
> thought frequently evokes a widespread sense of social incoherence, frag-
> mentation, chaos and disorder. The response is often despair and pessimism,
> panic and hyperbolic discourse, and desperate searches for solutions to the
> apparent crisis (p. viii).

Postmodern theory is a perspective for understanding the world and therefore does not lend itself to be tested easily. However, it is very useful to consider the world and its actors through its lens to help make sense of modern life with its array of familial arrangements. In today's society, daily survival is less of an issue for most in the Western world, and people can concentrate on building their lives in the ways they see fit. There is less pressure to live and behave a certain way, as our nation has become even more heterogeneous. The social order was first questioned through social changes, such as those brought about by the Women's Rights Movement, which have allowed many families to adopt new lifestyles that previously would have been lived only in secrecy or with the risk of stigmatization. In postmodernism, we choose our identities and our families, and create and re-create our lives.

There is relativism inherent to postmodernism, meaning that ideas are relational and no one idea (or family form or way of living) is better than another (White, Klein, and Martin 2015). Postmodern theory discusses multiple realities, identities, and ways of being, none of which are considered better than any other. Postmodern thought allows all situations to be considered real and equally valid. Pertaining to the family then, multiple family structures are held up as equal. There are many options and multiple truths.

Postmodernism can be used to explain why it is wrong to consider some family structures better than others. Under postmodernism, since all family structures are created by individuals and are equally important, voices that were previously subordinate (for instance, those of women of color) are given equal status to others (Hill Collins 2000).

Postmodern theory recognizes a diversity of realities operating at the same time. According to this understanding, all people experience their own individual and subjective reality, and all of these realities are to be equally valued. To relate to families and aging, each person experiences his or her situation of family and aging differently, and these realities are equally valued. Overarching, all-encompassing narratives and constructions of the way an aged person "should be" are not useful or truly representative of reality (Estes, Biggs, and Phillipson 2009). Individuals are left to construct their own identities as they age and designate their own roles within a family (Estes, Biggs, and Phillipson 2009). Complex social life is then made up of all of these realities.

One important part of understanding postmodern theory is being aware of and critically assessing who the producers of knowledge are. In science and academia, traditionally it has been male, especially white male, scientists and faculty who represent social discourse. It has been much the same in the media and politics, as well as in most aspects of social life (Hill Collins 2000). Now, as there are more previously underrepresented minority and female professionals, including in academia and the social sciences, multicultural sensitivity and cultural competence are seen as vital when studying diverse family situations (Boswell 2015). Diverse scholars ask diverse questions reflecting their own experiences, more suitable research methods are being developed, and new research and theories will emerge. Thus new truths will be named, and it will not always be just through the scientific route. In addition, new forms of social power, such as blogging or tweeting to large numbers of followers, will create new truths. Social media allows anyone to share their reality and put it out to the world without having professional credentials (Bareket-Bojmel, Moran, and Shahar 2016). Thus we all have a social audience, which gives new powers to those who previously had weak voices (Janeway 1975).

As we settle into the twenty-first century, family theory accepts these multiple realities and the relativism of different families, but believes that theoretically we can still draw upon an assortment of theories to understand family life (White, Klein, and Martin 2015). In other words, while not denying the veracity of postmodernism, we should not eliminate all ideas of theory and structure, or scientific research.

In sum, postmodern theory allows individuals and families to live and name their identities, family options, and realities of experience as equally valid to all others. Lived out, while all this diversity of family is experienced, future research should examine how it will play out both as families age but also as older cohorts are replaced by younger cohorts of individuals (Silverstein and Giarrusso 2010).

Increasing Diversity of Families

Modern versus Traditional

Families and family structure have changed considerably over time. Some are panicked over the changes and speak of the demise of American families (Coontz 2016). As stated in the above lengthy quote about postmodern theory, dramatic changes in society can lead to crisis, panic, and pessimism. Those who are worried about the retreat of traditional nuclear families are feeling this postmodern quandary. A debate in family research, as well is in the media and politics, is ongoing between those who are traditionalists and those with more liberal interpretations of family (Powell, Bolzendahl, Geist, and Steelman 2010; Widmer 2016).

Traditionalists state that the changes in the structure and function of the modern family are causing serious social problems. They believe that the traditional family (a nuclear family, defined as a first marriage with biological children) is the most stable one and best for society. Popenoe (1993) was one of the most well-known writers on the topic, and his work is still used today. His frequently cited argument is that there has been an unprecedented weakening of the American family as an institution since 1960. He writes that the functions of the family have disappeared and that families are smaller in size, less stable, and do not stay together. He worries that the individual has become more important than the bond of the family.

Few can argue with the reality of the changing family. However, Popenoe defines family through the lens of structural functionalism, and as such his definition revolves around the traditional functions of the family, many of which are no longer needed. He is concerned about reproduction and socialization of children occurring outside monogamy and the traditional family. He describes five dimensions of family decline: number of children, marital roles, family structure and marital dissolution, marriage, and nonfamily living (Popenoe

1993). All of these family dimensions have changed significantly. People have fewer children, gender roles are more fluid, divorce is common, marriage has declined, family structures are complicated, and singlehood is increasing. Since fewer families are nuclear and traditional, there are more family roles and pathways for aging family members.

Those with modern family lifestyles or beliefs do not deny the changing demographic trends, but say that such trends represent change, not decline. They argue that qualifying them as "decline" puts a negative ideological spin on the changes. They also argue that many of the changes are good, such as women's increased freedom to leave abusive marriages. A major proponent of this perspective is Judith Stacey (1998), author of "Good Riddance to 'the Family': A Response to David Popenoe" (Stacey 1993). She shared Popenoe's concern about the future of American families and children but pointed out that his definition of family as "a positivist, empirical institution, amenable to a structural-functional definition . . . a heterosexual, conjugal, [preferably patriarchal], nuclear, domestic unit" is ephemeral and prejudicial to diverse family forms (Stacey 1993). Modern historians and family theorists show that many so-called diverse family forms have always existed, just not with the same prevalence or freedom to be public about their living arrangements (Coontz 2016; Stacey 2011).

In the context of families and aging, some of the concerns are that with all the singlehood, never-marrieds, and single-parent families, the support

systems that families traditionally offer will no longer be available. With much smaller families, the psychological and physical needs of our aging parents and loved ones may not be met, as well as our own needs as we age. Along with the end of traditional families is the loosening of norms and obligations that were present in traditional kinship structures but that now must be negotiated in modern kinship.

Increasing Diversity of Realities

Much of late-twentieth-century and now twenty-first-century sociology of the family examined the changes from the so-called ideal nuclear family of the 1950s, and the beliefs it upheld, to the reality of modern families (Coontz 2016; Hill Collins 2000; Powell, Bolzendahl, Geist, and Steelman 2010; Stacey 1998; 2011). Sociologists began to point out that, already before WWII but especially after the post-war baby boom, families were not anymore simply a mother, father, and two or more children. Rather, the divorce rate began to climb, with a small peak post-war as the troops returned and couples who married rashly just before the war found out they did not get along. They also showed that we had a good deal of abandonment, in which there were single mothers living alone, as their husbands left and never returned. The social zeitgeist was still that of the traditional family, but social life had changed. The multiplicity of family realities, beyond the traditional first-time married couples with children, had expanded, and achieved greater—though certainly not total—acceptance (Coontz 2016).

Acceptance of the new family reality varies by type: for instance, delayed marriage and childbearing is generally lauded as a wise choice for many young people today. Young adults increasingly experience an extended and prolonged adolescence, in which they do not have children or get married at an early age. They are encouraged to pursue education and careers (Coontz 2016). Indeed, this experience too is a modern family form (delayed adulthood), and is promoted in U.S. society. As a consequence, some parents find themselves continuing to parent actively for children into their twenties. Thus the expectations of what is an ideal family and the ideal way to arrange family life has changed and is more open to many alternatives. Postmodern theory recognizes that every family arrangement is socially constructed and situated within the experience of those who live it.

Family life today, including cohabitation or same-sex marriage and partnership, is subject to a variety of opinions in terms of acceptance, and legal recognition (Powell, Bolzendahl, Geist, and Steelman 2010). Similarly, divorce and remarriage are very common, and LGBTQ experience is more accepted in U.S. society, and the associated stigma is gradually decreasing. One landmark study examined changes over time as to what Americans viewed as "family" (Powell, Bolzendahl, Geist, and Steelman 2010). It found that in studying people's attitudes toward eleven different types of families (such as two women with children; two women without children; woman with children; man with children; husband, wife, and children; and so on) there were three types of ways of thinking about families—exclusionists, moderates, and inclusionists. Exclusionists (38 percent in 2006) believed that only heterosexual married couples were family (but permitted exceptions for single parents to be considered family). They had much ambivalence regarding cohabitors with children, and did not allow other same-sex options to be included in what counts as family. Moderates (29 percent in 2006) allowed any relationship that had children to be a family, and finally inclusionists (33 percent in 2006) allowed each relationship structure to be a family. Thus about 60 percent of Americans were moderates or inclusionists. What was especially interesting about this study was the change from just three years before. The number of exclusionists dropped considerably just from 2003, and the number of inclusionists increased over these same years. Thus this work is prominent in showing large-scale changes over just a three-year period, leaving us to wonder how it will change in the next decades.

The Baby Boomers, who were born from 1946 to 1964, experienced the social norms and expectations of the 1950s' nuclear family (though it was not always the reality) (Coontz 2016). They also experienced the changes of the later twentieth century, namely the sweeping reforms of the Civil Rights Movement, the Women's Rights Movement, and the sexual revolution. They witnessed the integration of Blacks and Whites in American society, women entering the workforce en masse, the proliferation of divorce, and the legalization and availability of birth control, to name just a few changes that dramatically affected family life. As they age, many of these baby boomers see their own families living a contemporary lifestyle with loosened expectations of traditional family roles. Many have undergone dramatic shifts in their own family lives, such as Cathy and Julie from the beginning of this chapter. This generation had lower fertility rates than the generations before, and higher rates of divorce and remarriage, cohabitation, and prolonged singlehood as well. The next part of this chapter discusses the main trends that have changed the social landscape of families, and their implications for aging families.

Major Trends in Intimate Relationships: The Impact on Aging Families

In this section, major developments and trends in intimate relationships in the United States are reviewed. This chapter focuses on those trends that are most relevant to an aging society and discusses how they will affect families and family members as they grow older. Such trends include divorce and remarriage, stepfamilies, single parenthood, cohabiting, LGBTQ families, lifelong singles, childless couples, and a relatively new family form among older people in particular, **LATs** or those who are "living apart together" (Stewart 2007). There is increasing individualization of types of families (Widmer 2016). When reviewing all of these different family forms that are becoming increasingly common, it is useful to borrow an older term from Cherlin's (1978) concept of the family as an **incomplete institution**. Cherlin

iStock/myrrha

referred to remarriage and stepfamilies as an incomplete institution because they lacked the norms implicit in a first-married family. As discussed below, as families emerge in multiple forms, all interactions within a family need to be negotiated when traditional gender roles and/or family roles are not followed. These new family configurations require new roles (Widmer 2016). In families in later life, clashes between the "old" and "new" ways may occur more frequently than in the past.

Divorce

Divorce is common in the United States. By all accounts, the divorce rate peaked in the late 1970s and early 1980s and has remained relatively stable since then (Cherlin 1992; 2010a; Stewart 2007). There is some indication that the divorce rate is decreasing slightly, with the current estimate ranging between 40 and 50 percent of all unions (Cherlin 2010a). As such, there will be many older adults who have experienced either their parents' divorce or their own divorce. These families will create new bonds with new family members, while keeping ties with old family members. After a divorce, men and women experience different realities.

For women, the aftermath of divorce typically leads to the woman shouldering most of the childrearing alone and both partners experiencing a decrease in their household earnings (Stewart 2007). Estimates show that about 115,000 American women per year lose their private health insurance in the months following divorce (Lavelle and Smock 2012). The decrease in earnings and the stress of single-parenting can take a toll on women.

For men, divorce may offer more freedom. Rarely do men have custody of children. More typically, they are paying child support through much of their work lives, but they are not guaranteed a close relationship with their children. They are also more likely to start new families that have a higher likelihood of dissolution than a first marriage. Men are more likely to lose contact with their children over time (Goldscheider 2000).

Divorce affects aging families in many ways. It not only affects the couple who divorced, but also their parents, their children, their siblings, and so on. After a divorce, the parents-in-law often lose interaction with their son- or daughter-in-law. Sometimes this is met with relief, other times it is met with sorrow. More than once you may hear from family members: "I liked her [the daughter-in-law] more than I liked my son!" When a couple had children, the divorce is more complex and affects the parents-in-law more, as they are still grandparents. This results in negotiating whether and how often grandparents and grandchildren will interact. Since children usually go with the mother, there is usually greater interaction with the maternal grandparents. Grandparents help with instrumental and emotional support after divorce, and many grandparents also help with the financial aspects of childrearing (Goldscheider 2000). Aging parents of sons struggle in an attempt to maintain contact with their grandchildren. This is especially difficult when the former daughter-in-law remarries (Goldscheider 2000; Stewart 2007). In that case, the grandchildren now have a new stepfather, and access may be further limited. Ultimately, due to various divorce situations there are increasing generations of men with weak links to their biological children after divorce (Goldscheider 2000). As men age, the lack of bonds with children can be problematic because of regrets and loneliness. As Goldscheider (2000) wrote, "The only enduring family tie many [divorced] men have is to their own parents, while women create new, enduring bonds—to their children" (p. 530). These trends may change as fathers' roles continue to change to more active parenting. More men have taken custody of their children after divorce, and that will affect families differently in later life. Grandparenting is discussed in greater detail later in the book.

Another rising trend is divorce among middle-aged and older adults, the so-called gray divorce. The divorce rate among those aged 50 and older has doubled between 1990 and 2010 (Brown and Lin 2012:731). There are many reasons for the rising divorce rate in this age group. Some documented reasons include the following: more people in less stable, higher-order marriages (second marriages and beyond), shifting cultural norms and the weakening of marriage as an institution, more women in the labor force (thus with more autonomy), economic disadvantage, marital quality, and finally increasing life expectancy, which means more years of exposure to the risk of divorce (Brown and Lin 2012; Lin, Brown, Wright, and Hammersmith 2016). While men and women are about equally likely to divorce, there are some differences by race and ethnicity. In their article, Brown and Lin (2012) find that African Americans have the highest likelihood of divorce in later life, followed by Hispanics, and then Whites. They did not examine other groups. Interestingly, they point out that while the national trend of divorce is decreasing, it is rising among those aged 50 and over, a cohort that previously had very low rates of divorce.

Remarriage and Stepfamilies

There has also been an increase in remarriage and the reconstitution of families (Cherlin 1992, Stewart 2007; Lin, Brown, and Cupka 2017). With the high divorce rate comes a high level of second, third, or higher remarriages. We are optimistic about remarriage. Though cohabitation has already been around for many years, moving in with a new partner (cohabiting) is on the increase as well (Cherlin 2010b). When women have younger or school-age children, they typically bring their biological children into their new marriages; it is rare for men to bring their biological children into the new marriages (although this too is happening more frequently than before). Subsequently, many experience a birth with their new partners after the remarriage, thus increasing the members of the stepfamily and creating half-brothers and half-sisters. Since men are less likely to be with their children, it affects them differently. Stepfamilies are thus a very common occurrence in U.S. society: an estimated one-third of children will live in a stepparent home before the age of eighteen (Parke 2007), and 50 percent will have a stepparent at some point in their lifetime (Stewart 2007:21). In sum, stepfamilies come together and experience a new realm of family possibilities. Many older adults have remarried or repartnered. According to the study by Lin, Brown, and Cupka (2017), two of every five couples with individuals aged 51 years or older are in stepfamilies. Many bring children from first marriages and prior relationships into the marriages.

Men are more often nonresidential fathers (Goldscheider 2000). They may have biological children from previous unions, and then they may have children in the next marriage as well from birth or through their new partner. This complexity of family relations ultimately affects the fathers' choices and their children's choices over time (Hofferth and Goldscheider 2010). Fathers may decide to stay geographically close to their children, provide financial support, and continue parenting children from their first marriage or relationship. In a remarriage, men also become stepparents to children that are not biologically their own. The level the father actively parents in the new relationship then varies by age of the children, expectations of discipline, amount of parenting by the biological parent, and stepchild's gender, to name a few factors. Depending on the constellation of circumstances, fathers and stepfathers continue to actively engage in the lives of their children and stepchildren. However, this is variable based on many factors including financial support, geography, emotional attachment, ability of the mother to raise children, and so on. For women, it is much more common to remain engaged with children over the entire life course.

In most relationships, women generally are the primary caretaker of children in divorce and remarriage. They also take on most of the emotional and kin-keeping labor in their new family. They often coordinate and balance the needs of their ex-husbands and the ex-grandparents' desire to see the children. This walk between their new and their old family is difficult and can be a strain on women and families in general. While this puts stress on women, it also provides them with many social connections and relationships that can be protective in later life. Older women with children are less likely to be isolated due to these family connections.

Stepfamilies create a greater complexity of family relationships, financial strains, and lack of norms—problems that disproportionately fall on women and lead to stress (Avison, Ali, and Walters 2007; Cherlin 1978; 1992; 2010b; Stewart 2007). They also offer a chance of hope, happiness, and stability in life. As time goes by, in these new unions, men and women sometimes successfully and sometimes unsuccessfully maintain ties with their children and extended families. Visitations and custody must be negotiated when children are involved. Figure 2.1 shows a hypothetical divorced couple in which both partners remarried. The biological father from the first (focal) marriage remarries, and continues to be active in his daughters' lives. In this family tree, starting from the bottom, the focal mother has three children, two daughters from the first marriage, and one son from her remarriage. The daughters are half-sisters to the son. When examining the middle row, that is, the parent generation, we see the focal union that ended in divorce, as shown by the equal sign with a slash ≠. Each parent remarried. The focal father did not have more children. Now, when you look at the top row, we see all the grandparents. In this scenario, there are four sets or eight grandparents. Think of the complexity of arranging family reunions. This is a time when children with four sets of grandparents may be requested to attend two or more Thanksgiving dinners in order to visit all families. It is plausible that for a daughter's major event (such as a wedding), all eight grandparents could attend. Certainly grandparents 3–6 would be in attendance, and likely grandparents 1–6, while grandparents 7 and 8 would be

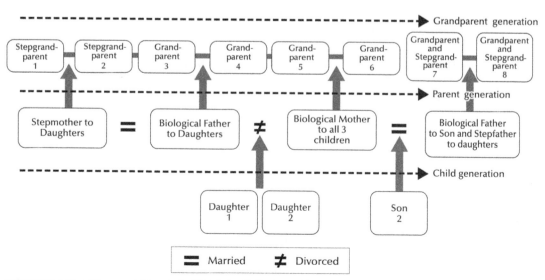

FIGURE 2.1 One Divorced Couple in Which Both Partners Remarried

invited if the daughter/sister was close to the half-brother. Does this sound confusing? It should, and this is a fairly simple diagram of a remarriage.

All of these complexities in family arrangements affect later life. Most notably, new constellations of family arrangements develop in which family calls upon one another more by choice, rather than need, obligation, or tradition. This concept is known as the **latent kin matrix**. This matrix refers to all the relationships that one has in their family that spans over many generations and various kin structures (Riley 1983; Riley and Riley 1993). The matrix of family relations is latent, and the ties can be enacted for support. Varying levels of closeness emerge among all the different possibilities of stepchildren, half-siblings, stepparents, and so on, and people decide which connections to mobilize. Increasingly, older adults also find themselves in more complex sets of family relations (Sweeney 2010). In addition, the emotions and sense of obligation vary depending on factors such as how the family got along, how long they lived together, and their geographic proximity (Stewart 2007). For instance, some half-siblings may have known one another since they were two years old and never considered themselves anything but siblings, whereas others may be spaced twenty years apart and have very little in common. These are the types of issues that come to bear in later life when people may seek out family or may simply need help (Carstensen 1992). Older people will have less clear family obligations and connections. Pursuit of family relationships will need to be more enacted or purposeful for those who lived in stepfamilies, experienced divorce, cohabited, or remained single. One can no longer rely on the traditional norms and obligations of a family who only experienced one lifelong marriage.

Single-Parenting

Single-parenting is very common today. For those born in the 1960s and before, single-parenting was often due to a death in the family (Coontz 2016). The divorce rate had not yet peaked, and most older people of today grew up in two-parent families. Those born in the twenty-first century, however, will have lived in a very different society, with many more single-parent households. Of the 11 million families with children under age 18, and no spouse present, the majority are single-mother families (8.5 million). Single-father families comprise the remaining 2.5 million of single-parent families (U.S. Census Bureau 2016b).

About 40 percent of all births today are to unmarried women (and this varies greatly by race and ethnicity). For unmarried women the statistics are as follows: Hispanic (53 percent), Black or African American (70 percent), American Indian or Native American (65 percent), Asian and Pacific Islander (16 percent), and White (36 percent) (Martin et al. 2017). Thus the experience of single-parenting is much more common among some groups as opposed to others. This means that living in a single-parent household for some time during childhood has become a mainstream experience, and we know that about 50 percent of children will have a stepparent at some point in their lifetime (Stewart 2007:21). Teachman, Tedrow, and Crowder

(2000:1240) found that among African American families in particular, nearly one in three women may never marry. In addition, while the proportion of children ever living with a single parent has increased, the number of African American children who live with two parents (biological, adopted, or stepparents) dropped from under 60 percent in 1970 to 36 percent in 1998. Also, nearly 50 percent of White children and two-thirds of African American children are likely to spend at least part of their childhood in a single-parent family. Thus, there are differences in the experience of living as a single-parent, and/or living in a household as a child with only one parent at home.

Most older adults of today were not raised by single parents, nor were they single parents themselves (Martin et al. 2017). However, not long from now, we will have cohorts of individuals who were raised by single parents and/or are aging as single parents. This may lead to a stronger connection with, and dependence on, the immediate family member—that is, the child (or children) who were in the household—as there may not be a partner on whom to rely for support. In addition, there will be more single-parenthood generations within the same family, resulting in predominantly maternal kinship networks of support. This is especially true among African American women (Hill Collins 2000). Additionally, growing up in a household without a father makes it much more likely for both men and women to become parents earlier in life (Hofferth and Goldscheider 2010), thus perpetuating this cycle.

Single parenthood can be stressful. It is associated with psychological distress (Mirowsky and Ross 2003a) and poor subjective health (McMunn, Bartley, and Kuh 2006), in large part because of economic hardship (Avison, Ali, and Walters 2007; Mirowsky and Ross 2003a). Those who were single mothers are more economically fragile in older age as well, due to a lifetime of disadvantage (Loue and Sajatovic 2008). Families should think about older women in this position, as they are less likely to have the financial reserves that a married woman would have in old age.

Cohabitation

Cohabitation has always been practiced to some degree in the United States; people have been living together without marrying since the country was formed. Common law marriage regulations directly address cohabitors. What has changed is the growth in cohabitation. Many single parents are actually cohabiting (Cherlin 2010a). About 20 percent of nonmarital births experience the support of cohabitation (Cherlin 2010a). With or without children, there has been a major rise in cohabitation. **Cohabitation** involves two unmarried individuals, either of same or opposite sex, who reside together in an intimate relationship. Currently, about one-half to two-thirds of the young population (aged 19–44) have cohabited (Kennedy and Bumpass 2008). Among older people, marital unions are decreasing, as marriage is no longer the only option for people who want to live together in an intimate relationship. In 2007, more than two million older couples (aged 50 and older) reported to be cohabitating (Stepler 2017). That number has risen to 4 million older adults, which equates to about 4 percent of the population aged 50 and over cohabiting. Thus, while still not a large share of cohabitors, the trend is increasing. Most of these older adults who are cohabiting have been divorced (Stepler 2017). Among those aged 65 and older, 3.3 percent of women and 4.6 percent of men were in cohabiting relationships (Cherlin 2010a), showing that cohabitation also does occur in this oldest demographic group. Figure 2.2 shows trend data of the increase in cohabitation among those currently cohabiting aged 55–64, compared to all ages of cohabitation. In this later middle-aged group, we see a steady rise of those cohabiting from 1996 to 2012 from 1.1 percent to 2.8 percent. This rise is in tandem compared to all cohabitors, which rose from 3.8 percent to 6 percent (those who were currently cohabiting at the time of the survey). Thus, regardless of age, cohabitation is on the increase in general.

Cohabitation is not simply the same as marriage. Marriage buffers stress, and provides a path for social connections, among other things. In short, marriage fulfills many social-psychological needs of humans (Waite and Gallagher 2000). Cohabitation does not appear to fulfill these roles in the same manner, with cohabitors having worse health on average and more depressive symptoms (Brown et al. 2005; Brown et al. 2006; Cherlin 2013; Liu, Reczek, and Brown 2013). There are substantial differences between cohabitors, remarried couples, married couples, divorced couples, never-married individuals, and widowed individuals in relation to demographics, economic resources, physical health, mental health, and social ties (Brown et al. 2005; Brown et al. 2006). Research shows that cohabitors exhibit greater

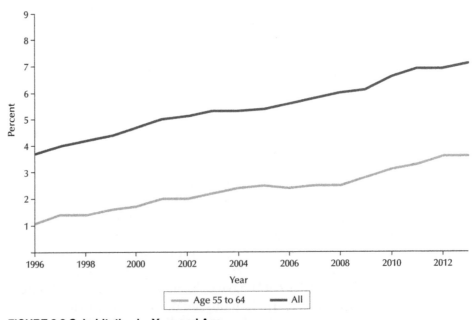

FIGURE 2.2 Cohabitation by Year and Age
Source: Based on microdata from Current Population Survey, Stanford CPI

levels of depressive symptoms than married couples but fewer than divorced couples (Brown et al. 2005), mostly mirroring the depressive symptoms of the unpartnered. Between genders, women in cohabitating relationships derive substantially fewer benefits than men, but men report higher scores of depression (Brown et al. 2006). Since research suggests that cohabitors are not receiving the same psychosocial benefits as married couples, the question arises as to what the differences between the two populations are. Of course, one factor to consider is the potential **selection bias or effect** regarding who cohabits. A selection bias is a nonrandom event or pattern that occurs among people, leading to a misleading conclusion. For instance, a classic example of selection bias is in survey research. In a survey, a sample is selected. This group of people will be asked a series of questions. In our example, when these people are asked about their income, let's say those with the lowest 10 percent of income refuse to answer the question. As a result, the results from the sample are biased. The sample appears to have a higher average income because the poorest people in the sample did not include their income. Applying selection effect here then, in marriage versus cohabitation, there is a nonrandom group of people who are more likely to cohabit than to marry. Those who are more liberal and less religious are more likely to cohabit. Younger people compared to older adults are more likely to cohabit as well (Stepler 2017). In addition, those with poor mental health may be more likely to cohabit than marry (DeKlyen, Brooks-Gunn, McLanahan, and Knab 2006). However, it is not cohabitation that causes behaviors or outcomes (for example, greater depressive symptomatology) but rather that those who cohabit may come into the relationship with more depression, or that they are not as attractive on the marriage market and are pushed into cohabitation. Indeed, Brown (2005) found that among middle-aged and older adults, male cohabitors are in poorer health, suggesting that women may be willing to live with, but not necessarily marry, men in poorer physical condition. Trends of cohabitation also show ethnic and racial differences, with African Americans being more likely to cohabit than their White counterparts (Brown et al. 2006). Among older people, cohabitation is sometimes used for economic reasons, for instance, keeping Social Security benefits intact. Sometimes cohabitation replaces marriage in older adults due to emotional reasons, such as not wanting to move or create a new home life, or let adult children know there is a new relationship and so on. As the cohabitating population continues to grow, the diversity within it will increase as well.

A new relationship style is emerging beyond marriage and cohabitation, especially for older people: living apart together, or LAT. The term was first introduced in Denmark in 1978, but has taken on more interest in recent years (Silverstein and Giarrusso 2010). A LAT is a couple of same or opposite sex who has an intimate relationship but lives in separate homes. At times they may live together, but they always maintain separate homes (De Jong Gierveld and Peeters 2003). Sometimes the homes are close by, as in the same city, and sometimes they are not. However, the individuals in the relationship are perceived as a couple and treated as such (Trost 2010). LAT relationships are common among those who are older and were previously married (Stewart 2007).

Research finds that no-longer-married older adults (aged 55 and over when their marriages ended) are three times more likely to form LAT relationships than younger adults (De Jong Gierveld 2004). People over fifty may choose a LAT relationship because they don't want to introduce children to new homes if there are still children at home. In later life, they may not want to co-reside because of their caregiving situation (either giving care to or receiving care from family members) or because they do not want to physically combine the contents of their homes into one (Trost 2010). They may also want independence in their day-to-day activities or be concerned about combining finances or losing pensions, inheritances, or Social Security benefits (De Jong Gierveld and Peeters 2003). Some of the issues of LATs overlap with those in divorce, stepfamilies, aging, independence, career, and the complexity of finances in retirement. LATs even speak to our Western lifestyle, in which aging is associated with such an accumulation of stuff that much of the work in the end-of-life is the transference of wealth and accumulated goods to other people and generations. Some LATs choose to live apart to avoid physically combining their possessions.

While almost no research exists on the topic, some evidence points to LATs' relationships being less happy and supportive, compared to marriage, remarriage, and cohabiting (Lewin 2017). In this comparison of relationships, it may be because LATs have the easiest potential dissolution (they already live apart) that they are the least committed. This is a new area of study, and we will learn more about LATs in the future. When examining all the different types of families, it is always useful to examine how they fare in terms of mental health and relationship quality.

Singlehood

While a small percentage of the population has always remained single, historically this has been attributed to something considered undesirable on the marriage market—such as disease or mental health problems. Some women became "spinsters" and some men remained "bachelors" due to lack of interest, choices, or desirability. Even geography and isolation mattered—as with, for instance, the isolated fisherman of the Northeast or the daughter of a farmer in Iowa with few men living around her. Lifelong singlehood was an option (and still is) for some clergy and for very wealthy individuals who have the financial means to remain single. Historically, in the days of slavery, many African Americans remained single during slavery because in some cases they were not allowed to marry (Meadow and Stacey 2006). Some who considered themselves gay did not marry—but most did marry and even had children back then. Finally, among a few upper-class men and women, some eccentrics and intellectuals chose to live a life outside of the norms of society. For instance, a few famous late-nineteenth- and early-twentieth-century female artists, writers, explorers, and scientists remained single. However, most people married and had children.

It is estimated that about 10 percent of the population is remaining single (Wang and Parker 2014), as defined by being never married. However, by 2030, an estimated 25 percent of those aged 45–54 will be single, based on current trends. This is truly an abrupt change and this demographic is growing quickly. With the legalization of same-sex unions, perhaps more will get married than was anticipated. As the expectation of marriage has decreased, the acceptance of remaining single for one's entire life has increased (Marsh et al. 2007). It is socially acceptable and desirable by some not only to *not* marry, but also to not cohabit with anyone.

As always, some people will remain single because they are not highly competitive on the marriage market. What is new is the proportion of people who will remain single by choice. Additionally, sometimes singlehood occurs by circumstance, as when people never find someone with whom they want to share their life, or if they have low education and skills, which suppresses job and marriage prospects. With the stigma of remaining single waning, some may choose singlehood in order to fully devote their lives to their work. The contingent of African American professionals remaining single has been termed by some sociologists as the "Love Jones" cohort, after the movie and television shows highlighting the new demographic trend in the African American middle class of being single and living alone (Marsh et al. 2007), which is seen as an avenue to middle-class and upper-middle-class standing. On the other hand, some African Americans choose not to marry due to poor prospects and a society that disadvantages African American men in particular (Hill Collins 2000; Raley, Sweeney, and Wondra 2015).

Remaining single for a lifetime has profound implications on the aging family. Many who remain single will also be childless. Most people who age and develop health issues receive support from family members, in particular a spouse or partner and children. This support may include phone calls and visits, but may also include instrumental help such as trips to the doctor and the grocery store. Those with few family ties have to seek help from others—friends, neighbors, or siblings. If we think about family trends such as reduced fertility, childlessness, and increased singlehood, we get a picture of an increased number of old people with very few ties to family who might provide social support and assistance. One consequence of singlehood is lack of caregiving in later life. We know that the most likely nursing home residents are those with few to no familial attachments (Buys et al. 2013; Luppa et al. 2010).

Childlessness

Being childless is not a new phenomenon. There has always been a proportion of the population who was either voluntarily or involuntarily childless. What has changed is the increasing percentage of those who will be childless in the future. One study analyzing the National Longitudinal Surveys data found that in 2002, 12 percent of women ages 40–44 were childless, as compared to 9 percent in 1982. These women were more likely to work full-time and to have higher education (Abma and Martinez 2006). Currently,

Childfree by Choice

Some people choose to be childless and are happy with this choice. Several such groups exist on the internet. This is how one of them describes themselves:

> We are a group of adults who all share at least one common desire: we do not wish to have children of our own. We are teachers, doctors, business owners, authors, computer experts—you name it.

We choose to call ourselves "childfree" rather than "childless," because we feel the term "childless" implies that we're missing something we want—and we aren't. We consider ourselves childFREE—free of the loss of personal freedom, money, time and energy that having children requires.

(http://www.childfree.net, retrieved October 13, 2016)

about 18 percent of all U.S. women aged 40–44 are childless (Monte and Ellis 2014). This percentage is expected to grow as more women feel free to remain childless and to pursue careers and other interests with less stigma than ever before. The term *childless* is the most commonly used; however, more recently the term *childfree* has been introduced. Childfree better expresses the voluntary nature of remaining without children. The internet has several places for those who choose a childfree lifestyle to congregate. As the box above shows, those who are childfree express clearly their comfort with such a decision. They do not want to be pitied. They are not sad they will not have children. Rather, they value their freedom and enjoy being childless.

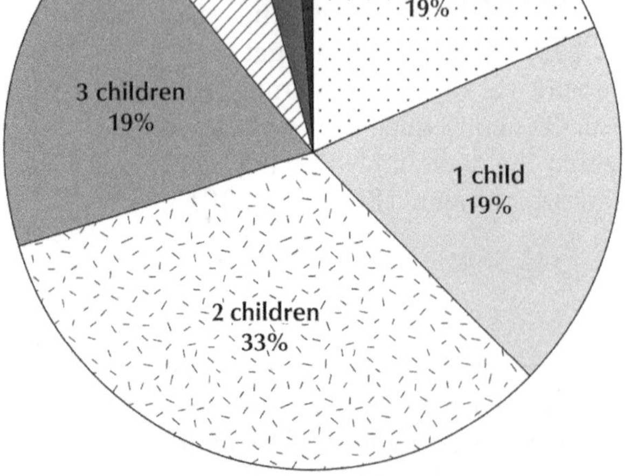

Those without children may love children, but still not have their own. Sometimes this is by choice, as described in the box. Other times it is by circumstance, for instance, when a couple waits so long to have children that when they finally try they are unable to get pregnant. Involuntary infertility may also be a result of being separated over the years, as in the case of military families in which a soldier is on multiple deployments for many years with infrequent visits back home, or when couples have jobs that keep them in different geographical locations.

Figure 2.3 shows 2010 data from the Current Population Survey 2010

FIGURE 2.3 Number of Children Ever Born to Women Aged 40–44, 2010
Source: Based on data from U.S. Census Bureau, Current Population Survey, June 2010

and shows the number of children ever born to women aged 40–44. Most childbearing has been completed by these ages. Nineteen percent of the female population was childless at this time, and 18 percent had only one child. Thirty-three percent of the population had two children. Thus, 70 percent of the female population had two children or fewer. An additional 19 percent had three children. After that, the total number of children drops significantly, with the remaining 11 percent having four or more children (with most of those—7 percent—having four children).

DINKS

The term Double Income No Kids (DINKS) is a popular way to convey the idea of wealth that couples amass when they do not have children. DINKS are typically younger, high-SES couples with professional jobs. When both partners work and do not have children, they are able to use all their income for themselves or put it away in savings. Many couples who are now DINKS remain childless, and this can pay off financially. One study (Plotnick 2009) found that married couples without children had slightly more income in later life, and about 5 percent more wealth than married couples with children. Among unmarried men and women, there was an even greater difference in wealth between those unmarried individuals without children compared to those with children (Plotnick 2009). Remaining childless is a strong predictor of wealth accumulation (Keister 2007; Koropeckyj-Cox 2007; Plotnick 2009), and can pay dividends in nicer homes, greater savings, and more economic freedom in later life. However, transferring one's wealth is an issue, as there are no heirs. It is likely that special-interest groups and charities will become the recipients of the estates of childless people who have no heirs and no immediate family to whom they may leave their possessions.

When a larger proportion of a population remains childless, this raises questions about who will care for older adults, since children typically help their parents in later life. As with those who remain single, those without children are more likely to be alone when they need assistance in old age. Traditionally, having children was a form of insurance that someone would be there to act as a caregiver. One may picture a lonely widow or widower without any family. However, research shows there is a selection effect and that childless individuals are not more depressed, lonely, or isolated. It appears that those who don't have children are better at forging nonfamilial ties throughout their lives, including later in life. They also have more disposable income (Silverstein and Giarrusso 2010). Thus, they create

Family decals are popular and show various family compositions. This person understands what it means to be a DINK. This sticker depicts a couple together with lots of money rather than showing them with their children and pets. Photo by the author a social support network to counteract the fact that they don't have children. Indeed, research shows that in later life, empty-nesters (whose children have left the home) do not benefit from having had children. For example, they do not have less current depression than nonparents (Evenson and Simon 2005; Zhang and Hayward 2001). This is likely due to the adaptability of nonparents, who have a broader social network than parents. However, research has found a possible gender difference. Childless divorced, widowed, and never-married men were more depressed than childless women in these same situations (Zhang and Hayward 2001). As will be discussed later in the book, women are better than men at creating and maintaining friendships and a social support system. Thus, perhaps it is more important for men to have the social insurance of children, unless they become experts at creating and maintaining social networks.

LGBTQ Families

LGBTQ is an acronym that stands for lesbian, gay, bisexual, transgender, and queer. "LGB" represents a continuum of sexualities and preferences with which people identify—lesbian, gay, or bisexual. These identities can shift over the life course. One's sexual identity is considered fluid, and a very individual experience. Young people may know from early on that they are gay, or they may identify always as heterosexual or cisgender. They may engage in same-sex intimate relationships, but still not identify as gay or lesbian. Or they may engage in same-sex intimate relationships and identity as lesbian or gay. Still others do not limit intimate relationships to same or different sex relationships, and identify as bisexual. Transgender refers to someone who has or is transitioning from male-to-female, or female-to-male, or who is transitioning to something other than what they were assigned at birth (Cruz 2014). Finally, queer has multiple meanings but can represent anyone who rejects the gender binary and sees themselves on the continuum of sexual identity and expression. It also means questioning to some, meaning someone is trying to figure out their sexual identity. While the common norm and experience for families in most of U.S. society is a heterosexual union, the possibility of living and publicly being out in an LGBTQ family has increased greatly, and is growing. Same-sex marriage as a right-to-marry was embraced in the executive office during Barack Obama's presidency. In his second inaugural speech in 2013, President Obama stated:

> Our journey is not complete until our gay brothers and sisters are treated like anyone else under the law—for if we are truly created equal, then surely the love we commit to one another must be equal as well.

While many Americans applauded this bold statement, others sat stunned and felt that it was not honoring their religion or their belief that marriage is only intended as a union between one man and one woman (Camila 2013). It was the first time a sitting president publicly supported legalization of same-sex marriage (Gates 2013; Liu, Reczek, and Brown 2013). No one could deny the boldness of the president making a pro-gay statement regarding legalized unions. Then in 2015, the U.S. Supreme Court decided that same-sex marriages would be legal throughout the United States (Gay Marriage 2015). Celebrations quickly ensued across the nation, with the slogan "Love Wins!" posted on social media and about one million Facebook users adopting a gay pride color flag wash across their pictures within the first hour of the Supreme Court decision (Matias 2015). Same-sex marriages are on the rise, and policies are changing across workplaces, granting economic rights to same-sex unions. Equal rights under the law allow gay and lesbian couples to enjoy more freedoms, including marriage, childbearing, adoption, and legal rights at death. However, cultural changes have lagged, with couples reporting trouble getting marriage licenses in some states, families still not supportive, and adoption agencies refusing to work with LGBTQ couples, to name a few of the problems encountered.

Individuals are more likely to live in a family life of their preference. As awareness and acceptance increases, transgender individuals will have more freedom, both to transition and to continue to live and work in the same areas where they lived and worked before transitioning. However, transgender individuals still experience the greatest amount of discrimination and higher-than-average rates of both violence and suicide, especially among people of color (Stotzer 2009).

Research finds that lesbian and gay relationships are not that different from heterosexual relationships in terms of creating and sustaining the relationship (Patterson 2000). In addition, the legal status of a civil union is helpful for the mental health of same-sex spouses (LeBlanc, Frost, and Bowen 2018). However, among LGBTQ individuals age 50 and older, many have previously had heterosexual relationships. With changing social norms, some people are transitioning into other relationships that better represent their sexual identities (Moore and Stambolis-Ruhstorfer 2013). For instance, they may move from a heterosexual marriage with children to a same-sex partnership and marriage. With each decade of change, more people are able to openly live the life they choose. These trends in social change underscore postmodern ideas of multiple options and choices for the identity that one is creating. Younger people are more open to accepting same-sex unions as families than their elders (Powell, Bolzendahl, Geist, and Steelman. 2010). As each subsequent age cohort replaces the next cohort, more acceptance toward same-sex marriage is expected.

Based on current knowledge and a review of the literature, Fredriksen-Goldsen and Muraco (2010) have tried to estimate the proportion of the older population that identifies as lesbian, gay, or bisexual. They estimate that about 1 to 3 million LGB individuals in the United States are older than sixty-five years of age. Estimates then project 2 to 6 million LGB individuals by the year 2030 (Fredriksen-Goldsen and Muraco 2010), so there is an expected increase. Currently it is difficult to estimate the number of LGBTQ individuals in the United States.

Aging LGBTQ individuals experience many of the same aging family issues as those who have not lived an LGBTQ experience. However, older LGBTQ individuals do encounter some specific issues. Since they historically did not have access to all of the financial, social, and other support services available to heterosexuals, they may be a population needing special assistance. LGBTQ adults experience higher levels of discrimination, and there is still the possibility of stigma and trouble with social support services for older LGBTQ adults (Fredriksen-Goldsen and Muraco 2010; Grollman 2014). Some of these problems—such as lack of health insurance, nonautomatic same-sex partner next-of-kin status for hospital visits, and medical decision-making—are beginning to be addressed as laws change. Others are more informal, such as being treated respectfully at a restaurant. Transgender and gender-nonconforming individuals may be especially likely to postpone health treatment due to stigma and discrimination (Cruz 2014). This becomes more problematic in older adults who may need more medical care.

Older LGBTQ adults tend to have fewer adult children who can eventually engage in caretaking, compared to their heterosexual counterparts. They are more likely to be at risk for greater isolation, and may not have as many potential family members to care for them (Hash and Mankowski 2017). They may also have special social support needs in later life. As a consequence, there is a call for more LGBTQ retirement communities (Fredriksen-Goldsen and Muraco 2010), especially for the oldest LGBTQ adults who were raised in a time when they may have lived most (if not all) of their lives "in the closet." Some of these communities already exist, such as developments in Boston, San Francisco, Santa Fe, and Palm Springs (McHugh and Larson-Keagy 2005). These communities facilitate social lives and social support among an accepting community. LGBTQ older adults are often good at creating families of choice (described in the next section) and, as such, since these are discretionary and not obligatory family roles,

iStock/StephM2506

caregiving may not be as much of a burden (Hash and Mankowski 2017). They have also been found to participate in more formal and informal end-of-life planning, in part to offset any possible discrimination within their families or legal trouble (Thomeer, Connelly, Reczek, and Umberson 2017).

Families of Choice

All of these trends—remaining childless, living apart together, staying single, divorcing, remarrying, living as DINKS, and forming same-sex unions—point to a surge in families of choice; that is, people are constructing families with those they want to be with, regardless of blood or marriage. In the LGBTQ community this is typically called **family of choice** (Weston 1997), whereas more traditionally, and especially in African American families, the term **fictive kin** has been used to underscore what many people may have considered family (Hill Collins 2000). In African American families in particular, fictive kin have been relied upon, sometimes due to historical oppression and a lack of availability of mothers, fathers, or grandparents, to take care of a child. Fictive kin, that is, neighbors or friends, have become family and have taken care of children, providing love, shelter, structure, a home, financial support, and nourishment (Hill Collins 2000). Families of choice is a similar concept, but it better describes how obligatory ties toward family have eroded. Families of choice are created when people choose their families based more on love and friendship than obligation. Thus, families of choice also describes LGBTQ families that have social support networks, and that share holidays and life's milestones together. Family of choice is different from one's **family of origins**, that is, the family into which a person is born. As obligations loosen, and families are more transient and flexible, families of choice may become more important than families of origin. In the aging family we will see many more open renditions of various family arrangements. Since the family is a major place for caretaking as people grow older, these family structures and processes will become relevant in later life. With the increase of families of choice, in matters of caretaking we will see an expansion of the definition of family beyond blood, marriage, and adoption.

Biracial and Multiracial/Multiethnic Families

As discussed in chapter 1, the fastest growing group in our population is that of biracial and multiracial families (Jones and Bullock 2012). One cannot write a common theme about these families. Their experiences of aging differ greatly. Sometimes they forge new family ways and traditions, blending cultures and experiences from different families. Other times, it is a difficult melding of cultures and frustration, as families try to stay emotionally close amid geographical distance, different religious traditions, and different cultural beliefs. In multiracial and multiethnic families, there are risks of not sharing beliefs regarding how to raise children, how to take care of parents, what level of interaction with grandchildren is appropriate, and what religious beliefs and customs are important. Race and ethnicity and related cultural and religious practices provide a framework for the organization of family life. Shared cultural understandings help people organize their thoughts about how often to visit and see family, how involved family members should be in each other's lives, and the likelihood of their living together. In multiethnic families, little can be taken for granted in terms of traditions and expectations (Maynigo 2017).

These changes will be difficult for some older couples, as it is increasingly common for their children to have partners, spouses, and grandchildren from diverse races and ethnicities, cultures, and religions. Adopting a multicultural outlook will help with adaptation (Dilworth-Anderson and Cohen 2009). They will need to adjust to new ideas to maintain positive family relationships. All major family events, such as births, deaths, and weddings, are experienced with different traditions. This multiculturalism will aid in adapting and creating new family rituals, especially in an era of declining religiosity among younger people. In concordance with postmodern beliefs, no one culture is superior to another.

Religiosity

The United States is experiencing decreasing religiosity (Pew 2015). The Pew religious landscape survey shows that the Christian share of the population is declining, with an increase in those stating they are atheist or agnostic. While the drop in religiosity is most apparent among the younger population, it is occurring across all age groups, among African Americans, whites, and Asians, and for both men and women. The survey finds that our nation is still predominantly Christian, with about seven in ten Americans identifying as such, but the change over time reflects an overall decrease in Christianity. There is a generational difference between younger and older family members and religion that will affect family life. Much of the change we will see in the future will be due to cohort replacement, in which the younger generation replaces the older generation. One countervailing trend is that the Muslim population is growing around the world, and increased immigration to the United States from Muslim countries is also noted. Muslim families generally have more traditional attitudes toward families and women (Pew 2011; 2015). We may also see increasing polarization of the religious versus the nonreligious in the United States (Pew 2012).

Traditional Pulls

Concurrently, there are some traditional pulls on families that will counteract the increasing diversity of the United States. The movement toward traditionalism will affect the way families interact and age in the future. One such trend impacting families is intensive mothering, and the increasing emphasis we have put on parenting children into their midtwenties.

Intensive mothering requires families (especially mothers) to invest their time and resources into creating "superchildren" who are competitive and exposed to many different activities and sports. The phenomenon of intensive mothering puts undue stress on women and children (Hays 1996). As children get older, they are driven around to multiple activities and sports, doing their homework between activities and late at night. It has become so common that the American Academy of Pediatrics (AAP) has taken note, recommending that parents be careful not to overschedule their children as such stress restricts the imagination and results in stifled creativity during adulthood (Ginsburg et al. 2007). Children are overburdened with activities and lessons. Over time, intensive mothering may turn into helicopter parenting, in which older parents continue to actively parent their older teens and twenty-something children, even engaging in their college education. This trend of extended parenting will be discussed later in the book. Many grandparents have also become involved in helping grandchildren get to all of their activities, while single parents and dual-earner parents struggle for time to do it all. Lower fertility rates also give grandparents more time to invest in their fewer grandchildren. Not many grandparents in the future will find themselves dividing their time among a lot of grandchildren—realistically, they can expect to have anywhere from zero to four or fewer grandchildren, based on current fertility trends of about two children on average per family.

Summary

This chapter examined the changing nature of the family and the implications of such changes as families grow older. Family continuity and stability are not a given, and we will see more of the described trends, especially singlehood, childlessness, and LATs. It is unclear if rates of divorce and stepfamilies will change substantially. After all this discussion of how much family is changing, it is important to keep in mind that many in the United States do not want families to change and are leading traditional family lives with strong conservative beliefs (Powell, Bolzendahl, Geist, and Steelman 2010).

The chapter began by discussing the postmodern theory of families, according to which families define their own reality, with all realities considered equally relevant in society. In the twenty-first century, we should continue to see that Millennials (those born after the 1980s) and the generations after perceive marriage and family differently than do older generations. Being immersed in relativity, they exhibit more acceptance toward different family forms and will redefine what is socially acceptable for future generations. It is also noteworthy that traditionalists—that is, those who believe that the new family developments are problematic and are ruining the social structure and moral fabric of the nation—will likely be more represented in the older cohorts. Simultaneously, more accepting attitudes will arise as people who have experienced the restructuring of family lives based on choice rather than legal ties or obligations will increase in number (Powell, Bolzendahl, Geist, and Steelman 2010). Aging families will need to be open to all family members and changes in order to absorb all these trends in flux. The nexus of family relationships will come together with multicultural backgrounds and multiple roles in the family, and negotiating change will be important for a positive family future.

Critical Thinking Questions

1. Where do you place yourself along the traditional versus modern continuum? Where do you place your parents or grandparents? How do you think societal changes impacted any differences?

2. Which family forms would be most conducive to taking care of older adults? Why?

3. What are some challenges that multiracial families will have in later life? How does biracial or multiracial identity come into play?

Chapter 3

Changing Gender Roles
Effects on Aging Experience

CHAPTER OBJECTIVES

1. Review the six propositions of feminist theory as they relate to the aging family.

2. Understand the gendered lives of older adults in terms of spouse, parent, and worker.

3. Learn about dating and sexuality in the older population.

4. Consider how widowhood is different for men versus women.

By age fourteen, Dan was living in a boarding house and was pretty much on his own. When he grew up, his major expectation in marriage was that he wanted a family, in fact, a big family, and he wanted to celebrate holidays. He explained that he never had Christmas trees or other holiday celebrations, so that was his one big wish—"I just wanted a Christmas tree, and an Easter dinner!" His bride, Evelyn, agreed to the idea. They married forty-nine years ago. He was thirty-two and she was twenty-six—late for the 1960s. He owned his own successful business and she taught at a school. He now enjoys retirement and volunteering.

Once their two children came along, she decided to continue teaching and shared a babysitter with a group of teachers. He considered this quite natural. "She is a very smart lady, and I couldn't imagine her being at home. It would be a waste of her mind," he said. With that, he supported her, even when she decided to go for her MA and then her PhD in education, in her fifth decade. He said that while his hours were flexible, her hours were pre-dictable school hours and the arrangement was manageable. Then, their alma mater called and asked her to become a professor . . . and so she did . . . for the next twenty years. She was a professor throughout her children's middle school, high school, and eventually college years. While Dan said he never expected this, he was always really supportive. The children (by then in their teens) could get themselves in the door after school, make a snack, and knew mom would be home soon. If she was out of town, they knew he was a phone call away, and that he would be home by dinnertime. The teens also had lots of friends, and could rely on friends for occasional rides during the work day. So he looks back on this past life as fairly easy and very natural. The main changes he could remember was having two dinners. He said they always got together the kids' dinners by 6 PM, and then he and his wife would have a second dinner later in the evening. Sundays were sacred for the family dinner all together. He also recalls putting a stool in the kitchen so that when a student from her college would call, she could have a quiet place to advise them. Back then, at this particular college, professors were to be available 24/7. The busier she got, the more he made a point to check in with his kids each day.

But what was interesting in this interview was how harmonious it all was. He never considered having her not pursue the opportunities she was given. He knew others in his age group who had wives who went to work, moved up the career ladder, and then their marriages ended in divorce. He said that was not for him. I asked if she was swayed by the feminist movement in all of this. "No, she really didn't subscribe to all that because she never felt put down or held back by a man." Indeed, in this relationship it didn't sound like that was an issue. He finished the interview stating, "I'm the kind of guy who will leave with the girl I brought to the dance . . . She's my partner. We're always there for one another." His wife lived up to her end of the bargain. They celebrate every holiday, and make a big deal out of birthdays. "She has plates for every holiday—we have Christmas plates, Thanksgiving plates, New Year's, 4th of July plates, and so on." She rotates decorations for holidays throughout the year. Their children, now with children of their own, continue these holiday traditions. With nearly fifty years of a happy marriage, he maintains he was lucky by being in the right place at the right time, many times over.

Feminist Theory

Feminist theory is a framework, or lens, one can look through when examining the social world. Feminist theory has many variations and can be very complex. For the most part, it is divided into individual-level theories, such as the role of socialization, and structural-level theories, such as the gender stratification of society. When studying gender, we often use theories of gender inequality, interactional theories, structural theories, conflict theories, and critical theories.

Current feminist theory is also informed by race, intersectionality, and queer theory, and scholars have tried to understand inequality from multiple social locations. Each theory seeks to understand the unequal power between men and women, and dominant white heterosexual male privilege compared to all others. There are many variations of feminist theory, thus it is impossible to list them all. Below I focus on the six propositions of feminist theory (or theories) put forth by White, Klein, and Martin (2015:220–223). Their work is one of the clearest and most recent works in family theory. As they discuss in their book, each proposition listed could be considered controversial and has a counterargument due to the various strains of feminist theory. However, these propositions seem the most logi-cal and agreed upon within the discourse of feminist theory (White, Klein, and Martin 2015). Basic to the argument is the difference between sex and gender. Sex is the biological characteristics of being male or female. Gender is the cultural manifestation of sex. How a society reacts to individuals is based on sex, and expressed in people's gender. Gender is different depen-dent upon time in history, geographical space, and cultural background of the area or group.

Six Propositions

Below is the listing of the six propositions and how they relate to family and aging (White, Klein, and Martin 2015). I discuss how things are now and how they may change in the future as each successive cohort of men and women grows older.

1. Gender structures our personal life experiences.

How we experience social life is in part structured by the cultural mean-ings ascribed to our biological sex in our societies. Our culture shapes how we dress, speak, behave, and experience social life. Thus we express our gender based on our culture, and experience life through this gendered experience.

In the context of family and aging, gender structures how we experi-ence the obligations, duties, and rewards of family life. For example, gender affects activities such as kin keeping, caretaking, and having and managing financial resources. We have carried our own gender with us throughout our lifetime so, by later life, we are a culmination of our gendered experience. Often this means that older women are more attuned to their families than older men, older women do more family work than older men, and older women are more supported by their families than older men.

2. Gender structures all societies.

Every society structures its resources, space, and social relations by gen-der. We socialize children into their gendered categories early on. This social-ization becomes part of individuals' identities, and then is reified by society. Even when people stand up against their gender socialization, and do not accept it as part of their identity, the society in which they live will sanction the members of society for acting out of their gendered expectations.

In the family and aging context, society structures gender differently for those who are now in older cohorts (generally more traditional) than those who are in younger cohorts (generally more open and gender flex-ible). Older cohorts of women were less likely to work in high-powered careers and older cohorts of men rarely provided much childcare. That is not to say that younger generations do not experience a gendered society, but those raising children in their twenties now have much more gen-der flexibility than those who did so one hundred years ago. Women are much more likely to work full-time; men are more likely to take more active care of their children. Gender structures Americans' experiences in different ways.

3. Women as a class are devalued and oppressed.

Across the world in the gendered hierarchy, women are placed below men in importance. This hierarchy is further delineated by other oppressions, such as race, skin tone, ethnicity, language, sexual identity, social class, and so on. Thus intricate hierarchies exist in societies, with white men generally at the top of the hierarchy and women of color at the bottom.

In the family and aging context, men's advantaged position is perpetuated throughout life. Starting at young ages, boys have greater self-esteem than girls, and this is amplified in their teens. Given their socially advantaged position, adult men do not take the brunt of inequalities in income or carework. Moreover, they are more likely to commit acts of domestic violence compared to women, and are less likely to care for sick family members. They also have more financial resources. Thus, while most older people are in good financial shape compared to young people, a subset of older women—especially women of color in America—are especially disadvantaged and live in poverty. The structure of women's work lives further disadvantages women because state-based assistance from Social Security still assumes a male-breadwinner role. Thus, women who didn't marry and women who weren't married for at least ten years do not receive spousal benefits. In comparison, women who were married for at least ten years are eligible to receive spousal benefits in addition to their own Social Security benefits (Harrington Meyer, Wolf, and Himes 2006). Additionally, women's jobs still pay less than men's jobs, and women are more likely to take off time from the workforce to raise children, which ultimately affects their Social Security benefits.

4. As a result of sex, gender, beliefs, and historical and continuing sexism and oppression, there exists a female culture.

Women throughout the ages have formed female-centered spaces and rituals, in part as a celebration of women and in part as a reaction against patriarchy. African American females in particular have a tradition of female-dominated culture (Hill Collins 2000). This female culture is a place in which they work, attend to children, and handle family issues. The female culture may be within neighborhoods, within the family, within their children's schools, and in friendship networks. The female culture is sometimes liberating, in that women are more likely to be their authentic selves with the absence of men in control. But all female spaces are also a way of reifying gender segregation. These female-centered spaces and rituals may be frustrating as well. Female-centered culture will often be a place where children are taken care of and such spaces likely do not provide the opportunities to reap the same rewards as men in the male-dominated circles of business and financial well-being.

In the context of family and aging, women have experienced some level of continuing sexism and oppression, whether they realize it or not. Women still earn less than men, and are much less likely to be in STEM fields or leaders in business. The female culture in the aging family is especially palpable because of caregiving issues (that is, both men and women are typically more comfortable having a woman take care of them physically). Women are much more likely to provide care, connect to family, and help

iStock/shapecharge

with grandchildren. Moreover, because of the age differences in male and female mortality, as women get older they are more likely to be in increasingly feminized places. Nursing homes, in particular, have high female-to-male ratios.

5. The family is not monolithic.

Family is portrayed in society as an ideal. Young men and women are led to believe that family is generally a nuclear family consisting of a married couple with children. Feminist theory has pointed out that there are many types of families, and one is not better than the other. In addition, even in the past, diverse family forms (such as gay and lesbian families, single mothers, etc.) existed, they just were not as common or openly acknowledged in society.

Within a family and aging framework, while many of the older cohorts of families did experience a rather traditional family structure, their children and extended families have likely branched out a lot in terms of variations in family structure. Young people are much more likely to marry outside of their religion or geographic area. They have fewer children as well. Same-sex marriage is now legal in the United States. The divorce rate is still high, and many simply do not ever marry. An increasing number of people stay single or cohabit with their partners. Thus aging families live with fewer guarantees of siblings and children, and many have more tenuous relationships with ex-in-laws, new in-laws, half siblings, and other stepfamily members.

6. The family is a central institution for the reproduction of oppression.

Within the family, patriarchy and oppression is exercised. Women still do more housework than men, and most childcare. Intimate partner violence is predominantly male against female violence—emotionally and physically.

As such, feminist theory recognizes the potential oppression of family structure and family process, and tries to reconcile how family should be re-created to be more equitable. Again, many variants of feminist theory exist, ranging from creating female-only spaces of power to gaining equal rights with men, and so on.

In an aging context, the family is still a central institution for the reproduction of oppression as well. Older women and men in particular were raised during a time with more rigid sex roles. The division of labor was historically more divided by gender. This disadvantaged both men and women. For men, there was and still is a more narrow range of appropriate (masculine) gender display and behavior. Many religions support men as head of the household and the church. For women, emotional display and caring is tacitly expected within marriage and family, and this is one reason women do much more of the caring work in old age. But, as men and women age, they often become more **gender flexible**—especially men who become more open to helping with chores around the house. The reality of an aging woman with health issues means that the husband is more likely to have to help with housework or caretaking.

In sum, feminist theories provide a framework for viewing the family as a site of perpetuating inequality and oppression, as well as a place of heterosexual privilege. Feminist theory also tries to reconcile these inequalities by suggesting alternative ways of acting to counter the institutionalized sexism in the family. Among older people, the inequalities may be more pronounced, as many of these people were born and raised during a time with more traditional gender roles. In the future, we expect some positive changes among younger men and women since gender roles have diversified to some degree.

Changes in Gendered Lives Over Time

Women's lives have changed dramatically in the last century as more women entered the workplace. Modern women, including those of the baby boom generation, came of age during a time of rapidly shifting changes for women. Women work, and sometimes out-earn men. They have children, but many are choosing to remain childless. Many women are single parents. Men's lives have also changed in that they are much more likely to be in two-wage-earner relationships. As we saw in Dan's experience in the beginning of the chapter, these changes to women's roles significantly affect men's lives as well. Men have become more active in family life. For the most part, men are now expected to be more emotionally available to and supportive of their families than in previous generations. They have a different experience than their fathers or other older male relatives. Both men and women now are concerned about work-family conflicts and how they are going to handle their time-greedy work lives (Gerson 2010). In this chapter we will review major roles—such as those of spouse, parent, and worker—and how they are changing.

Spouse

Expectations for spouses have changed over time. Men are now usually more active as parents and do more housework than in the past. Despite a growing segment of the population who are stay-at-home fathers, women are still expected to be the primary caregivers for children during the parenting years, and they are also often expected to contribute to the household budget through paid work (Galinsky, Aumann, and Bond 2009). Studies have shown that men's share of housework does not change much over the life course and remains relatively low compared to women's (Baxter, Hewitt, and Haynes 2008). In the future, women will increasingly expect men to do more housework and more actively parent children (Gerson 2010). There will be less rigidity in gendered expectations for spouses, and this should carry into old age. With more changes in gender roles, the sixth proposition of feminist theory, that family is the site of oppression, will hopefully be alleviated to some degree. When young people of today are older, it is plausible that there will be much less gender oppression.

However, among the older cohorts of women today, a great number of traditional attitudes prevail as well. Women feel more responsible for families. For instance, Locher et al.'s (2010) research examines the gendered responsibility of feeding the family, and how it transitions in later life. Their study found that females were frustrated with not being able to fully participate in feeding activities—which was central to their self-identity. Males were frustrated at not being able to provide food that met their wives' expectations. In other words, because such a major part of women's identities (especially from earlier cohorts) centers on caring for others, and cooking for their families, when they are no longer able to do so, they (and their husbands) are frustrated by this change in their lives (Locher et al. 2010).

Parenting

Declining fertility has changed the roles of parents dramatically because they parent fewer children. They spend more time and effort in parenting these children and have more resources available in their smaller families. This section focuses on those who parent, rather than parents who are no longer in frequent contact with their children. Overall, the generational gap between adolescents and parents during the 1960s, 1970s, and 1980s was much greater than the gap between children and parents now (Taylor and Morin 2009). We are closer to, and get along better with, our children now than before. While Hays (1996) wrote about intensive mothering in the 1990s, what is expected these days is intensive *parenting*. Baby Boomers in particular have been known to be overly involved in their children's lives and are accused of helicopter parenting and can be extremely caught up in their adolescent child's personal life, school, and future plans (Padilla-Walker and Nelson 2012). Intensive parenting seems to show no signs of abating and with fewer children in a family, even more attention can be focused on a child.

In smaller families, men in dual-earner couples have become more active parents and, as such, will likely be closer to their children in the future. Men today often perform mundane tasks of parenting such as changing diapers, putting children to bed, driving school-age kids to activities, and so on. These daily life experiences can help to forge a closer relationship between older men and their adult children as they have experienced many years of simply being together. Thus, modern family life involves fewer children with greater attachment and dependence.

Worker

Men and women are now in the labor force for an extended amount of time. Most women born post-1950 have been employed for most of their lives. Indeed, ever since World War II, the proportion of working women has increased. The movement of women into the marketplace was greatest during the 1970s and 1980s (Mosisa and Hipple 2006). For women with children aged 6–17, labor force participation peaked in the early 2000s at almost 80 percent. Percentages declined a little throughout the subsequent ten years of the 2000s, with about 76 percent of women in the labor force (BLS Reports 2014: table 7). There is also racial variation in labor force participation rates for women. Most African American women have always worked, though their employment may not have been officially documented if they were domestic laborers (Hill Collins 2000). In contrast, overall labor force participation for men has declined. In 1948, among civilian men over sixteen years of age, 83.5 percent worked; by 2012, this number had declined to 64.4 percent (BLS Reports 2014: table 2), and the decline is steeper for African American men (Mosisa and Hipple 2006).

iStock/DGLimages

Changes in work histories will affect women's and men's earnings in later life—with more women having more savings, pensions, and so on. In old age, there are three main sources of income: Social Security, private pensions, and savings (Harrington Meyer and Herd 2007). Thus women who have worked consistently, continuously married women, and women who have not had children are often financially advantaged (Harrington Meyer and Herd 2007; Keister 2007). Men are more advantaged than women with more continuous work histories, greater Social Security benefits, and greater likelihood of pensions. However, there are other disadvantages for women based on the current Social Security system. For instance, as a woman's likelihood of being married for ten years is declining (especially among African American women), so too will retirement benefits via Social Security decline because she will be ineligible for spouse and widow benefits (Harrington Meyer, Wolf, and Himes 2006). For the most part, women's earnings have not reached the equivalent of men's earnings, and African Americans have lower earnings on average as well as much lower levels of wealth (Harrington Meyer and Herd 2007). Overall, we can expect that women will have more money from pensions and Social Security than in the past, but it will still not equal that of men's. Moreover, whites and Asians earn more than African Americans and Hispanics on average. Consequently, in later adulthood these differences will be perpetuated, with women more likely to experience economic hardship because they work less and earn less over a lifetime (Harrington Meyer and Herd 2007). The proposition of women being devalued over the life course shows major financial differences in later life. However, we also anticipate that women will enjoy more financial independence than they have in the past. This large cohort of women have worked most of their lives, and they have their own work histories and bank accounts.

Gender, Dating, and Sexuality

Dating and Intimacy

Older Americans seek and enjoy intimacy and companionship in later life. Some of the strong sexual desires of youth wane, but a desire for intimacy, touch, and companionship remains and may become more important than a sexual relationship. Both men and women seek intimate relationships, including those who are unmarried, older adults who are divorced or separated, and those who are widowed. Some are simply looking for friendship while others seek intimacy and/or a sexual relationship. Later adulthood is frequently punctuated by loss. People experience loss of spouses and partners, as well as loss of friends. The need for intimacy continues and thus it is also a time to renew friendships or seek new ones. Many aging individuals continue to engage in nonsexual touching as well (Galinsky, McClintock, and Waite 2014; Lodge and Umberson 2012; Karraker, DeLamater, and Schwartz 2011). One especially detailed study that examined relationship satisfaction found that most men and women who are in relationships feel they can rely on and open up to their partners, though this declines slightly in the older age groups (Waite and Das 2010). Another study showed that adult women (both lesbian and heterosexual women) seek to lessen boundaries and work hard to maintain intimacy between partners whereas gay and heterosexual men did so to a much smaller degree (Umberson, Thomeer, and Lodge 2015). Some older adults (especially men) try to find a spouse in later life. There has been a general increase in online dating websites, but also an increase in volume within those sites (such as eHarmony and match.com) for senior dating matching. There are also websites devoted to seniors, such as OurTime.com and AARP's own dating website.

It is difficult to get a sense of the dating scene in later life. Brown and Shinohara (2013) conducted a study to give us a "national portrait" of dating relationships in older adulthood. They found that among older unmarried adults, 14 percent were in a dating relationship; however, the percent within the group differed by gender—27 percent of men were in a dating relationship in this group, while only 7 percent of women were in a dating relationship. Much of this imbalance can be explained by the feminized sex ratio of women to men in later life. The researchers also compared daters to non-daters and found that daters were more advantaged socially, physically, and economically. Specifically, they found that daters were more likely to be younger, male, and divorced or separated (as opposed to widowed), to have higher SES, better health, and more confidence in their driving, and they were more socially connected (Brown and Shinohara 2013).

Men and women also appear to date for different reasons. Men and women both are interested in dating after widowhood, especially if they lack

iStock/Tomwang112

social support (Carr 2004; Carr and Boerner 2013). However, men were more interested (and more likely to date) in large part due to partner availability, but also to compensate for low social support, whereas women can more easily find companionship without men. Older women may have more social norms against dating and remarriage after widowhood, and may not actively seek men for a relationship. Older women are also wary of getting into a situation in which they are caretaking for a man. Thus in dating at older ages, men are more active as daters, and are more likely to remarry. Women want companionship, and sometimes seek it through dating, but they have more possibilities for intimate relationships with friends and family (Carr 2004). In the future, it is likely that there will be more interest in dating in old age. New cohorts of older individuals will have less gender-stereotyped lives. Men in particular may be less likely to seek a helpmate for cooking, cleaning, and caretaking (as compared to their older counterparts), and women will have experienced a youth with more sexual freedom, as well as career freedom (and may be more assertive in dating than their older counterparts). Women may be more comfortable actively seeking men for romance and companionship. Partner availability will still benefit men substantially more than women.

When seeking an intimate relationship, people often become more aware of their physical appearance. Both men and women experience bodily changes as they age. These changes can be distressing. Skin loses elasticity and age spots begin appearing, and frequently weight gain occurs. Men and sometimes women lose their hair, and it usually turns white or gray. Women by far experience greater social control, social stigma, and perceived loss of attractiveness with age (Clarke 2011). With extended life come more bodily changes and affronts to what is considered socially attractive.

For both men and women, there is pressure to try to maintain a youthful appearance. Certainly the pressure is greater for women. Many middle-class women often experience what Nora Ephron called maintenance. In her midsixties, she wrote about how much time and money she had spent on hair (both taking care of it and removing unwanted hair), nails, skin, and so on, in an effort to keep her looks together, while wistfully and humorously looking back at her youth (Ephron 2006).

As women age, they are pressured to keep their looks as youthful as possible (Clarke 2011). They often dye their hair to cover the gray, use makeup and teeth whiteners, and select clothes to flatter their appearance. They may use Botox to smooth wrinkles or laser treatments to get rid of unwanted hair. Dermatologists offer skin resurfacing to create smoother and more evenly toned skin. Some turn to plastic surgery for tummy tucks, liposuction, face lifts, and breast lifts. Men too are engaging in some of these beauty regimens that enhance physical attractiveness. For instance, they also dye their hair, use Botox, have laser hair removal (and waxing), and use teeth whiteners and skin resurfacing as well as liposuction, eyelid, and nose surgery, to name a few. Men may begin or continue to lift weights to maintain muscle mass.

Standards of hygiene and beauty continue to be raised, and the gendered expectation of doing the "beauty work" is no longer relegated only to women. Undoubtedly, women still have much more pressure on them to look

Gender and Attractiveness

The amount of maintenance involving hair is genu-inely overwhelming. Sometimes I think that not hav-ing to worry about your hair anymore is the secret upside of death.

From Nora Ephron (2006), *I Feel Bad about My Neck: And Other Thoughts on Being a Woman*, pg. 32.

good than men do. One study found that among those aged 62–90, women who were partnered in later life were more likely to work on maintaining a sexually attractive appearance, but it was not the same for partnered men. Rather, it was the unpartnered men who were most likely to work to present a sexually attractive appearance (Galinsky, McClintock, and Waite 2014). These findings demonstrate gendered lives. Women feel they must maintain their appearance within relationships more than men do. Unpartnered older men, likely emboldened by the skewed sex ratio, work to retain their sexual attractiveness because they know they might find partners. In the future, adults who were raised with these new standards of hygiene and beauty will likely carry them into later life.

Sexuality in Later Life

For both men and women, sexuality continues to play an important role in later life (DeLamater 2012). Many older adults are married or partnered, and continue to have a sexual life with a partner into their eighties, and even later. Sexuality in later life has been described as more free (no worries about pregnancy, for example), and the privacy of being alone together may bring about more relationship warmth and comfort (DeLamater 2012). However, intimacy remains important for aging individuals, and many continue to engage in nonsexual touching as well (Karraker, DeLamater, and Schwartz 2011). Studies show that sexual activity declines for most people with age (Bancroft 2007; DeLamater 2012; Lodge and Umberson 2012; Waite and Das 2010). This is related to issues such as changes in their bodies, loss of a partner, depression, medication, or health issues. Some evidence shows sexual touching is more important to men compared to women (Galinsky, McClintock, and Waite 2014). One qualitative study showed that while frequency declined in later life marriages (that is, sexual frequency), quality improved (Lodge and Umberson 2012). These older adults discussed knowing their partners better, maturity, and growing together sexually over time (Lodge and Umberson 2012). Unfortunately, we know very little about same-sex intimacy and the aging experience, though new calls for research and new data should change this in the next ten years (Fredriksen-Goldsen et al. 2011; Fredriksen-Goldsen and Kim 2017; Umberson, Thomeer, and Lodge 2015; Umberson et al. 2015).

There are several reasons for diminishing sexual experiences with age. Women and men may suffer from a lack of interest in sex in part due to the societal expectations of virility and masculinity for men, and youth, beauty, and thinness for women (Calasanti and Slevin 2001). Women are pressured to remain youthful and beautiful and say they do feel aging anxiety as their hair, skin, and bodies change (Barrett and Robbins 2008). In their study, Barrett and Robbins (2008) identified a racial component, noting that white women had more anxiety over their changing looks than African American women. These changes affect women's self-esteem, feelings of femininity, and sense of sexual attractiveness.

Another reason for the decrease in sexual activity is the biology of aging. Men experience conditions such as erectile dysfunction (ED), in which they have an inability to develop and maintain an erection that is adequate for intercourse (Eardley et al. 2010). While we do not know how many men experience this disorder (because many do not seek treatment or may not respond truthfully in surveys), it is estimated that between 20 and 30 million individuals in the United States are currently affected (Eardley et al. 2010). Some men seek treatment and are prescribed Viagra (sildenafil) (Jackson, Gillies, and Osterloh 2005). FDA-approved in 1998, Viagra dramatically changed the sexual landscape for many older men. The patent for Viagra expired in 2012, and now there are more choices for generic forms of sildenafil, making it more affordable and widespread. Using sildenafil is considered useful to continue sexual relationships among older men and women (Lodge and Umberson 2012).

Females also experience sexual dysfunction, and it is estimated that approximately 40 percent of the female population reports some type of sexual problem (Palacios, Castaño, and Grazziotin 2009). Some issues aging women face include menopause, hysterectomies, treatments for diseases (such as radiation for cancer), depression, and the effects of medicines such as SSRI (selective serotonin reuptake inhibitors) used to treat depression, among other biological and medical reasons for a waning libido.

Marital status also affects men's and women's sexuality differently. Since women are often widowed, there is a precipitous drop in sexual relations, especially among older women who have lost their spouses. Physical touch is important for humans and it is helpful for widows and widowers to maintain some type of touch with others. Some research examines frequency of touching, including hugs from neighbors, adult children, friends, and so on. Even interaction with pets can provide older people the experience of touch after a loved one dies, and studies show that the role of touch is very important for well-being (Waite and Das 2010).

As noted earlier, studies indicate that sexual activity declines with age for most people (Bancroft 2007; DeLamater 2012; Waite and Das 2010). One major reason is widowhood; thus, women are less likely than men to have a sexual partner. But more specifically in the Waite and Das study (2010), among those with partners, reasons for not having sex are quite different for men and women, and by age. For instance, men—and especially older men (those 75 to 85)—were most likely to say that it was due to their health problems and limitations, and women concurred that it had more do to with their male partner's health than their own. Women were less interested in sex overall. Among those without partners, not being interested (more common among women) and not having met the right person were reasons for not having sex. Also, some cited not having the opportunity or having religious beliefs that prohibit sex outside of marriage, however, these two reasons were less frequently cited by both men and women. The study also reported a high prevalence of nonsexual intimacy indicators, such as touching a pet, embracing someone, cuddling with a grandchild, and so on. Overall, these patterns diminish with older age, and women have more nonsexual intimacy overall (Waite and Das 2010).

Another study (Karraker, DeLamater, and Schwartz 2011) showed that men are more likely to remain sexually active into their early seventies compared to women. In fact, in terms of monthly frequency of sexual activity, men aged 44–59 years reported an average of 6.18 times per month, and women 4.68 times per month. Among men aged 57–72, men averaged 3.11 times compared to women's 1.74 times per month (Karraker, DeLamater, and Schwartz 2011). From this study, we definitely see how partner availability truly impacts women. Once a husband dies, many women do not have opportunities or desires to be sexually intimate with another person.

STIs and Aging

Traditionally, older individuals were not thought of as being at a high risk for acquiring HIV (human immunodeficiency virus) and other STDs/STIs (sexually transmitted diseases/sexually transmitted infections). In fact, the common stereotype of older individuals is that of asexuality. However, since older adults are sexually active, they are at risk. Two reasons are: (1) there is some evidence that use of ED enhancers (like Viagra) promotes riskier behavior among men; and (2) there is less condom use among older adults who have sex (Imparato and Sanders 2012). Because individuals do not see themselves and their partners as being at a high risk, and because health care providers don't see them as at risk (or they don't feel comfortable talking to them), many older people do not get tested for STIs, which makes it difficult to accurately determine the rates of infection among this population. However, recent research indicates that individuals over the age of fifty are increasingly at risk of STDs/STIs and HIV, and researchers are arguing that medical professionals should pay more attention to the sexual needs of older patients (Minichiello, Hawkes, and Pitts 2011). While qualitative studies indicate a desire among older adults to communicate with their caregivers about sexual health, older people are aware that society does not see them as sexual beings and are thus further discouraged from initiating discussions about sexual health and risk behaviors with their primary caregivers (Gott and Hinchliff 2003). It is likely that with more senior dating, there will be more STDs/STIs among the older population.

Widowhood

Widowhood is the marital status denoting the death of a spouse, without remarriage. All couples who remain together will eventually undergo the death of a spouse and the subsequent stressful adjustment period after the loss. Widowhood is known as a time of sadness, depression, and bereavement. Most adjust to widowhood over time, without the need for professional help (Williams 2014). However, losing one's spouse is one of the most stressful experiences one will have, and it is very hard on the surviving families. After the death of the loved one, people generally go through stages of grief including denial, anger, bargaining, depression, and eventually acceptance (Kübler-Ross 1969). Though these stages, first proposed by Kübler-Ross, are well known, they are merely an outline of the array of emotions entailed in a major loss. They may or may not be experienced, and they may present in a different order than above.

When one becomes widowed in later life, many emotional, social, and physical aspects of life change (Williams 2014). There is sadness surrounding the loss, and most people go through stages in accepting the death. There is the change of not having someone around to talk to, to eat meals with, and to sleep next to. Loneliness frequently sets in (Utz et al. 2014). There may be fewer or less frequent visitors after the initial weeks following the death as family and friends who come for the funeral go back to their daily lives. Sexual or intimate behavior stops abruptly, and widows and widowers must adjust to this end of sharing touch with a loved one. There are physical changes also, for instance, if one is used to getting help carrying in groceries or getting down steps, the widow or widower loses this extra help. This may make them more at risk for falls or other problems. If the surviving spouse or partner counted on the other for driving, there is a sudden change in mobility. Another change that occurs, especially for men, is that they may not receive cooked meals anymore. Virtually everything changes, from morning routines and trips to the store, to mealtimes and sleeping arrangements.

Later in life, women are more likely to be widowed and alone, and are much less likely to remarry compared to men (Cornwell and Waite 2009). Help and support from family is especially useful, and perceived support is very important to well-being in later life (Holt-Lunstad, Smith, and Layton 2010). Women are usually better at maintaining close friendships with other women and being in touch with their children, which is useful in later life. Men, on the other hand, are more likely to have trouble adjusting after widowhood, in part because they are not as connected to others. Men who are closer to their children (both geographically and emotionally) benefit from these close ties (Holt-Lunstad, Smith, and Layton 2010). Ultimately, men are much more likely to remarry after the death of a spouse. Partner availability is strongly skewed in their favor, and men may want to seek the intimacy and household labor that a wife can bring.

Overall, more women than men are widowed, and those who are older are more likely to be widowed. One pattern not examined in previous literature is widowhood status by educational levels. Thus, figure 3.1 examines the percentage of those who became widowed in the past twelve months by education level and sex. Overall, those with only a high school education were the most likely to be widowed, and those who had college and graduate school education were least likely to be widowed. When examined by sex, however, men with less than a high school education and men with college degrees or graduate school education were more likely to be widowed, thus indicating a pattern in which the wives of those in the least educated and most educated groups are more likely to die first. This pattern is surprising; at the less-than-high-school level, this may reflect the hard lives these women in particular usually lead, and it may also reflect smoking habits. However, it is unclear why those with college degrees and above also have more female than male deaths. In the groups with high school and some college education, we see the expected pattern showing that women are more likely to be widowed.

One phenomenon after widowhood is what social scientists call the widowhood effect. That is, how the death of a spouse leads to an increased likelihood of an earlier death by the surviving spouse (Elwert and Christakis 2008). Evidence points to the reality of this effect across many countries (Hu and Goldman 1990). In the United States, some research shows that the widowhood effect is most common among white couples, as compared to their African American counterparts. It may be because the benefits that African American married couples receive (such as extended social support, kin support, healthy habits, and so on) last after the death of a spouse. For white couples, who tend to have less-extensive kin and support networks,

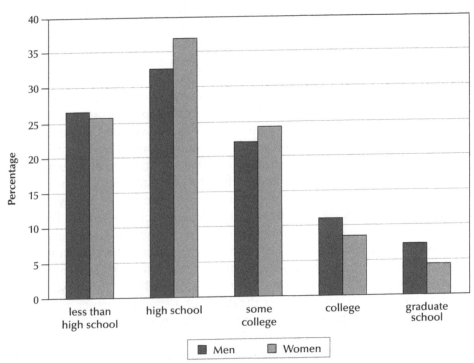

FIGURE 3.1 **Percentage of Widows/Widowers by Educational Level and Sex**
Data are for 2009, calculated for those who were widowed in the past 12 months.

the positive effects of marriage do not continue into widowhood (Elwert and Christakis 2006). Indeed, Elwert and Christakis (2006) found that for white couples, mortality is highest in the first month after the death of a spouse, and declines by the first six months to one year, whereas they found no such widowhood effect for African Americans.

What leads to easier adjustment after the death of a spouse or partner? Certainly, having supportive networks and family, adequate income, and proper housing are all key to an easier adjustment to widowhood. Some research has found that for women, those with work histories have lower depressive symptoms than those with no employment history (Pai and Barrett 2007). Presumably, women attain positive outcomes from working, including a broader social network, more income, a more well-rounded identity, and self-esteem. Other research shows that being extroverted is helpful, especially when one knows that a death is imminent because this personality trait may help people to marshal social support (Pai and Carr 2010).

Widows and widowers also lose the help (or tasks done) by the other person after their spouse's death (Elwert and Christakis 2006). Men in particular, if they are used to women cooking, may be especially disadvantaged in later life in terms of nutrition. In fact, one reason African Americans are less likely to experience the widowhood effect is that they share household tasks more, which leads to an easier transition after the death of a spouse (Elwert and Christakis 2006). Locher et al. (2005) found that not driving anymore, not attending religious services, being limited in mobility, and being afraid to go out alone in their neighborhood were all associated with greater nutritional risk. Examining racial differences, they found that single African American women were most at nutritional risk, followed in order by African American men, white women, and white men. African American women were very isolated and had little interaction and support from others, and African American men were most threatened by violence (and discrimination), which kept them homebound and alone (Locher et al. 2005). As gender roles change, men will be more likely to cook for themselves compared to cohorts of older men now (Locher et al. 2010), but other circumstances for the elderly are less likely to change, such as improved neighborhood safety or a greater likelihood of marriage among African American women. Older African Americans who have been widowed are more likely to experience health declines than older whites (Kelly-Moore and Ferraro 2005). In short, widowhood is a time of adjustment and affects men and women differently due to race, mobility, perceived social support, and neighborhoods.

Social Roles, Sex Roles, and Mental Health

Life circumstances and experiences are gendered and have an effect on the emotional lives of individuals. Later in life, family roles, which are often gendered, may affect mental health—both positively and negatively. For instance, women's attachment to others, including family and friends, often leads to greater social support later in life. Men's more precarious attachment to family can leave them vulnerable in old age—especially if they are not close to their children. Women experience more depression and anxiety in their lifetimes compared to men, and men experience more anger and substance abuse. Figure 3.2 shows adult men and women with psychological distress over the past month. As we can see over many years of data, women consistently have routinely higher levels of psychological distress than men.

Most men have work histories whereas women may have sparser or more interrupted work histories—especially among older cohorts of women. Work is often associated with better mental health while not working leads to more potential isolation, lower sense of control, and higher depressive symptomatology (Mirowsky and Ross 2003a; Pai and Barrett 2007; Drentea 2002). Most women have mothered and, as such, have attachment to their children in later life. However, not all men have been active fathers, and later life linkages to biological children are more precarious for men (Goldscheider 2000). In short, men and women experience different sets of roles in life. In later life, these multiple roles affect their mental health. Below I will discuss some of the major roles and mental health outcomes in later life.

Higher levels of perceived isolation (that is, loneliness as measured by feeling you lack companionship, are left out, and are isolated from others) had the strongest effect on mental health. Perception is important here: it is not necessarily that you lack these things. It is your *perception* of loneliness that matters, and loneliness is highly subjective (Cornwell and Waite 2009; Holt-Lunstad, Smith, and Layton 2010). Perceived social support was also important, and both perceived social support and perceived isolation were associated with poorer physical and mental health (Cornwell and Waite 2009) and a higher mortality risk (Holt-Lunstad, Smith, and Layton 2010).

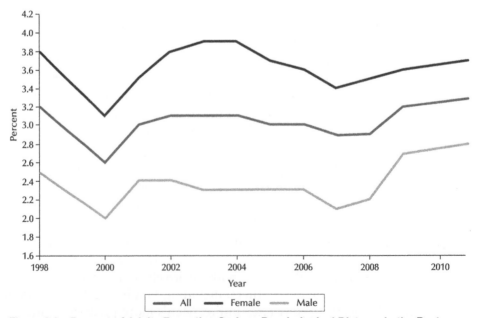

Figure 3.2   Percent of Adults Reporting Serious Psychological Distress in the Past Month
Source: National Center for Health Statistics

In sum, women are more likely to be widowed for longer amounts of time, and loneliness is a greater threat for women (with regard to being exposed to being alone). Some evidence indicates that women experience more mental health issues associated with loneliness (Cacioppo et al. 2006); however, other studies have shown that because men are not good at making friends and are more likely to be estranged from their children, they are especially at risk in widowhood (Goldscheider 2000). This is most pronounced for childless men (Zhang and Hayward 2001).

Having a spouse or partner is protective against depression (Waite and Gallagher 2000). Having social support is crucial to mental well-being, and the effect is often greater for men (that is, the marriage bonus for men) because a spouse can sometimes be their only source of support, whereas women have greater support from multiple places. Marriage and long-term partnership also give individuals an intimate partner, which is protective against depression. Not surprisingly, widowhood—and especially recent widowhood—is associated with greater sadness and depression (Utz et al. 2014).

One would assume that having children is protective against loneliness and depression in later life. Indeed, it appears that children do provide support to their aging parents. Some studies show that parents are happier than those who are childless, and that children's support in later life is very valuable (Nelson et al. 2013). On the other hand, research also shows that having children does not bolster social support when one is in ill health. Rather strong and supportive ties to a spouse outweigh having a child, in terms of guarding against loneliness (Holtfreter, Reisig, and Turanovic 2016). However, some studies have shown no difference between those with children and those without for depressive levels because those who are childless have formed strong relationships outside of parent-child relationships (Zhang and Hayward 2001). The main pattern appears to be also related to marital status and reasons for childlessness. Those who chose to be childless and are married have equally good mental health as married people with children. However, those who are childless not by choice and are divorced or separated have poorer mental health, and this is especially true for men (Koropeckyj-Cox 1998; Zhang and Hayward 2001). Another interesting pattern shows that childless adults have lower levels of depression than those who have children, and not surprisingly women who outlive their children had higher levels of depressive symptomatology (Bures, Koropeckyj-Cox, and Loree 2009). With more people childless in the future, this will be an interesting area of study. Our prediction is that both childless and single older adults will have more opportunities to socialize because there will be more people like them, and they can find similar others through social media.

There are also gender and race differences in old age and mental health, with older widowed African American women and men having the poorest mental health compared to whites (Locher et al. 2005). In a study of women aged 52–81, it was found that African American women have higher levels of depressive symptomatology throughout life, and into late adulthood. This was in part due to poorer physical health and lower socioeconomic status (compared to white women) (Spence, Adkins, and Dupre 2011). For similar reasons, they also experienced more anxiety surrounding aging (compared to white women) (Barrett and Robbins 2008). Thus, the concept of triple jeopardy—that is, old, African American, and female—comes to light regarding mental health. Minority status, which is strongly related to socioeconomic status and opportunity throughout one's lifetime, makes older individuals more vulnerable. Religion and church attendance can mediate this relationship and serve to protect many older African American women (Drentea and Goldner 2006). Interestingly, these women fare better in later life than whites when they are caregivers, due to myriad reasons including church attendance, the normative experience of caring for family members, and a strongly knit, usually female-centric kin system (Drentea and Goldner 2006; Goldner and Drentea 2009).

Summary

This chapter examined feminist theory and how social roles are experienced and have changed for men, women, and with regard to family issues. The family is a central site for experiencing inequality, gendered situations, and gender enactment. The family is also a place of gender change, and men and women have and will continue to adjust to new gender roles over time. This chapter began with Dan's description of his lifestyle, and how his wife earned a PhD and continued working during a time when it was not as common for married women with children to do so. Six major propositions of feminist theory were reviewed, and some major changes over the past several decades in society due to the feminist movement were discussed. Changes in expectations for spouses, parenting, and working were also examined. The chapter then addressed intimacy, sexuality and dating, and how it varies by sex. While sexual activity generally declines for most, there is evidence of continued quality of sexual relationships and intimacy. Finally, gender differences in widowhood and mental health were discussed. In most cases, predictions for the future include fewer gender differences as men and women become more gender flexible. One possible exception may be fatherhood and the experiences of men in later life: there is little evidence that men will be more active with children in later life after divorce. While many fathers are becoming more involved in parenting, especially if they are living with their children, still other fathers lose touch with their biological children and experience little social support from family in later life. Thus, the experiences of societal change with fathers are bifurcated. Some men are becoming more invested in their children's lives and are more hands-on parents. As such, we expect payoffs in later life when their children are grown. However, those men who lose touch with their children after divorce or separation will be more likely to be lonely in later life.

Critical Thinking Questions

1. Relate one feminist theory proposition to older male and female parents. How will parenting differ for them?
2. How will gender continue to shape attitudes toward social roles in later life? How will later life roles of parent, worker, or spouse continue to change?
3. Should health care professionals begin screening their older patients for STIs? If yes, why? If no, what could they do instead?

Chapter 4

Parenthood in Later Life

CHAPTER OBJECTIVES

1. Understand the life course paradigm and identify the four Ts.

2. Explain ART and positive and negative ramifications of later-life births.

3. Consider boomerang children and how young adults are less independent than in previous generations.

Jeff first married when he was twenty-three years old after learning his girlfriend was pregnant. He explained that this was not uncommon in the late 1970s and early 1980s, and that many of his friends had similar experiences. He was a Catholic and accepting the responsibilities of having a family at that age seemed normal to him. He felt prepared to raise a child, had lots of energy, and was busy both living on and caring for a farm, and then doing graduate school studies at night. Over a decade later, when he was in his thirties, he and his wife decided to have two more children. Jeff was ultimately a husband with three daughters, and also a scientist with a demanding career. As time went on, his wife became depressed, inconsistent, and angry. After handling some extremely tough circumstances living with her mental health issues, they divorced when he was in his late forties. His oldest daughter was on her own, and his teenage daughters lived with his ex-wife. Jeff moved on with his life, and within a year or two found himself in a new relationship with a younger woman. He was fifty, she was forty. Clara had been divorced herself for a few years, and the two quickly found love and stability in their new relationship—both had endured previous relationships with spouses with mental health issues. However, more inconsistency, anger, abuse, and depression ensued at Jeff's ex-wife's house, and one of the teen girls moved in with Clara and Jeff. While Jeff and Clara tried to create a stable home for the girl, they also decided they wanted to try to have a child of their own. This would be Jeff's fourth child, and Clara's first. At age 42, Clara found herself pregnant, learning to be a stepmother to a teen girl, and in a very demanding science career herself. After the baby was born, the new household struggled with a teen, a baby, and parents with two time-greedy careers. The next few years were rough as they tried to manage it all. However, Jeff states, "having more children was never an issue—children enrich lives." At age 52, his science career was going strong and he was aspiring to really contribute to his field with cutting-edge work that would be internationally recognized. But he also found himself slipping behind. He was still helping the two teen daughters (the one who had lived with him moved out and was finding her way in the world, the youngest daughter was in college). Their needs included time-consuming issues such as coordinating and buying telephone plans, buying cars, getting insurance, financial aid, and so on. The oldest daughter was having babies herself, so he had also become a grandfather. At the same time, his young son was a toddler and needed constant supervision.

He compared the differences between having a child in his early twenties, his early thirties, and then in his early fifties. He said he felt he has changed perspectives on discipline. As a young parent, he was heavier handed, felt a child should behave, and should even be spanked. Over the years, he realized that children do not always behave and he has become more flexible and mature in many ways in his parenting. When I asked him about the experience of having another child at an older age, he said, "Having a fourth child with someone I love who is mentally stable was an exciting prospect." It probably helped that he was one of ten children himself so he was used to large families. For Clara, it was a chance to realize a dream that she thought was forever dashed when she divorced in her late thirties.

Clara devoted her twenties and thirties to earning a PhD and to her career. She married in her early thirties and had hoped to have children some day. After the divorce, she thought children "were not going to happen for me," so she decided she could love her friends' children. Once Clara and Jeff decided to try to have a child, she was not worried about it. She said, "This may be due to an unusual set of women in my family. My mother, grandmother, and even my great-grandmother in the late 1800s had children in their thirties. So I was comfortable with the idea of older parents and had role models." She did not think about it being an unusual experience and noted proudly that it helps that she looks young so people don't notice it as much. (In comparison, more than once, people have assumed Jeff's oldest daughter was his wife). She describes the advantages of having children later in life as being able to draw more on her own life experiences, having more access to knowledge and resources, being more relaxed and patient, and not being as insecure. She often wonders how a twenty-year-old parent draws on life experiences. Her main downsides are how difficult it was in the middle of a successful career to suddenly become a mom to a baby and a teen at the same time. She couldn't just focus on the baby, and there were financial burdens which she had never experienced before. (Jeff paid both alimony and child support, and now they needed childcare.) She knows she doesn't have the same energy levels that she had in her twenties and thirties. She also noted that if she had had a baby in her early thirties, she would have had more time to catch up in her career. In her forties, at the height of her successful career, there was no time for catching up. Finally she worries that, with her mother growing older, she will get stuck in a predicament in which both her mom and her young child will need her at the same time.

The Life Course Paradigm

Life course theory is guided by the notion that earlier life experiences affect later life outcomes. Its central premise is that "no period of life can be understood in isolation from people's prior experiences, as well as their aspirations for the future" (Mortimer and Shanahan 2003:xi). Another major aspect of the life course paradigm is that age-graded patterns are embedded in social institutions and history (Elder, Johnson, and Crosnoe 2003). The life course assumes a logical chronological order, such as childhood, adolescence, adulthood, and old age. What happens during those times is sometimes easily predicted or located in a certain time frame (such as biological changes like menopause), but many of the transitions are social, such as launching your last child out of your home. Thus there is also variation in the order in which major life events surrounding age and family occur. The life course perspective then assesses how the order and timing of events affect later life outcomes. For instance, as discussed in chapter 2, many people have children, before or without marriage. This perspective can examine how the timing of the birth, combined with or without marriage, may affect the later life outcome of the mother or father. Or it may examine under which conditions one typically marries first and then has children, or has children and then gets married. By examining these types of questions, we begin to see which issues may be related to biological age, time in history, and the order or sequence of events. Moreover, timing of birth and marriage may affect later life outcomes for parents with adult children, when these parents seek assistance in old age.

Most consider life course research as a paradigm rather than a theory. A paradigm is a lens through which one views social phenomena. As such, the life course paradigm provides a very broad way to examine the world. We can use this framework in research to examine changes over time. The life course is based on five principles: life-span development, human agency, historical time and geographic place, timing of decisions, and linked lives (Elder, Johnson, and Crosnoe 2003). For the purpose of this chapter, and in understanding parenting in later life, the four Ts of the life course paradigm will be discussed (Elder, Johnson, and Crosnoe 2003). These include:

1. Trajectory
2. Transition
3. Turning Point
4. Timing

One's trajectory is the way in which one's life course unfolds over time. Most people have long-term patterns of stability and change. The trajectory is the sequences of roles and experiences. Trajectories take on patterns, though there can be changes to the trajectory that are either subtle or severe (such as in the case of severe illness). One's trajectory may take them from being an honors student in high school, to college, to a promising career, to having children later than the average age at first birth, and then to work-family conflict in later life. On the other hand, in a more disadvantaged scenario, the trajectory may take a person from inadequate schooling, to being unprepared for college, to early parenthood, to a series of unsatisfactory jobs, and to heavy reliance upon grandparents to help raise children. Both of these trajectories are plausible and disparate examples. Every person follows their own trajectory, but trajectories also tend to have social patterns.

Transitions are changes in status or identity. Becoming a parent is a common transition that alters the course of one's life, friendship networks, family life, sense of self, and so on. Once the transition has occurred, it changes the roles one has in life. One cannot go back to where they were before the transition. The transition to parenthood still occurs for most people in society and, when done "on time," it is a normative experience in one's friend and family network.

Turning points are dramatic transitions that mark a substantial change in direction. They are usually related to school or work, such as graduating from college or losing a job. Turning points are dramatic because they are at forks in the road of life. After college graduation, many move away from home, sometimes to new states, and begin careers. One's friendship network changes dramatically. While families stay relatively stable, one's connection to family sometimes becomes more distant as they no longer see family on a regular basis. Individuals have changing relationships with their families, which may or may not include frequent texting, phone calls, and visits to one's immediate family. A pregnancy later in life can be considered a turning point. Due to its off-time nature, it is not a shared experience with those having children in their late twenties and early thirties. Later parenthood then is a major turning point in society, and leads us to the last T—timing.

The timing of life events has strong effects on the outcomes one experiences. For instance, having a first baby is very different at age 16 compared to age 36. At sixteen, one is usually in high school and living with parents. Rarely are sixteen-year-olds married. At thirty-six, one is likely employed and may be married or living with a steady partner. At sixteen, the timing of an early baby affects educational achievement aspirations, and leads to an early need for steady income and increased responsibility. Decisions in life are made with the immediate new needs of the mother and baby in mind. It is rare to go from a teenage pregnancy directly into a highly demanding field, such as medicine, which would require years of schooling and long hours. Thus the early life experience precipitates later life outcomes such as lower lifetime income. At sixteen it is also rare that one's whole social network will also be having babies, thus the mother experiences a different lifestyle than her more carefree friends. On the other hand, at age 36, a woman has likely spent the last twenty or so years completing her education and working. She probably does not live with her parents but rather alone, or with a partner or spouse. Her pregnancy and birth may lead to a series of decisions about cutting back on work, or finding reliable infant care for her baby. Similar to the sixteen-year-old, however, many of her friends may have children entering middle and high school, so she is not experiencing a similar life stage as compared to what her peers are experiencing. In both of these situations, the mother is considered "off-time." She is experiencing a family transition, which may create turning points in work. They are not necessarily what is expected at that time in life. In comparison, had the woman had her first baby at age 26, she would be "on-time" because that is the biologically and socially normative age to have a child (Billari et al. 2011). Many of her friends would likely be in the same situation, and they would go through that life's passage together. Much of the research then on on-time versus off-time addresses whether the event is stressful or harmful if it is considered off-time. In this chapter I discuss several on-time versus off-time events. First there is a discussion of what is on-time in terms of having children, and how on-time parenting is coming later as the average age of first birth rises. Then, we discuss the off-time event of later childbirth—that is, those who fall under the label of advanced maternal age—over thirty-five years old, and the ensuing pros and cons of advanced maternal age. Other situations of older parents are discussed, such as boomerang children, which refers to the newer trend of children moving back into their homes in their twenties, after college or first jobs. Young adults are also living at home longer with their parents. Thus, throughout these sections, the notions of the timing of events is key. The chapter ends with a discussion of later-life issues in parenting such as intergenerational linkages, transfers of money and wealth to children, and dispossession—that is, when parents begin to downsize their homes and belongings in anticipation of old age and potentially moving.

Increasing Heterogeneity

Many researchers have found an increasing variation or individualization across the life course (Shanahan 2000). In other words, the standard trajectories that people are experiencing include many more possibilities with myriad patterns. For example, in the eighteenth century, a standard trajectory for those who did not die early of disease or accidents would likely be childhood, marriage, and having children. Taking care of children, home, and preparing food would have taken a lot of time. Death may have occurred by about age 50–60. Patterns in modern times are much more varied, including extended education, multiple sexual relationships, singlehood, possible marriage, possible children, jobs, divorce, and so on. The patterns and events can vary over time and can come and go at different times. With this increased heterogeneity of lives, the life course is more varied and unpredictable. Examining the constellations of these different life situations, and in what order they occur, is fruitful. Another phenomenon to consider when examining age-linked patterns is that there is even more variation in later life (Dannefer and Uhlenberg 1999). Indeed, the accumulation of advantage or disadvantage compounds over time, affecting later life outcomes.

The exposure to the same life event is expected to have different impacts for individuals at different stages of the life course because of their different needs, experiences, and resources (Elder, Johnson, and Crosnoe 2003). Thus having children in one's teens, twenties, thirties, forties, or beyond will present different life experiences. Having children at the most common age (that is, from the late twenties to the early thirties) is the current standard life course pattern in the United States (Billari et al. 2011). However, many are having their first children later in life, and the trend is growing, so we will examine this pattern.

Research shows that having children at a later age than most may be beneficial from a maternal health perspective (though not a biological fecundity perspective). Sociologist John Mirowsky mathematically modeled the best time to have a first baby in terms of the mother's health, and determined the optimal age to be about thirty-four years old (Mirowsky 2005). This is much older than the most fertile period of one's teens and twenties. Mothers who have children before about age 22 tend to be less healthy than nonparents of the same age, sex, race, and SES. Mothers who have their first child from age 22 to age 39.2 are healthier than nonparents who are the same age (Mirowsky 2002). Thus, while biologically it is not one's most fertile period, it is the time with the fewest health implications. We now turn to outcomes that occur when people have children at advanced ages.

Increasing Age at First Birth

In the United States, as in many developed nations, the average age of first birth has been rising. Since about 1970, it has increased by almost four years, from 21.4 years in 1970 to 26.3 years in 2014 (Mathews and Hamilton 2016). We expect this trend to continue to rise, especially as the upper boundary of fertility has been pushed with the use of donor eggs and injected hormones. Delayed childbearing pushes childrearing later into the life course. A later age of first birth has an impact on total family size, as there are fewer years to create a large family.

While all states have seen an increase in maternal age of first birth, some have seen more growth in age than others. Interestingly, there are strong geographic variances, with the Northeast leading in terms of oldest age of women at first birth, averaging closer to twenty-seven years old, and the Southeast states such as Mississippi, Alabama, Arkansas, and Louisiana having some of the youngest ages of first births (closer to twenty-three years old). Since we are discussing averages, that means that many women also have births before and after the average age. Teenage births, while still occurring, have been on a gradual decline since the 1950s, and have reached their all-time lowest rate on record (over seven decades of data) to 34 births per 1,000 (Hamilton and Ventura 2012). While all racial and ethnic groups experienced a decline, there are differences. Hispanic teenage women have the highest birth rate (56 births per 1,000), and African American women have the second highest level of teenage pregnancy at 52 births per 1,000 in 2010. Native American women fall next at 39 per 1,000, with non-Hispanic whites at 24, and Asian and Pacific Islander at only 11 births per 1,000 (Hamilton and Ventura 2012). Thus while we see this general decline, we also see Hispanic and African American women as most likely to experience these early births. Next, in keeping with the focus of this book, we consider those who experience later births and their outcomes. We see an overall decline in teenage births and an increasing age in mothers.

On the other side of the "average" equation are those who are having children later in life. Not surprisingly, the trend is growing, with major leaps in cohorts of women over thirty, over forty, and even over fifty giving birth. From 2000 to 2014, the increase in women having their first child over the age of thirty-five rose from 7.4 percent to 9.1 percent (Mathews and Hamilton 2016). The pregnancy rate going into one's forties represents the largest increase (70 percent) since 1990 (Curtin, Abma, and Kost 2015). The CDC reports that birth rates for all women are falling except for women aged 30 and over (since 1990) (Curtin, Abma, and Kost 2015; Martin et al. 2017). There were a reported 111,848 children born to women aged 40–44, and another 8,171 births to those aged 45 in 2015 (Martin et al. 2017). Additionally, 754 women aged 50–54 were reported to have had children in the United States in 2015 (Martin et al. 2017), for most of them their first or second child. Thus we see this dramatic increase of women at much older ages (than historically has been the case) bearing children. Typically, women who have children later in life have higher levels of education and income, and are more likely to be in a career. Many of these women chose their careers and education first, and motherhood second. They also may have delayed being in a long-term relationship, or they may be partnering with a man after his first divorce. Having children later in life often requires the help of medicine. In addition, many infertility services are not covered by insurance and thus are paid out-of-pocket—sometimes at enormous expense. As such, older women who have more economic resources are better able to use these services.

When cohorts of women have babies into their forties, many new issues arise. One is the energy needed for childbearing and childrearing. As one forty-five-year-old woman wrote of her pregnancy, "the only downside to being an older mom is *being* older. It's grunting when you get up off the floor" (Kizer 2009). She later explains that people always try to figure out if she is the mother or the grandmother. Older parents will generally overlap fewer years with their adult children.

Older mothers are more likely to experience difficulties with pregnancy, labor, and delivery. Also, there is some evidence that adult children of older mothers have poorer health outcomes with obesity and mortality (Myrskylä and Fenelon 2012). These authors controlled for SES and length of life-span overlap with the mother. Most of the negative outcomes diminished for problems such as Type 2 diabetes, psychological issues, heart disease,

More women are giving birth to their first baby in their forties. iStock/JPWALLET

stroke, cancer, lung disease, blood pressure, and arthritis, after the controls, except for those having children at age 40 and over. They also found having children in one's teens was detrimental to the child's health (Myrskylä and Fenelon 2012). Older age of the parents, and particularly if the father is over fifty and/or there is a large age gap between the mother and father, all appear to be linked to autism spectrum disorders (Sandin et al. 2016).

Below I discuss the pros and cons of having children at an advanced maternal age.

Advanced Maternal Age—Women Thirty-Five and Over

Advanced maternal age is a term applied to women who have children at age 35 and older. It is an increasingly common experience, with currently about one in ten babies being born to women 35 and over (Curtis and Schuler 2013). Curtis and Schuler (2013) further explain that much of how women fare with pregnancy in advanced maternal age has to do with how physically in shape they are before the pregnancy. As we age, fertility decreases significantly, with precipitous drops around ages 38, 40, and 42. While the number of women having children later in life is growing, it is still a popular belief that women should be finished with childbearing by age 40. In a study examining surveys in twenty-five countries regarding men's and women's beliefs about what they call a social age deadline for when it is no longer appropriate to have children, 57 percent thought women should be below age 40, and 46 percent thought men should be below age 45 (Billari et al. 2011). In addition to social costs, there may also be physical costs to both parents

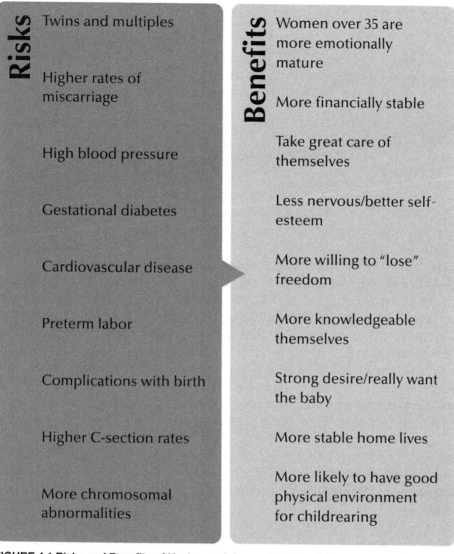

Risks

Twins and multiples

Higher rates of miscarriage

High blood pressure

Gestational diabetes

Cardiovascular disease

Preterm labor

Complications with birth

Higher C-section rates

More chromosomal abnormalities

Benefits

Women over 35 are more emotionally mature

More financially stable

Take great care of themselves

Less nervous/better self-esteem

More willing to "lose" freedom

More knowledgeable themselves

Strong desire/really want the baby

More stable home lives

More likely to have good physical environment for childrearing

FIGURE 4.1 Risks and Benefits of Having an Advanced Maternal Age

and child. Figure 4.1 is a risks and benefits table adapted from multiple sources. These are generalities; it should be noted that perhaps the greatest risk of having children later in life is what one doctor points out quickly: the biggest risk of advanced maternal age is not getting pregnant (Curtis and Schuler 2013). Looking at this figure we see that risks are biological in nature, whereas benefits are social in nature.

Reproductive Medicine and Technology

One of the reasons more families are experiencing major changes in childbearing and childrearing as they age is reproductive medicine and technology. Modern medicine is able to help those who wish assistance in childbearing. Extending the window of fertility for women means that they can (1) have

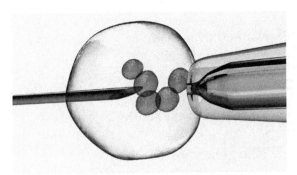

In IVF, sperm and egg are joined outside the body, then placed back into a woman's uterus. iStock/kali9

more children, because they have more years available to have children, and (2) further delay childbearing. Reproductive medicine includes the availability of sperm banks, the use of fertility drugs such as Clomiphene to stimulate ovulation in a woman having trouble conceiving, and the use of technologies such as artificial insemination. Assisted reproductive technology (ART) "includes all fertility treatments in which either eggs or embryos are handled" (CDC 2018). "In general, ART procedures involve surgically removing eggs from a woman's ovaries, combining them with sperm in the laboratory, and returning them to the woman's body or donating them to another woman" (CDC 2018). When the fertilized eggs are transferred back into the woman it is called in vitro fertilization (IVF). Usually the eggs are put back into the woman's uterus in hopes that she will become pregnant. Sometimes, however, the woman is a surrogate. The surrogate has IVF and then carries the baby to term. The surrogate mother then gives the baby to those for whom she was the surrogate. These types of procedures help those experiencing infertility to conceive. It also allows single people, gay or lesbian couples, and older women (and men) to have children. Thus fertility is being extended into the early forties and sometimes beyond, and is also available to those other than married heterosexual couples. It is estimated that 1.7 percent of babies are born through IVF (CDC 2018). It is also known that both the older age of parents and the use of ART and other reproductive medicine and technologies have been on the increase since the 1980s and that this is associated with multiple births (twins, etc.) and other outcomes (discussed below).

Down Syndrome

With advanced maternal age comes the increased risk of children born with chromosomal defects, the most common of which is Down syndrome (Natoli et al. 2012). Individuals with Down syndrome have an extra chromosome (47 instead of 46) beyond the normal 23 from each parent. The syndrome is marked by several common characteristics such as decreased muscle tone, developmental delays, generally mild to moderate impairment in cognitive functioning, a range of facial and physical features, and other health problems. Disabilities range from mild to severe. The risk of having a child with Down syndrome increases with age, with a steep increase in the later ages. Children with Down syndrome have special needs that require more services of physicians, nurses, physical therapists, and so on. They also require special help in schools, and lifelong support that varies depending on the severity of their condition. Below is a table of incidence of Down syndrome by age of mother (but note that in 25 percent of cases, the extra

TABLE 4.1   **Risk of Down Syndrome by Age of Mother**

Maternal Age	Risk of Down Syndrome
25	1 in 1,250
30	1 in 1,000
35	1 in 400
40	1 in 100
45	1 in 30

Source: Adapted from http://www.marchofdimes.org/complications/down-syndrome.aspx, retrieved April 23, 2015.

chromosome comes from the father and therefore is not due to the age of the mother) (Curtis and Schuler 2013). As one can see in table 4.1, the incidence increases rapidly the older the age of the mother. However, one should also keep the statistics in perspective. Even in the oldest age group, the odds of *not* having a child with Down syndrome are higher.

Many women now undergo prenatal testing for genetic disorders, which is generally recommended for pregnant women aged 35 and over. Some women who have such tests decide ahead of time that they will have the child despite any abnormalities that may be discovered but prefer to have the information so that they can be prepared. Others make a decision if and when an abnormality is found. Currently in most cases when a woman knows about a genetic disorder, she chooses to terminate the pregnancy (Natoli et al. 2012). In their meta-analyses of published termination rates from major studies, estimates of the percentage of women who terminated a pregnancy after receiving a prenatal diagnosis of Down syndrome varied depending on whether the studies were hospital-based (67 percent), population-based (85 percent), or anomaly-based (meaning that a major anomaly pointing to Down syndrome was found) (50 percent) (Natoli et al. 2012). Thus, even though the rates vary widely depending on the study, they are still the majority of cases. The decision to proceed with the pregnancy is a very complex one which pulls into question values, morals, religious beliefs, finances, age, social support, trust in medicine, career choices, and many more areas of one's life, identity, and being. Deciding to continue the pregnancy is deciding to take care of a special-needs child.

For older parents, concerns about their child eventually living without them become very real. Many people with Down syndrome now live to be older themselves, even into their sixties, which is a dramatic improvement from a life expectancy of twenty-five years in 1983 (NDSS 2016). Most people with Down syndrome can live productive lives given adequate supports, through families, agencies, job programs, and health care. Thus, parents who have children with Down syndrome need to plan for the future of their adult children who will likely need support (financial, social, housing, health, and psychological). Most older adults with Down syndrome also have multiple health problems as well as an increased risk of psychological problems, such as depression and anxiety, and Alzheimer's disease (NDSS 2016).

Twins and Multiples

Another consequence of both older mothers and the use of ART is the increase in twins and multiples. The U.S. twin birth rate has increased by 70 percent from 1970 to 2004 (Martin et al. 2009). Births of triplets and higher-order multiples had seen a rise of 400 percent between the 1980s and 1990s, then are now experiencing a leveling off and downturn. They peaked in 1998, then have fallen by 46 percent (Martin et al. 2009; 2017). This is due to recommendations to fertility specialists to avoid such higher-order births due to the inherent risk to mother and children (Martin et al. 2009; 2017). The novelty of twins is waning; the realities for parents of multiple children the same age—especially for those with triplets and more who struggle to meet the needs of all of their children—are sinking in. We will continue to see a strong showing of multiples with ART and the increase in

World's Oldest Moms

There are many news accounts of some of the oldest women known to have given birth. The most famous oldest mom is probably the Indian woman, Omkari Panwar, who, at the age of seventy, had twins in 2008. She conceived via in vitro fertilization and delivered a boy and a girl. She and her husband desperately wanted a male heir to carry on their name (they also had two grown daughters) (Russo 2008). Other accounts abound of women in their fifties and sixties having babies. For instance, in 2009, a sixty-year-old woman gave birth to twins in Calgary, Canada. In 2008, a sixty-one-year-old Japanese woman gave birth as a surrogate for her daughter and husband. She used the egg of her daughter and the sperm of her daughter's husband. In yet another story, a Spanish mom had twins at sixty-six years of age; she died three years later, leaving toddlers behind (MSNBC 2009). There are ethical implications of such births. In some of these cases, the fertility clinics report the mothers lied about their age. The ethical and practical implications are numerous. Women of advanced age do not enjoy the same levels of health on average as younger women, and many stories were filled with difficult pregnancies and deliveries. It is unlikely these older women will have the energy to handle their young children day in and day out as parents, especially after the physically draining experience of childbearing. And then, of course, there is the reality of the length of life—how much more time one has left. How many more of these children will lose their mothers at a young age? These off-time experiences of late childrearing are extreme. In a good situation, in which the mother lives a longer life, a twenty-year-old daughter or son would have an eighty-year-old mother. It is also plausible that many of these parents may die in their seventies, leaving behind children who are just entering their teen years.

Note: We could not find a scholarly source for all of these births and relied on news stories, verified on Wikipedia "Pregnancy over age 50," retrieved January 13, 2016 (https://en.wikipedia.org/wiki/Pregnancy_over_age_50). While admittedly not the best source, Wikipedia corroborated the news stories and we thought it worthwhile to review some of the cases to get a sense of how ART (assisted reproductive technology) has affected the extreme upper limits of having children.

older mothers, but perhaps we will not see as many cases of extreme multiples, such as the famous "octomom" in California who had octuplets with IVF, and who had previously had six other children via IVF. This case was so well publicized that it really brought the ethics and responsibilities of fertility doctors to the forefront.

Older Parents and Psychosocial Implications

Previously we examined some of the demographic trends and medical implications of older parents. We now turn to the psychosocial implications of being an older parent. Research indicates older parents typically have more resources, such as time and money. Of course, this is in part due to the **selection effect** that higher socioeconomic status parents are more likely to postpone childbirth (Powell, Steelman, and Carini 2006). Advanced parental age (for both mothers and fathers) is associated with more financial, social, and cultural resources (Powell, Steelman, and Carini 2006). After accounting for socioeconomic status, older parents are more likely to save for college, to start saving earlier, to use private schools for their children, and to have computers and educational objects in the home. They are also more likely to know their children's friends, help with homework, volunteer at school, and so on, all of which are associated with social capital (Powell, Steelman, and Carini 2006). The maturity that is associated with middle age and the accumulation of life experiences can enrich an individual, giving them a greater sense of well-being (Mirowsky and Ross 1992; Mirowsky 2013). In addition, people are more willing to share their time and energy with younger people after their own developmental needs have been met (Erikson 1964; Mirowsky and Ross 1992).

Many parents who have children later in life are neither launching children nor thinking about the empty nest. These parents typically range in age from their forties to their sixties. Sometimes they are in their first families, experiencing raising small children at a later time than most. Other times, they are in second or stepfamilies, sometimes having two distinct age sets of children, as in the opening vignette. In these cases (especially for men, who are more likely to remarry), they may have older children who are in their twenties and either in college, having children, or starting jobs (Sweeney 2010), and then they have their "young" families, often with a younger wife who is having her first child. Thus these parents may be handling parenthood, grandparenting, college costs, and possibly child support and alimony. As one can see, the economic strain on these parents is daunting, yet it is a common situation in the United States.

When parents who had children later in life launch their children into the world, they may be between sixty and seventy years old—a time we traditionally associate with retirement. Helping one's tweens negotiate middle school dramas is not typically what people think of doing in their fifties. Since the average age of death is between seventy and eighty, generally speaking, children of older parents will lose their parents while they are in their thirties and forties, a time when these children have likely begun families of their own. These children are much more likely to be sandwiched between their own young children and their aging parents. For instance, parents who had a daughter when they were thirty-eight years old will be nearly seventy years old by the time the daughter has her own children at age 30. Health and vitality issues may affect the grandparents' ability to help their daughter with physical aspects of childcare for their grandchildren. Thus these children will have the off-time experience of having older parents. In a way, it is similar to the early 1900s, when children lost parents at a younger age because of shorter life expectancies. In sum, we have examined the physical and psychosocial implications of parenthood later in life. When the age cohorts of the two generations are farther apart, there are dramatic implications with regard to the vitality, health, and life expectancy of the older parents. Older parents may be kept youthful by their young children, but as their children reach their own childbearing years, older adults may find it difficult to fulfill active roles as parents and grandparents.

Another trend occurring in the early part of the twenty-first century is that of grown children returning home. Parents who had their children relatively young (for instance, in their twenties) now find the nest is reoccupied by a returning child. For those who had children in their thirties and forties, the nest may once again become occupied when they are in their fifties and sixties. We turn now to a discussion of these so-called boomerang children.

Boomerang Children

The time spent in adolescence is increasing, young adulthood is growing longer since marriage and childbirth are delayed, and there are fewer economic opportunities for the young. Eighteen-year-olds may be launched out of the home to college, the military, or jobs, but then come back to their parents' homes. The emotional gap between the younger and older generations has narrowed. In contrast to the generation gap between adolescents and parents of the 1960s and 1970s, parents of today are far more likely to see their adult children as friends (Arnett 2015). The concept of a boomerang child refers to when a young adult has moved out of the home and then ends up coming back to their parents' home. It is estimated that three out of ten adults aged 25–34 have moved back into the home at some point (Parker 2012). Reasons for returning are varied and may include difficulty finding employment, not having enough economic resources to live independently, delayed marriage, divorce, and needing help with childcare. For older adults, the likelihood of an adult child moving back increases with a greater number of children, poor health, lower economic resources (in which the child helps), or higher economic resources (in which the child needs help from parents) (Peek et al. 2004; Parker 2012). There are also cultural differences in which African Americans and Hispanics are more likely to co-reside with their grown children (Fry and Passel 2014; Peek et al. 2004; Parker 2012).

After the 2008 recession, foreclosures became much more common and are part of the reason for the upturn in intergenerational households (Taylor et al. 2010). Other reasons include the growing immigrant population in which multigenerational households are more common. Additionally, research shows that post-2008 recession, up to one in eight children aged 22–29 moved back into their parents' home (Taylor et al. 2010). Among those aged 25–34, one in five moved back to their parents' home. Similarly, one in five of those 65 and older lived in a multigenerational household (Taylor et al. 2010). Researchers note a U-shaped relationship: In 1940, about 25 percent of the population lived in a multigenerational household; this figure then dropped to its lowest at 12 percent in 1980, and rose again so that in 2008, 49 million Americans, or about 16 percent of the population, lived in a multigenerational household (Taylor et al. 2010). Four years later, in 2012, a record 57 million Americans or 18.1 percent of the population lived in multigenerational households (Fry and Passel 2014). Young adults (ages 25–34) make up almost 25 percent of these multigenerational households (Fry and Passel 2014).

Multigenerational arrangements can be financially beneficial to both parents and their adult children. For the most part, adult children report being satisfied and upbeat about the arrangement and their futures (Parker 2012), indicating that the adult-child relationships are strong, and also that many adult children see this as a helpful stepping stone to get back on their feet. Many parents also receive help and companionship in return. Some older adults develop health issues and appreciate having the daughter or son around; others have financial strains and appreciate the pooling of resources. Finally, some are in their golden years, traveling and enjoying life while they turn their house over to their child while they are gone. Overall, the trend of boomerang children has been on the rise since the recession. Also, many young adults do not leave the home after high school, and live in multigenerational households with their parents and, at times, grandparents also (Fry and Passel 2014). Future economic trends and cultural aspects of living arrangements among those who are foreign-born in particular will likely play a large role in whether or not young adults will live with their parents. It may also hint of a less transient population in the future.

Intergenerational Linkages

Intergenerational linkages are the social relationships or social ties among the different generations in family life. Some of these linkages are straightforward, such as the linkage that exists between a mother and her child. We typically identify linkages to our parents, siblings, aunts and uncles, and grandparents quite easily. In a large family, there can be many linkages. For instance, take two parents who had four children. Within their own immediate family, each child has a linkage with each sibling and with each parent (thus fourteen linkages because each sibling links to their other siblings = six links, and then each child has two links to each parent = eight links) (see figure 4.2).

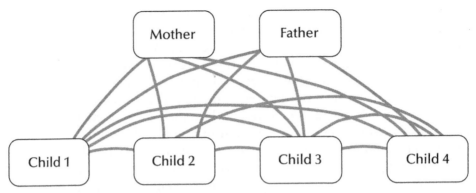

FIGURE 4.2 Nuclear Family: Mother and Father, 4 Children.

If the parents still have their own living parents, linkages multiply even more. Consider now if one of the children has two children of her own in her early twenties, and then divorces and remarries. She is connected to her immediate family still (that is, her parents, siblings, grandparents, aunts, and uncles, etc.), her new husband's immediate family, and possibly still her ex-husband's family. Depending on many factors such as geographic distance, interest, and quality of relationships, all of the links may be active for her and her children. Her children can easily have six grandparents (the mother's parents, the biological father's parents, the new husband's parents) —and that is just with one divorce. It is no wonder that kin-keeping can become a time-consuming and organizationally challenging endeavor during holidays or when remembering birthdays.

Intergenerational linkages can also be less defined and more unclear in today's society. For instance, Clara (from the beginning of this chapter) divorced Elliot when they were in their early thirties—they had no children. Elliot eventually moved across the country while Clara stayed in the same city as Elliot's parents. The bonds between parents-in-law and daughter-in-law were strong, and even after the divorce, Elliot's parents' sense of love and commitment to their now ex-daughter-in-law remained. Thus they continued their family ties, even though there was truly no link anymore except for an emotional one. Other linkages are also less clear. For instance, if a same-sex couple's children are the offspring of one but not the other parent, one partner will never have a direct biological connection to the children (Connidis 2010), and the legal ties may also be unclear if the couple does not share joint custody of their children.

As we grow older, the likelihood of intergenerational linkages both increases and decreases. Greater life expectancy increases the number of linkages, as people now live to see great-grandchildren and beyond. We will spend less time raising small children but more time as parents as we live longer (Stewart 2007). Moreover, as family members live longer, the ties continue for many more years than in the past. However, the number of linkages will also decrease in our society because of Americans' smaller families. Many more families are remaining childless today and will thus have fewer linkages that an extended family would bring. Also, with all of the stepfamilies of today, the norms of obligation to adult stepchildren will vary. Little research has been done in this area, but future research should examine what parenting means over time in stepfamily and cohabiting situations in which the expectations are more or less clear and the bonds more voluntary (Stewart 2007). It is plausible that unmarried adults with children may choose not to remarry to protect their children both from heartache and to protect their children's inheritances (King and Scott 2005). These two trends have implications for the types of obligations usually maintained through intergenerational linkages, such as transferring money to younger generations (and occasionally transferring money up to one's parents), grandparenting, and caregiving.

The Sandwich Generation

The sandwich generation refers to those middle-aged adults who have both children and older parents of whom to take care. The term was coined by Dorothy Miller to describe the stress middle-aged adults feel while caring for children and older people simultaneously (Miller 1981). It has become more prevalent as childbearing is increasingly delayed, and parents find themselves with their own parents getting older. Being caught in the middle of caring for both children and parents can cause considerable stress and burnout, especially for women who are often also in the workforce (Malach Pines et al. 2011). Longer lives, the high costs of health care, and the ability to do more home health care work (such as administering IVs at home) have increased the likelihood of a person taking care of loved ones' health needs. In some ways, however, the concept of a sandwich generation is considered outdated and falls short of the real model of care. For instance, it does not take into account that multiple generations and family members may care for a loved one. It also does not consider how much care can be transferred upward—for example, while an adult daughter may care for her mother, her mother may also provide childcare support and financial assistance (as discussed below in transfers) (Bookman and Kimbrel 2011). Intergenerational exchanges of care are complex and dynamic, involving multiple generations, and multiple goods and services.

Transfers

Older parents give a significant amount of help to their children. These are often called **transfers** in research, and involve a flowing of resources (also called flows) from one source to another among generations. Typically, the flow is from the older generation to the younger generation, and involves wealth and financial aid. This is called a downward flow. One recent study found that the average monetary transfer among those who had no marital transitions over a seven-year period was $11,137 in aid. About 63 percent of households made this type of financial transfer to their adult children (Shapiro and Remle 2010). Transfers usually involve monetary wealth such as inheritance, and regular financial aid. Parents and grandparents may give loans to their children, cosign loans, or otherwise help financially. They may also give homes, cars, furniture, and luxury goods. Transfers also involve the resource of time. Older parents babysit and take care of grandchildren and great-grandchildren. They help with shopping, cleaning, and cooking for busy young families.

Upward flows (that is, from children to parents) also occur, usually in cases of caregiving, or when older adults have few economic resources. Similarly, upward transfers of time are given by adult children and grandchildren to their aging parents. This may include the same type of activities such as shopping, cooking, and cleaning, but also involves more extensive transfers such as carework. The younger generation also may visit older family members and keep them company. Finally, when older adults have few economic resources, their adult children may help financially or provide housing for their parents or other older relatives (Taylor 2010).

Other social patterns in transfers indicate that a later-life marriage means parents are less likely to provide transfers to adult children, whereas later-life parental divorce and widowhood are associated with a slight increase in providing a financial transfer (Shapiro and Remle 2010). In terms of sex and race, females were more likely to give money, and underrepresented minorities were less likely to give money to their children (Shapiro and Remle 2010). Another form of transfers that typically moves from parent to child is that of goods as older adults get rid of their belongings in

It is not unusual for older adults to amass a great deal of belongings that eventually need to be given away. iStock/posteriori

anticipation of moving, death, or simply to downsize. I now turn to the concept of dispossession.

Dispossession

Another transfer involves what David Ekerdt (2009) coins **dispossession,** which is the movement of property away from the older generation, often to the younger generation. Ekerdt (2014) also uses the term material convoy to describe this collection of things that each person possesses that must eventually be dealt with after the death of the person. Those born during the Great Depression are known for keeping everything they can, just in case it might be used again. Those from the Baby Boom generation are not necessarily as likely to never throw anything away but rather have larger homes and also came of age with a staggering rise in consumer goods and expectations of middle-class life. Their life experience has been one of enhanced consumerism and surplus. As these generations age, they eventually no longer need all of their things. Sometimes they desire or must move into a smaller residence. Sometimes they need to move into a nursing home that does not have much space for belongings (Johnson and Bibbo 2014). Homes today are larger than ever and, as such, people accumulate more and sometimes they keep off-site self-storage as well. Among the wealthy, multiple homes may be involved. Often they are holding a lifetime of accumulated things (and remember lifetimes are now longer), possibly along with their children's things (especially since adult children are taking longer to establish their own homes). Thus part of the transition for older parents is the process of dispossession, in which belongings must be distributed to either children, charities, or other family members, or sold for profit (Ekerdt 2014). Older adults want to know that their belongings are going to good use and often want to pass their things down to family. Due to lower fertility rates on average, there are fewer family members to offer these items to and grown children are not always receptive to taking their parents' possessions, since most have already established their homes (Ekerdt 2009). The accumulation of life's objects ultimately needs to find a resting place when their owners move into a smaller home, an assisted living facility, or a relative's home in which they may only get a room. Eventually, after death, all objects must be dealt with and the necessity for this transition has given rise to companies, organizations, and individuals that help people hold estate sales. There are even "senior movers"—companies that help seniors downsize, such as a company called Move Seniors Lovingly, based in Canada—that assist seniors and their families with the moving process. They offer services such as decluttering, recycling, donating unwanted items, and help with selecting cherished items, and then assistance moving into a smaller place and setting up the smaller space (http://www.moveseniorslovingly.com). They also provide emotional support and guidance in choosing what stays and what goes.

Summary

This chapter introduced the perspective of the life course paradigm which examines the timing, transitions, turning points, and trajectories of people's lives, and how these are intertwined with history and when the transitions occurred. This chapter examined the experiences of parenting in later life. It considered what parenting is like when it starts off-time after the average age of having children in one's twenties and thirties, and it explored some of the compound effects of later-life children with regard to issues such as twins, Down syndrome, and the use of ART to have children. It also discussed the trend of more women having children later in life, and the advantages and disadvantages of this. Terms such as the sandwich generation and boomerang children were discussed. The social ties of intergenerational linkages were discussed. We investigated the transfer that occurs between generations as more help is needed by aging parents, and wealth and property are distributed. Finally, we discussed dispossession, in which older people begin to downsize and may move into smaller homes.

In the future we expect to see continued growth in delayed childbirth and advanced maternal age. All of the trends discussed in this chapter will likely continue, and the life course perspective will inform how the timing of the transitions and turning points affects how parenting in later life is experienced. Future research will continue to examine how the timing of different major life milestones (such as landing one's first real job or the birth of a first child) affects one's experience. Most research predicts a continuation of the trends of delayed first birth, later marriages, more time spent living with parents, and so on. The launching of children takes longer and, for older parents, that launch may coincide with retirement and health issues of their own.

Critical Thinking Questions

1. Identify one of the four Ts of the life course for one of your parents. Do you think the life course trajectory would be different for you under similar circumstances?

2. As women delay having their first child, what are some positive and negative outcomes expected at the population level?

3. What do you foresee in future families in later life in terms of transfers and dispossession? When your generation nears old age, will it have similar levels of transfers as the current older generations? Why or why not? What is something you will have to dispossess that your parents did not even have?

Chapter 5

Work and Retirement

Sonya is sixty-four years old. She is from Boston, and moved to Texas in the turbulent 1960s with her husband and three children. In Boston, though young, the children enjoyed visiting different neighborhoods, eating ethnic food, and being part of a thriving city. She was a nurse (LPN) and her husband was a lab scientist at a food company. As her husband's parents began ailing, they decided to move to Texas to help them. Once they arrived in Texas, she had several unexpected surprises—most associated with race. She had raised her children to be dynamic and cultured. However, in their new neighborhood, other people accused their family of acting white and thinking they were better because their children were cultured, active, and well educated. Over the phone, her husband was guaranteed a job at a large food company. She said:

> Almost immediately I knew things were different, once they saw my husband, the job offer disappeared with a vague "the position is already filled."

In their new African American neighborhood, they immediately became concerned about the schools. Sonya said she and her husband, Daniel, prayed together and decided she would quit the nursing profession because of the long hours away from home. This was the first major choice in her work career, and this choice launched a trajectory for so many other things in her life. Their core values surrounded family, and she said her kids were "my 100% responsibility; we had to make sure they became spiritually, economically, physically, and emotionally secure." She had always known how to sew, and took up a part-time seamstress job at a department store. Later, upon learning that her white counterpart, "who could not even put in a zipper," was earning more, she decided to take her clients with her and began working out of her house as a seamstress. From then on Sonya and Daniel decided she would stay home and take care of the children. Many years were spent raising children and doing alterations from her home. As her children grew, she also began working at the local youth recreation center, trying to help at-risk youth. She said,

> To this day, those children, now grown, still write and thank me for my guidance during their turbulent teens. Sometimes the problems had to do with their parents, sometimes I would send them to take a shower and teach them what a young lady is supposed to look like. So many of those children had troubled family lives, and looked to me for help.

Daniel ended up working construction for the rest of his work life, until two strokes led to his forced retirement. Sonya said she has no regrets about the decisions they made, though it has had lifelong consequences in terms of finances. She stated that they are feeling the consequences of the years of low income. With their health problems, they cannot afford medical care and now use a local charity hospital. In addition, she thinks of changes they had hoped to make to the house, and laments that they are considering selling their house for some extra money. But again, she said she has a blessed life, and the only regret is how hard her husband has had to work, often in the heat, at a *much* lower pay rate than he earned at his lab job in Boston. She wished he could have had it easier. They never for a minute regretted that she worked from home and took care of her kids. She proudly talked about the successes of each of her now-adult children, and how their strong family values helped to maintain a strong family now, adding that her six grandchildren and three great-grandchildren also were learning these values. When would Sonya stop work? "Never!" was the reply. She enjoyed life, her work, and people too much.

Age Stratification

Age stratification theory was introduced by Riley and Riley (1993) to understand how a society divides social experiences by age. It explains how people interact with both their cohort and the social structure. Each cohort is distinguished by their shared experiences. We often refer to the Silent Generation (those born from 1925 to 1945), Baby Boomers (those born from 1946 to 1964), Generation X (those born from 1965 to 1981), and Millennials (born from about 1982 to 2004). It is generally agreed that the youngest generation—still being labeled with no one name decided upon, called Homelanders (because they have only lived in a post-9/11 society with higher security risk) or iGen (for the iPhone) or Generation Z (as in Gen X, Y, and now Z) (born from 2004 to today)—is a distinct cohort in which people are used to customizing everything to suit their own needs. Each group's characteristics structure how they interact with society.

Society and time structure our daily pursuits, which are then experienced differently, depending upon our age. For instance, we have been made aware of the obesity epidemic and how we need to change our behavior. Young people are experiencing the change because school lunches became healthier under the Obama administration. Middle-aged people know they should be more active and reduce the amount of fats and sugar they consume. Older people of today, especially many Baby Boomers, are the first full cohorts experiencing this level of overweight and obesity. This impacts our health care system in myriad ways—from the increased prevalence of Type 2 diabetes, to the need for larger hospital beds, to the difficulty experienced by in-home caregivers in taking care of an obese spouse or adult children who are bedridden. Each generation shared work and family experiences. The Silent Generation experienced economic instability, but relatively rare divorce; Millennials experienced high levels of divorce among themselves and their parents, and are defined as much less loyal and more entrepreneurial than Generation X or Baby Boomers. Age stratification theory explains that when cohorts stay secluded in their age range, there is less intergenerational exchange that takes place. Age stratification also shows that patterns of activities and of daily pursuits are structured by the life course (Riley, Kahn, and Foner 1994; Riley and Riley 1993). When society is stratified by age, experiences are limited and compressed during certain times.

Age stratification theory presumes a common orderly life. There is support for a general pattern or standardization across the life course (Shanahan 2000). For instance, the young go to school, middle age marks a time of work and family, and old age is a time of leisure and retirement; this has traditionally been called the three boxes of life (Riley and Riley 1993). Townsend's (2006) twenty-fifth-anniversary paper about structured dependency argues that long-term economic and social policies (and market forces) have created an unneeded dependence of older adults on institutions. As such, these older individuals do not experience the full range of human rights because they have become dependent on others for care (Townsend 2006). Townsend's work supports age stratification theory, which leaves the oldest stuck in an unnatural dependency upon the state and health care institutions. He cites elder abuse examples, and suggests approaching the social problem of the dependency with a human rights perspective. The more people care for those older individuals with failing health, the more humane it will be. Clearly, younger adults can be involved in caregiving. For example, a humane intergenerational exchange might be arranged such that a college student receives free room and board for providing company, food, and care for an older adult.

Others, alternatively, including the Rileys, write about how this age stratification is loosening its grip on our aging society. For instance, some retire very early; military men and women may retire as early as thirty-seven years old. Many go back to school when they are in their thirties, forties, fifties, and even sixties to pursue higher education. Caring for children is moving into the later decades of our lives, as mentioned earlier, with some still having the nest not quite empty when they are in their sixties or finding their fledglings moving back in with them later in life after college or a divorce. Grandparenting can become similar to taking on another job later on. For those with higher education, work careers may not really take off until they are in their late twenties or thirties, and then may continue well into their later years. Scholars have found increasing variation or individualization across the life course, in which the order and time of life's milestones is becoming more flexible (Riley, Foner, and Riley 1999; Rindfuss 1991; Shanahan 2000).

Older adults do not necessarily have to be relegated to a dependent situation in their later years (Townsend 2006). There is no good reason to be limited by age in our life experiences. For instance, education does not need to be only for those under age 25: work does not need to cease at age 65. The Rileys saw age stratification as problematic because it is limiting to one's full range of experiences. The theory points out the problems with grouping together those of the same age all the time, and how that leads to less intergenerational sharing. Work is compressed from young adult life to around the age of sixty-five, but many people continue to work after that. More importantly, for those who live a long life, thirty years of retirement and leisure may be neither desirable nor affordable.

The Rileys introduced the concept of **structural lag**, which may be described as what happens when a society does not have the infrastructure, norms, rules, or laws to adapt to the cultural shift. In this case, the structural lag is not having meaningful roles for individuals later in life (Riley and Riley 1994). Thus they argued for more *age integration*, meaning that age

iStock/RgStudio

should not dictate which opportunities are available or not (Riley and Riley 2000; Uhlenberg 2000). All life experiences, including those considered biologically bound—for example, childbearing—are being experienced over a greater range of ages. Accordingly, we should do a variety of things (childbearing, working, pursuing leisure activities, going to school) with fewer age- and time-bound limits. Cohort and societal changes allow for more freedom, and we should take advantage of this. More age integration is taking place in society, and there are more social, cohort, and cultural exchanges when old, middle-aged, and young interact and share experiences. Facebook is a good example of age integration and how middle-aged adults and older adults are interacting more online, with a number of young people interacting with other age groups such as their grandparents as well.

Younger cohorts will be different than their predecessors because they will have higher levels of education, are more likely to delay childrearing and marriage, and are more technologically savvy. As these cohorts age in society, they will have more flexibility in later life to continue working or to retire, basing the decision on their finances, wishes, health, and the economy. The workplace would do well to adjust to them and to allow them to continue working in order to keep the Social Security system viable, as well as to keep talented and experienced workers. Many will want to continue working, however likely not at forty-or-more hours per week. Those in later middle age will have more roles in later life, as they may still be parenting, working, and potentially caring for their aging parents. Meaningful roles for older people, whether paid work or volunteer work, will benefit society.

iStock/Highwaystarz-Photography

Age-integrated experiences allow for reciprocity of knowledge and an inter-generational exchange of ideas.

Changes in the Dependency Ratio

The **dependency ratio** is the ratio of people under age 15 and over age 65 (the dependents who do not work) over those of working age. While tradi-tionally that range was considered age 15–64, more recently demographers have changed the working age to 19 or even older in developed nations. This accounts for a more realistic start date of people working, since most young people (68.4 percent in 2014) enter college after high school comple-tion, and usually take a while to find employment (National Center for Ed-ucation Statistics 2016). The dependency ratio allows countries to estimate how many people are not working per those who are working. The work of Myers (2009) shows the changes in the old-age dependency ratio over time. When he defined the working age as 25–64, there were about ten older people aged 65 and over for every 100 working-age people during the early twentieth century. However, by 2010, the ratio increased to 24 older people per 100 workers. What is of most concern, though, is the dramatic surge in this ratio that is expected from 2020 to 2040. By 2040 it is estimated that the dependency ratio will be 41 older people to every 100 workers (My-ers 2009). The U.S. government is concerned about supporting this number of nonworking people. Estimates of immigration of younger paid workers have become important. High immigration scenarios will decrease the de-pendency ratio, whereas low immigration would be difficult for the United States. We will see in the future how much actual immigration will affect the number of workers paying taxes, but we already know a large majority of current and new immigrants will be Latino, and in the future it is esti-mated that approximately half of the potential buyers of Baby Boomers' houses will be Latino or Hispanic (Myers 2009). What is not clear though is whether they will be able to afford these houses, given their lower levels of income (Gassoumis, Wilber, and Torres-Gil 2008). Similarly, the Trump administration's policies to decrease immigration and build a wall between the United States and Mexico has not yet been considered.

Changes in Estimated Work Life

Estimated Work Life

Many begin working in their late teens and early twenties, and can expect to work until they are in their sixties and seventies on average. The Social Security Administration has raised the age at which one can get full benefits without penalty to 67 years for those born after 1960. Partial benefits will become available at age 62. As such, both men and women can expect to be employed for forty to sixty years of their lives. As we live longer, and with economic changes such as the downturn of the economy (coinciding with a high U.S. deficit), we are working longer than we did twenty years ago (Johnson 2011). Following age stratification theory, older adults will have shared experiences of extended work life. There are concerns over when Social Security will not have enough money to cover the U.S. population. Americans become eligible for Medicare at age 65, and sometimes that is tied to the end of work life because people can transition their health care to Medicare. Fewer retirement pensions and decreased benefits to retirees have also led to older people working longer. In addition, as the population grows older and has an extended time in older age of good health, the prospect of continuing to work is possible. These are some of many factors that predict how long Americans will work on average (Johnson 2011).

Work in Later Life

Many people express a desire to continue working, though sometimes they wish to work fewer than forty hours a week as they get older (Sterns and Chang 2010). Some older paid workers want to continue working for financial and personal reasons (Johnson 2011). Few Americans have saved enough for retirement and few have pensions. Underrepresented minority older adults are much less likely to have enough savings, assets, or pensions, and are more likely to rely on Social Security in retirement (Rhee 2013). As such, cohorts of older Americans may need to work longer in order to avoid economic hardship (Johnson 2011; Leicht and Fitzgerald 2014). Most everyone needs to make a decision as to how much and what type of work they will do in later life. Individual factors such as health, hobbies, grandchildren, spouses, skills, and finances play a role in these decisions. In addition, market-based factors such as demand for particular skills and jobs also affect an older worker's job prospects. Some older people's jobs are being phased out with technological advances and changes in consumption levels. For instance, repair services for items such as televisions and watches have become almost extinct in our current throwaway culture. The people with the best chance to continue working are the highly educated and those in service jobs. People in manufacturing jobs (especially men) are the least likely to continue working, in part due to fewer work opportunities in the economy in general (Sweet and Meiksins 2013).

Figure 5.1 shows the percent of people aged 65 years and older in the civilian labor force (as a percentage of total population 65 years old and over). The figure includes data from 1950 to 2010. From this graph we notice a general downhill trend that shows that people were leaving the labor force earlier until about 1985–1992. In 1950, about 27 percent of people aged 65 and older were in the labor force; this percentage went down to about only 12 percent around 1985. After 1992 or so, we begin to see the steady increase of people aged 65 and over who were still in the labor force, leveling off to 18 percent or so still in the labor force in 2010. Interestingly, when looking at these data over sixty years, the Great Recession does not show a spike in people still in the labor force. Rather, it is a gradual incline from about 12 percent to 18 percent. It is unlikely that the number of workers will return to 1950 levels. While more people need to stay in the labor

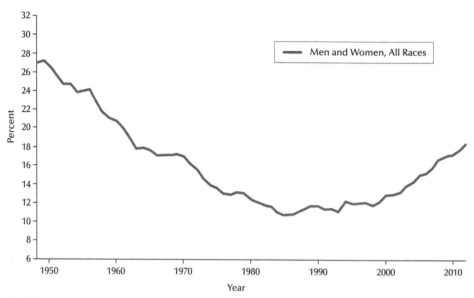

FIGURE 5.1 Percent of People 65 Years Old and Over in the Labor Force
Source: Based on data from U.S. Bureau of Labor Statistics

force later, many do have savings and other forms of income that will allow them to quit work by age 65.

Even though older Americans may wish to continue working, they sometimes cannot due to a myriad of reasons. Sometimes older paid workers are not able to keep up with changes in technology. Companies may choose to phase these workers out of their jobs rather than retrain them, hiring younger workers who do not need retraining. Additionally, sometimes jobs are being replaced by technology; for instance, the increase in self-checkouts has replaced the need for multiple cashiers at large stores. Some older workers experience cognitive impairment to the extent that they cannot continue working due to confusion or memory problems (Clouston and Denier 2017). Other older workers have physical limitations that prohibit them from working, including problems with ADLs (activities of daily living) such as trouble walking, climbing stairs, or seeing. Those who do heavy manual labor or outdoor work may also not be able to continue working due to the physical demands of those jobs. Older professionals can be very expensive for employers to retain due to their long work history and seniority; sometimes they command large salaries, which can make them vulnerable when there are cutbacks in the business. Workplaces sometimes offer older workers appealing retirement packages to entice them to retire early so they can hire cheaper, younger workers to replace them. All of these changes in work life affect older adults and their families, and extended life expectancy means people must prepare for longer lives.

Age bias, which is stereotyping people's work skills and abilities based on their age, rather than personal experience, still exists. Age bias may come into play when the workplace desires young, beautiful workers to sell products or to greet people at a company or in public. Age bias therefore not only affects who may be let go during layoffs (firing someone due to age is illegal but still occurs) but also may affect who gets promoted and who gets hired. The Age Discrimination in Employment Act (ADEA) forbids age discrimination against those forty years old and over (McCann and Ventrell-Monsees 2010). Specifically, according to the Equal Employment Opportunity Commission (EEOC):

> The Age Discrimination in Employment Act of 1967 (ADEA) protects individuals who are 40 years of age or older from employment discrimination based on age. The ADEA's protections apply to both employees and job applicants. Under the ADEA, it is unlawful to discriminate against a person because of his/her age with respect to any term, condition, or privilege of employment, including hiring, firing, promotion, layoff, compensation, benefits, job assignments, and training. The ADEA permits employers to favor older workers based on age even when doing so adversely affects a younger worker who is 40 or older. (EEOC 2017).

While it states we cannot discriminate on age alone, in reality in the United States, we do have some mandatory retirement. The anti-age-discrimination laws have been more accepting of differential treatment of older workers, compared to other forms of discrimination. For instance, Congress allows mandatory retirement for large groups of workers such as public safety and law enforcement personnel. Similarly, airline pilots must retire at age 65. There has been growth in age discrimination cases since the 1990s (EEOC 2017). Even though it may be desirable to hire older workers, many perceptions still exist that allow age bias to occur (Earl, Taylor, and McLoughlin 2015).

Age discrimination is legally treated differently from other discrimination (such as racial discrimination) because it is not something people experience as a "history of purposeful unequal treatment" (McCann and Ventrell-Monsees 2010:362). As such, while it is not legal to discriminate solely on age, and it is not legal to make way for younger workers by laying off or firing older workers, in reality people still hold ageist beliefs (Earl, Taylor, and McLoughlin 2015; McCann and Ventrell-Monsees 2010). Age bias also occurs when a whole society views older people as dependents. Focusing on health issues, and even the dependency ratio, can lead others to assume older people *are* dependent, thus leading them to dependent situations (Townsend 2006). In sum, there are many reasons that older workers may continue or discontinue work. They may want to cut down on work hours. While illegal, age discrimination still occurs. Next we will turn to family reasons for ending one's work life.

Work and Family in Later Life

We often think of middle-aged and younger adults juggling family and work. One study examined well-being across the life course and found that it is greatest in midlife (Mirowsky and Ross 1999). The researchers examined social factors such as marriage, education, income, jobs, work status, and children, and how these contribute or serve as protective elements for physical functioning and against physical impairment. They found that, unlike young people, those who are middle-aged have more education, higher income, better jobs, and higher marital satisfaction (and indeed are more likely to be married). Moreover, those between forty and sixty years old have not yet experienced the higher level of physical impairment that can occur later in life. Their children are older and more independent, and many in middle age launch their children and experience a renewed sense of freedom both in terms of time and money. Thus middle age is a busy time with work and family, but also a time with psychological payoffs (Mirowsky and Ross 1999; Drentea 2005).

However, work and family issues are very relevant in later life as well. Older workers consider their spouses, partners, parents, children, grandchildren, and other family members when deciding how to organize their work lives. Many couples have plans for how they want to spend their future together, which may involve working fewer hours, especially among those who have more economic security. A person will consider the health and expectations of their loved ones when considering later life work. Not surprisingly, women usually plan to stop working earlier than men (Szinovacz, Davey, and Martin 2015), possibly due to gender roles centered around the care of others.

For many women, and some men, the decision to stop working can be largely swayed by one's caregiving activities. When a parent, spouse, or sibling requires a lot of care, paid work is stressful and hard to fit into the schedule. Older women in particular often consider the care they give to their grandchildren in their work decisions—especially if they live geographically close (Harrington Meyer 2014). As we saw at the beginning of the chapter, Sonya quit her nursing and seamstress jobs to work out of her home so that she could be available to her children and to her husband's parents. Spousal retirement also affects one's decisions regarding work. Some couples decide to retire at the same time whereas others stagger their retirements. Hobbies and volunteer work are also considered, especially when a couple has a shared hobby, such as travel, that they plan to do together in retirement. There does appear to be a decline in both mental health and cognition after retirement (Clouston and Denier 2017; Drentea 2002).

Moving also may be part of the decision. Some decide to move closer to their loved ones as they get older, and finding a new job in a new location may prove difficult. Health problems lead to more help needed, and adult children typically cannot move their jobs and families. Those who are usually more financially stable may decide to move to a retirement destination, such as Florida, Nevada, or Arizona, to enjoy their final years in warm weather. Finally, some of the young-old, that is, those in their sixties and seventies, may still have children in the house and feel they cannot quit work until they have paid for their children's college, saved for retirement, and launched their children into the world. All of these trends are discussed at length throughout this book.

The work of Angel and Torres-Gil (2010) examines Hispanic Americans' special issues in later life. In the current cohorts of older Mexican Americans, for instance, many rely heavily on their children and families for financial support because few receive Social Security or private retirement monies. They are more likely to have spent much of their lives outside the United States in difficult conditions such as working in the heat, with polluted water and air. Many worked in the maquiladoras (factories) on the U.S. border in substandard work and living conditions. The cumulative disadvantage of this lifestyle often leads to chronic health problems later in life, such as Type 2 diabetes and heart disease, which means these individuals may require more hands-on assistance to accomplish the basic activities of daily living. Younger family members usually take care of their older relatives, as it is culturally not acceptable to put aging relatives in long-term health care facilities (Angel and Torres-Gil 2010). These factors cause strain on Mexican immigrant families.

It is worth mentioning that in discussing reasons for retirement, it often sounds like people make reasoned choices, planning their later lives and deciding when to retire. In reality, plans and decisions are not always so clear-cut. Things happen in life, and in later life they can happen more randomly and less controllably because health issues are more likely to surface. These life circumstances then create a situation in which changes are made. Sometimes the changes are clear and abrupt—for instance, if at age 64 you have a massive heart attack and you realize that you cannot return to work. If at age 57 you get cancer, and the next year will bring a series of doctors' appointments and hospital stays as you fight for your life, your dream of becoming the boss is thwarted. Sometimes changes happen more gradually.

iStock/DarioGaona

For instance, perhaps you notice your back hurts a lot and you get very tired each day after work, and then your husband retires and starts suggesting that you retire. You decide to work just one more year, but then your granddaughter has a child at age 20 and you are called in to become the main caregiver for her baby so that the young woman can finish college. These life changes then become the shaping forces of your new circumstances. You reduce your work hours, spend more time with your husband, and take care of the baby on your off days—now your back hurts even more, so you decide to quit your job so that you feel better. Your life is now devoted to taking care of a baby and resting on Saturdays and Sundays so that you have energy to be a caregiver Monday through Friday. It is easy to see how even the best-laid plans can change and are interdependent with family situations.

Much of the later adult years involves losses. People lose spouses, partners, jobs, health, and sometimes cognitive ability. Sometimes our mobility is limited, sometimes we lose the ability to drive, or have restricted times that we feel safe driving. It can be a difficult period of adjustment to many things that are out of our control. Even in old age, we balance work and family responsibilities, and consider family changes.

Retirement

Retirement is defined as a time when we are no longer working or seeking employment and begin to draw upon other sources of income for sustenance (such as savings, pensions, and Social Security). Retiring between the ages of sixty and seventy is most common. People talk about retirement and look forward to this time in their lives. Many older people do not wish to work at all; currently only about 40 percent of those 55 and over work, compared to 81 percent of those aged 25–54 (Rix 2014). Many workers have a defined time they plan to retire. Other workers simply stop working without officially retiring per se, but for one reason or another, they quit a job, are asked to leave, or are no longer putting in as many hours. A health event may also lead to leaving work such as when Daniel, in the opening vignette, had two strokes. Those who don't have pensions or sufficient savings may plan to work until they can't anymore. Retirement for women can be unclear as some are homemakers who haven't been otherwise employed for many years. They may eventually describe themselves as retired, rather than as homemakers, often at the point when their husbands retire. Thus despite how life circumstances may influence a person's views, retirement always involves ending work and getting living expenses from other sources.

Many are eager for retirement. It is something we look forward to in large part because of the leisure associated with it (Ekerdt 1986). For instance, we get a lot of fulfillment and autonomy in retirement (Drentea 2002; Ross and Drentea 1998). We associate retirement with rest, recreation, and free time, something we have earned after a lifetime of work. Ekerdt (1986) described it as the one legitimate time for leisure. According to the Protestant ideals of hard work and industry, we earn our retirement after years of toil.

Duration and Reasons for Increase in Length of Retirement

Traditionally, the retirement age has been sixty-five. Since average life expectancy is now into the late seventies and early eighties, we can expect to be retired for ten to fifteen years. Of course, this varies considerably with age of retirement and age of death. For those who live to be eighty, ninety, or one hundred or more, much longer periods of retirement are experienced. Also, many people end or dramatically reduce their working hours by their early sixties, and so the duration of retirement is growing. This time in the life course as one transitions out of work and family responsibilities generally subside has been called the encore adulthood, which is a time of change and renewal before old age and health issues become more salient (Moen 2016).

There are four main reasons for the increase in retirement. The first is our longer life span. People used to die earlier, but now full cohorts of the population are expected to spend up to one-third of their lives retired. Moreover, it is possible that we will spend most of this time relatively healthy. Second, there is a greater proportion of old people in the U.S. population. The Baby Boomers are ending their work lives during this time in history. By the year 2040, it is estimated that about 21 percent of the entire U.S. population will be aged 65 and over (USDHHS 2012). Third, there are more women than ever before in the labor force. Women's participation grew during World War II, and the rate has increased steadily since then. Before 1900 only about 15 percent of women were in the paid labor force and the majority were unmarried (Coontz 2016). Currently the percentage of all women sixteen years old and over working in the labor force has increased to 57.7 percent (U.S. Bureau of Labor Statistics 2014). Younger women are even more likely to work, even when they have children. Thus, ultimately more women will retire in the future. Fourth, while retirement age is traditionally sixty-five (or sixty-seven for those born after 1960), many retire earlier. Prosperity, changing norms, and organizational and firms' pension policies have all led to earlier retirement.

More retirees in the future will be comprised of underrepresented minorities. It is estimated that by 2050, one in four older people will be from an underrepresented minority group such as Hispanic, African American, or Asian, and at a much lower percentage, Native American (Angel and Torres-Gil 2010). Some groups, such as African American, Hispanic, and female seniors, are more likely to experience earlier retirement due to a forced exit from the labor force (Flippen and Tienda 2000). Early exit for many, including these three groups, is due to cohort differences such as lower educational levels, insufficient technological skills, or poor health. This is evidenced by a report showing that among unemployed adults aged 55 and over, limited schooling was associated with much higher unemployment rates, and the surge of unemployment nearly tripled to 11.4 percent for men, and 8.9 percent for women, compared to college graduates whose unemployment rate only doubled from 2007 to 2009 (during the recession) (Johnson and Mommaerts 2009).

Financial Planning for Retirement

iStock/adrian825

A basic formula for retirement savings estimates that you need to save 80 percent of your annual expenses for each year that you will live retired. Thus, say you plan to retire at age 65. First estimate your projected earnings and multiply that number by .80. That gives you 80 percent. For instance, if at age 65 you think you will earn $60,000, then 80 percent of that is $48,000. Now estimate how long you will live. Multiply the number of years by the estimated annual amount needed for each year of retirement. If, for example, you think you will live to age 78, you will have to cover thirteen years at $48,000, thus requiring a lump sum of $624,000 to cover those years.

In sum, we see changes in retirement trends as people live longer and spend more time retired, with many years of free time available to them for discretionary, obligatory, and committed activities. I now move into a discussion of some of the issues that affect families.

Phased Retirement

The workplace is increasingly offering more **phased retirement,** that is, when workers reduce their work hours and/or responsibilities before experiencing full retirement. Older workers may appreciate opportunities to transition gradually from full-time to either part-time or contract work, or to mentoring younger employees. This is especially attractive if they can live off their own or their spouse's benefits, and/or Medicare (Johnson 2011). Phased retirement is often offered in educational settings such as school districts, colleges, and universities; although they may not actually designate it as such, many companies are willing to work out a type of phased retirement (reduced hours, etc.) with older white-collar workers (Sheaks 2007; Johnson 2011). Older workers sometimes cycle in and out of work for a year or two after they retire, or they pick up a part-time job. Some (mostly white-collar employees) retire from their companies and then are hired back as contract workers. Some move into self-employment. Thus phased retirement is a catchall term that means reducing work hours in later life.

Savings in Later Life

Savings in later life affect people's decisions about when to quit work, when spouses or partners can quit work, and how to meet the expense of rising health care costs, prescriptions, and assisted living. The sources of income available to seniors in later life predict how comfortable they will be economically and whether or not they will experience financial hardship. Generally speaking, as we get older, more of our money goes to health care costs. Many older people have their homes paid off or live with relatives, so mortgage or rent expense is not as common as it is for younger and middle-aged adults, though many adults still pay monthly sums for living expenses. People usually have less money coming in, but their expenses are typically lower, with much of their money going to food, utilities, and health care. When there is financial hardship, these payments become difficult. A growing body of research is examining foregone care—that is, not purchasing the health care items, prescriptions, or services that are recommended or needed as people prioritize and try to do without in an attempt to cut down on expenses (Kalousova and Burgard 2013).

Savings vary by race and ethnicity, and whites typically have the highest level of savings and assets. Many Asians also have more savings. Similar to Hispanics, African Americans are less likely to own assets and are less likely to have pensions and savings for retirement (Rhee 2013). Moreover, when they do have savings, the amount for African Americans and Hispanics is much lower than that for whites (Rhee 2013).

Workers and individuals are urged to begin saving early for their later years, though most Americans have not saved the recommended amount (Rosnick and Baker 2010). Those with higher incomes can afford extra insurance to help offset health care expenditures. They may buy long-term care insurance, which can cover the costs of assisted living and home health care, if needed. However, it is not very common to have this insurance (IOM and NRC 2014). Most people cannot afford assisted living and rely on family members. Medicare can pay for some rehabilitation costs but, generally speaking, by the time someone enters a skilled nursing facility, they must rely on their personal finances, spend down their savings, and eventually turn to Medicaid once those are depleted (Eskildsen and Price 2009; IOM and NRC 2014). Medicaid allowances vary from state to state, with some much more generous than others. Reliance upon family for care is therefore more common when incomes are low.

The Great Recession and the Effects on Working

The Great Recession began in late 2007 and ended by early 2010. During that time, 8.8 million people lost their jobs (Goodman and Mance 2011). This recession is known to have eroded the economic status of older middle-class people in the United States (Leicht and Fitzgerald 2014; Rosnick and Baker 2010). Older workers experienced a decrease in the equity in their homes and reduced savings (Munnell and Rutledge 2013; Rosnick and Baker 2010). Older workers who were contemplating retirement at that time were not sure what to do, and felt ambivalence toward stopping work (Szinovacz, Davey, and Martin 2015). Some people made a conscious decision to continue working after they saw the changes in the economy. They felt it was not a good idea to stop work when there was so much uncertainty (Szinovacz, Davey, and Martin 2015). Others lost their jobs during this time and had a hard time finding new jobs. Some of these people remained retired, while others eventually found work (Rix 2014). Among the older population, the recession had the greatest effect on Baby Boomers who were getting ready to retire, as they saw decreases in their savings and their home equity (Rosnick and Baker 2010). That said, when comparing older workers to younger workers, older workers were actually less likely to be laid off than younger workers. However, it took more time for them to find new work if they were laid off (Johnson and Butrica 2012).

Debt

Post-recession surveys show those fifty and over carrying more credit card debt than their younger counterparts (Traub 2013). This reflects a change in the characteristics of who is in the most debt (historically the youngest) (Drentea 2000; Traub 2013). In the Traub report (2013), some of the reasons cited were health expenses (mainly prescription drugs and dental expenses), job loss, and covering the basics such as food, rent, mortgage, utilities, and helping other family members. Having debt in later life is associated with no plans to stop working (Szinovacz, Davey, and Martin 2015), and is associated with more symptoms of depression, anger, and anxiety (Drentea and Reynolds 2012; 2015). In later life, people seem to recognize they cannot retire when they still owe money, and they may still have a lot of financial responsibilities into old age (Leicht and Fitzgerald 2014).

Unemployment

"Unemployment" indicates that one has a desire to work and is actively looking for work. Unlike younger workers, older workers have different issues when seeking work. They are likely no longer raising a family, and have the knowledge that they can draw upon Social Security once they are past age 62, thus they have to weigh financial needs with other life circumstances. Older workers

may be less flexible when looking for work, in that they need to find a good match for their skills, abilities, health issues, family, and caregiving responsibilities. They are not necessarily seeking a lifetime career in which they must climb up a hierarchy, and so may be open to more opportunities and more willing to take a step down in employment if needed. Or, as with the case of Daniel in the opening vignette, they may *have* to take a lower-status job. They may be more flexible than younger workers because they have more discretionary time. Older workers may consider early morning work shifts because the natural rhythm of their sleep cycle often involves earlier morning wakeups, and they usually don't have to get children out the door to school. Similarly, they may not take evening and night shifts because of fatigue or not wanting to drive after dark.

As the economy worsened and changed over the past decade, more older Americans became job seekers. Rates for unemployment increased post-recession for the well educated and even more so for those who did not finish high school (Johnson and Mommaerts 2009). Unemployment rates for the 65 and over age group were highest in 2009 and 2010, with between 6 and 8 percent unemployed. But by 2014, the rates were lower and close to their prerecession rates of around 4.5 percent unemployment (Rix 2014). Overall, the picture for working in later life was better than during the Great Recession and near the prerecession rates. Currently, the rates are about 3.9 percent for the 65 and over age group (U.S. BLS 2017). Those who are well educated have the best opportunities to continue work. With many older workers, when they are unable to find work, they eventually stop looking work and "decide" to retire. Unlike younger workers, their ability to draw upon Social Security allows them more flexibility, even though taking Social Security early has a financial penalty over time (Johnson and Butrica 2012). Older workers also have other potential sources of income, use Medicare, and may use the equity in their homes (either by selling their home or getting a reverse mortgage), which provides a financial cushion that younger adults do not have. Within the aging family, financial decisions, and decisions about work and retirement can affect the larger kin network.

Summary

In the final years, one's mental and physical health is to some extent a culmination of one's entire life as well as contingent upon current life conditions. People take pride in the work they have done throughout their lives, whether as a school custodian, a homemaker, or a bank president. In adulthood, we often define ourselves by our work. Later life is thus a time of reflection, and a major area of reflection is how one spent many of one's days. Many eventually stop working and spend more time with their family, on hobbies, or both. Others spend much of their time taking care of others, or themselves if their health deteriorates. Those who live to be eighty, ninety, or one hundred or more have even more time off from working. What everyone has in common, though, is defining our identities and making sense of what we did in life and who we are. In our twenties and thirties, we are launching work careers, starting families, marrying (and divorcing), and trying to set up our own lives (Gerson 2010). Ideally by middle age, we have settled into a good routine for ourselves, spending our days in our chosen field (whether paid or unpaid). In later life, we become freer from family and work. Age stratification theory discussed the frustration with regard to these three boxes in life, noting that the third box is becoming larger (due to longer life spans) with too few social roles to fill it. It is not surprising then that healthy seniors can spend a lot of time taking care of grandchildren or helping their adult children who are so pressed for time. In tandem with the structural lag theory, this offers more intergenerational interaction as well. The end of work is abrupt for some, and blurry for others who cycle in and out of jobs and opportunities. Some work up until the day of their death, especially if they do not have either chronic health problems that prohibit work or obligations to take care of others. Others enjoy many years with a lot of discretionary time that is devoted to families or to themselves. Over time, with our increasing life span, more work opportunities for older adults makes sense. Having larger numbers of older workers provides a larger work base to help with the dependency ratio. It provides meaningful activity to those still healthy enough to work. It will also help with a Social Security crisis as funding is expected to run out by the 2030s, based on current models (OASDI Trustees Report 2015). Age integration would alleviate some of these strains, and in the future, we can expect to work beyond age 65 for several reasons, including increased life span, changes in Social Security rules, generally good health, higher levels of education in each successive cohort, and financial need. Families should plan on their loved ones working longer.

Critical Thinking Questions

1. As Millennials enter the workforce, and advance in their careers, they are replacing Baby Boomers. Do you think we will see more age stratification or less age stratification in the future? Why? Also, will there be more structural lag or less structural lag in the future? Why?

2. Should U.S. jobs offer more phased retirements? How would this affect the family, the dependency ratio, the economy, motivation at work, and so on?

3. Consider your own retirement. Under which conditions might you retire early? Consider government programs, salary, career, family, goals, and dreams.

Chapter 6

Activities in Later Life

CHAPTER OBJECTIVES

1. Familiarize oneself with the concept of activities, and theories surrounding activities.

2. Appreciate the many ways to think about activities in later life.

3. Learn in-depth about styles of grandparenting, types of grandparenting, and reactions to grandparenting.

4. Consider activities in later life such as internet usage and travel.

In 2017, Sandra and Adam had been married for fifty years. With their four children grown and moved away, they are enjoying a simpler life. Sandra says that, after so many years in which they both worked and things were always so busy:

> I was running the minute I put my foot down from the bed. Now I get to have the delicious naughtiness to stay in my pajamas until after lunch. I deserve that.

And yet, neither of them tends to stay in their pajamas very long. By having made the long-term commitment to exercise in the mornings three times a week, they make sure they get out and get going early. They have purposely chosen a retirement lifestyle that includes activities such as exercise, socializing, regular involvement in community service, and frequent outings. During the week, on an exercise day, Adam wakes at 4:15 AM and is working out by 5:00 AM at the YMCA. Sandra wakes up at 7:00 AM and does 8:00 AM aerobics. In the late morning, while Sandra is getting home and getting ready for the day, Adam tends to his garden around their Dallas, Texas, home. Both aim to be inside before the hottest part of the day. In Dallas, these hot days are much of the year. During the school year, Sandra works twice a week running the tutor program at the local elementary school. Once a week, Adam works at the food pantry. Both read voraciously throughout the day, with breaks for lunches, dinners, mail, paying bills, errands, and a round of computer solitaire. After dinner, they may read more, watch

TV, or view what Netflix has sent them. Weekends are more relaxing, they may sleep in, socialize with friends and family, cook a big meal, or shop for household items. Also, about every other weekend, they stay at their lake house. Once a month, Adam goes to his book club. Adam and Sandra are a good example of aging well. Over the year, they can get busy with various community projects such as their interfaith coalition service committee or with the community civic association. They visit family regularly, including traveling annually for Thanksgiving to visit one of their adult children. Often they travel at Christmas as well to visit another adult child, or their children visit them during the holidays. Sandra has a yearly girls' weekend with her daughters, grandchildren, and now great-grandchildren. Each of their four kids (and their families) either visits or is visited by Sandra and Adam at least once a year. With lots of chosen activities, enough financial resources, and good health, they have been able to carve out a satisfying leisure life in their seventies.

What are activities and leisure going to be like as we witness the aging of the population? In the future, families will change because we expect more years of healthy living. Moreover, longer life expectancy will lead to more years of free time. For instance, one could end paid work at sixty years of age and live to be ninety, leaving thirty years of free time available for self-care, leisure, family life, and hobbies. One might also spend that time with increasing frailty and health care needs, especially when in the oldest age ranges, such as eighty-five to one hundred years old. Health problems may elicit major changes such as moves. Aging parents may move closer to an adult child. A child's family complexities may become an issue, such as when a divorce leads to the need for childcare from a grandparent. In the future, longer lives will yield many older adults engaged in a vast array of activities. Moreover, changes in health, finances, and family composition may precipitate changes in daily activities in later life.

Activity Theory, Continuity Theory, and Selective Optimization with Compensation Theory

Sociologists and gerontologists have long believed that activities in later life are important for individual well-being. Maintaining interests and productive activity is considered helpful, although the types of pursuits change across the life course for many reasons including health, varying opportunities and preferences, changes in family patterns, decreased social activity, and finally financial status (Harris and McDade 2018; Mirowsky and Ross 1999; Ross and Drentea 1998; Shanahan 2000). Below three early-generation theories related to activity are reviewed—activity theory, continuity theory, and selective optimization with compensation theory. These theories contested the dominant theory of the time that older adults disengage from life and attempted to show that activity is good in old age. Activity and continuity theory are classics in the field. Selective optimization with compensation brought back the idea that there is some disengagement in later life. That is, older adults generally cannot do what they did earlier on, thus they compensate by changing their activities to fit their interests, mind, family, and body strength. All three theories are still important and useful for understanding the roots of the study of activities in later life, though the actual theories are not used much today. Many more recent aging theories are based on life course theory (Bengtson and DeLiema 2016). After each theory, we discuss their implications for families in later life.

Activity theory, in its most basic form, stresses the importance of individuals remaining active, vital, and engaged (Havighurst 1963). The theory states that in order to experience normal and healthy aging, older adults must maintain interests and begin new activities. Therefore, older adults should remain physically and cognitively active, maintain social relationships, and have productive social engagement. Older adults, then, must substitute new roles and meaningful activities for those lost with paid work (Passuth and Bengtson 1988). Older adults have more discretionary time to choose what they want to do. In the aging family perspective, older adults may begin new activities such as taking care of grandchildren, caretaking, or beginning to cook. Many of our American beliefs about individuality and growth support this perspective. We should continue to grow and change in older age.

Continuity theory states that in the course of growing older, people are predisposed to maintain stability in the habits, personality, associations, preferences, and style of life that they have developed over the years (Costa and McRae 1980). It is concerned with the personality of individuals, and how individuals construct their "selves" (Atchley 1999). According to continuity theory, there is a great deal of carryover of early life interests that occurs throughout one's life. In other words, people's main interests usually do not change that much, but the theory does allow for individuals to continue to change and grow in later life as well (Atchley 1999). This theory has the advantage of offering many different paths of adjustment to patterns in later life. In its original form, continuity theory suggests that how one interacts with their family (based in large part on their personality and lifestyle) affects how they interact with their family in late life. Atchley (1999) has argued for a less static theory of continuity in which individuals are not bound by their prior personality. He suggests that in late life, individuals attempt to replace their work and family activities with other meaningful activities, although they do not always succeed (Atchley 1999). In a similar fashion, Ardelt (2000) argues convincingly in her landmark article that individuals' personalities do change over time, and that we must consider the environment one lives in as well. As such, activities will change as personalities change over time, and exposure to different environments can lead to different interests and activities. An example of continuity in the aging family is as follows: If one has always enjoyed taking care of children, they may continue this activity in the future by looking forward to grandchildren. However, since we must allow for change in context and environment, we must consider the alternative. For instance, if one enjoyed family ties for many years, but then outlives their own children and relatives, they likely will not be able to continue having strong family ties. Thus they would need to replace their family get-togethers with other types of activities.

Another theory related to continuity theory and activity theory that reflects how older people modify their activities to suit their aging bodies is the selective optimization with compensation theory (Baltes and Baltes 1990). According to this theory, older adults use selection to find what they are interested in (and are more *selective* in what they choose). As such, they optimize their abilities by modifying the task using practice, and then compensate for what they cannot do anymore. One mode of compensation then is finding other ways to accomplish the goal (Baltes and Baltes 1990; Riediger, Freund, and Baltes 2005). For instance, perhaps someone has always volunteered at a food pantry, unloading trucks and helping families. As the years go on, this person may find that unloading the truck is best left to younger people. However, they still may want to be active in the food pantry. They decide that they still value the goal of providing food for those in need and thus they decide to help with the coordination and organization of volunteers to unload the truck and fill the pantry. In this way, they are still optimizing their ability—here, the knowledge of how the food pantry works—and then compensate by not engaging in the physical labor of unloading the truck. In the context of the aging family, one may have been an active parent, running around with their children and playing sports. As a grandparent, they may still value physical activity but cannot run around as they once did. A selective optimization could be to go bowling with their grandchildren, which would not have the same wear and tear as a sport like soccer.

In sum, these three theories attempt to explain how we continue with activities in later life. They are individualistic and psychological for the most part, and sociologists have largely gotten away from them, using life course theory instead. We have moved to focusing less on how later life is related to general decline and disengagement and moved to more positive understandings of new activities such as socializing, grandparenting, and participating in community (Johnson and Mutchler 2013). The theories reviewed here helped us move to thinking about successful and productive aging (Rowe and Kahn 1998) and beyond the negative notions of aging as a downward spiral.

Activities in Later Life

In order to understand what we do in our daily lives, scholars have attempted to classify activities into different domains (Putnam et al. 2013). Doing so makes clearer how we spend our free time. One classification system segments people's lives into **committed, obligatory,** and **discretionary activities.** Committed activities include productive roles such as paid employment. Obligatory activities include those required to live, such as sleeping. Finally, discretionary activities include free-time pursuits such as socializing

Committed	Obligatory	Discretionary
• paid work • housework • yardwork • home maintenance • shopping/food • carework	• sleeping • eating • personal care • grooming • managing medicine • managing health care paperwork • paying bills	• socializing • reading • playing cards • watching TV • hobbies • exercise • religious attendance

FIGURE 6.1 Three Types of Activities

(Verbrugge, Gruber-Baldini, and Fozard 1996; Sau et al. 2014). These three domains cover the range of activities that affect a family (see figure 6.1).

Another common classification divides time among social, leisure, and productive activities. Most activities of older adults fall in these three domains (Adams, Leibbrandt, and Moon 2011). Social activities include family gatherings and dinners, leisure activities include hobbies or going to a movie, and examples of productive activities are shopping for food, volunteering, and so on. Other common classifications for activities include physical, spiritual or serving others, intellectual and cultural, and solitary activities (Adams, Leibbrandt, and Moon 2011). Creating domains of activities has become important as we have realized that over time people do not simply disengage from active life but rather replace old activities with new ones as they age, and this is helpful for mental and physical health (Putnam et al. 2013). There is no one best way to measure how people spend their free time. Researchers choose the classification system that best works for their research questions.

When examining work and activities, the tradition is to measure basic characteristics that promote greater well-being (Kohn and Schooler 1983). With aging, **autonomy**, that is, the ability to do what one wants to do, when one wants to do it, increases (Drentea 2005). As such, figure 6.2 shows a simple graph of age with how much autonomy we experience. There is a general increase in autonomy in the oldest age groups. Because autonomy is measured here by how often someone tells you how and what to do, it is not surprising to see the increase. The larger confidence intervals in the youngest and oldest age categories are due to smaller numbers of people in those categories.

Adults in their twenties to fifties are juggling their jobs along with raising children and readying them to leave the home, as well as possibly dealing

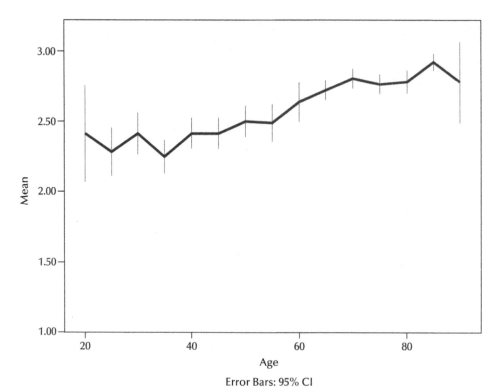

FIGURE 6.2 Relationship between Age and Autonomy
Source: Based on Aging, Status and Sense of Control data, 1997–1998.
Note: N = 1,365. Vertical lines show 95% confidence intervals

with divorce, remarriage, and new partnerships. As work and parent roles subside, we have more autonomy with regard to what we can do.

With more time available, discretionary activities increase over time. Generally speaking, these are known to lead to better health and well-being. Social activities such as visiting family and friends improve physical and cognitive function over time, and are a pathway to greater happiness. Moreover, socializing leads to more leisure activities that are associated with greater psychological and physical well-being (Chang, Wray, and Lin 2014). They also appear to have a protective effect against mortality (Menec 2003). Spending time with family and friends fosters intimacy, combats loneliness, and may lead to more social support. Social disconnectedness (that is, having a small social network and infrequent participation in social activities) is associated with poorer physical and mental health due to perceived loneliness (Cornwell and Waite 2009). While solitary activities such as hobbies also are associated with greater happiness over time, they do not seem to hold the same protective effect in terms of mortality and functioning (Menec 2003). Thus, while important and better than very passive activities (because solitary activities keep one potentially creative and interested), they may not lead to the same payoffs that interactions with others do. Having a high degree of engagement, fulfillment, and meaningful activity is especially important to psychological well-being (Matz-Costa, Besen, James, and

Pitt-Catsouphes 2014). Another avenue for many older adults alive today is to become more active in religious services and attendance. Previous research has found that church activities can increase social networks, social support, and enhance self-worth and self-esteem (Ellison, Schieman, and Bradshaw 2014; Krause and Hayward 2014). Additional research shows that emotional experiences both increase and improve as we age (Carstensen et al. 2011).

Of course, over time types of activities change. Following continuity theory, activity theory, and selective optimization with compensation theories, healthy aging is associated with continuing and modifying activities and adjusting them to our interests and our limitations. However, many older adults will not be able to choose how to spend their free time (Katz and Calasanti 2015). A disadvantaged life is associated with a disadvantaged old age. For instance, women with a low economic status may be food insecure and spend a lot of time watching television in their apartment. They may be asked to watch children for little or no money. Longer life brings encroaching health problems and later life can become a series of doctors' appointments, treatments, and times of rest as one tries to get better or as one nears death. An inordinate amount of time may be spent chair- or bed-bound, watching television or surfing the internet most days (Baker, Bodnar, and Allman 2003). Thus while there is emphasis on healthy aging, we must also understand that not everyone shares the same aging experience. Social inequalities affect choices, lifestyles, circumstances, and health (Katz and Calasanti 2015), despite the fact that, overall, a growing number of individuals maintain relatively good health and plenty of free time until very late in life.

More Leisure Time and Opportunities

As we move into the second decade of the twenty-first century, there is a widening spectrum for discretionary activities for the aging brought about by changes in technology and senior learning opportunities. As paid work decreases, time spent in other productive activities such as volunteering, civic, and religious participation can increase. Older Americans also spend time keeping up with family, and the families of their children. Activities associated with the family include watching and babysitting children and sometimes even raising children. In 1986, Ekerdt convincingly argued that modern society in the United States lives with a "busy ethic." Stemming from a belief in the goodness of work (indeed related to the Protestant work ethic), this is then transferred into later life with a belief in staying active through exercise, traveling, eating out, taking care of oneself, and the like (Ekerdt 1986). "Busyness," he argues, is like a status symbol for those who were raised in the Great Depression, and staying busy and engaging in hard work is virtuous. Furthermore, they believe that retirement is the one normative time in which individuals have *earned* their leisure after working hard for so long. This attitude is reflected above in Sandra's words, where she states that after hitting the ground running for so long, she really appreciates being able to spend a long morning in her pajamas.

Consumption: America's Favorite Hobby?

For many older Americans with lots of free time, much of it is dedicated to consumption. That is, time is spent eating out at restaurants, shopping for goods, and using services. Even with the economic downturn of the first decade of the 2000s, it is predicted that lifestyles in America will continue to center on consumerism and consumption. Some of the increase is in service needs. Restaurants and eating out are very popular. Older adults consume health care at higher rates than young people. They often need help doing household maintenance that they used to be able to do on their own. Moreover, they get help with personal services such as beauty work. For instance, an older woman may begin to visit the salon for a weekly shampoo and styling, or a man who lives alone goes to a nail salon to get help with cutting his toenails. Self-care that used to be easy becomes more difficult.

Another trend in U.S. society is that purchasing has become a part of personal identity. America has a love for "stuff" and with the changing demographics will come a market for more goods and services geared toward older Americans. Luxury items are popular among wealthier Baby Boomers (Danziger 2011; Schor 2004). Overall, Baby Boomers have come of age during a time of more wealth among the middle class. They did not live through the Great Depression, as many of their parents did. As such, they have grown used to lifestyles with ample clothing, multiple cars, many electronics, larger homes, and the like. They are beginning to downsize their homes as they age and are moving past their peak collecting years. There will be more interest in experiences over things among the well-to-do. Generation X (born about 1965–1981) is following suit, acquiring things, though there is a cultural shift of less collecting, more desire to purchase green and fair-trade products, and more interest in philanthropy and having varied experiences (Danziger 2011).

Thus, a major utilization of leisure is consumerism and shopping. Indeed, the United States and other developed nations have historically gone from societies focusing on producing to cultures of surplus and consumption (Bauman 2007). Additionally, the amount of goods available to consume is unprecedented (Hyde et al. 2009). We enjoy comfort. For many, from every socioeconomic class, shopping has become an activity of fun and leisure in which the emphasis is turning from simple fulfillment to self-expression and individualism (Danziger 2011), and to shaping our values and daily activities (Schumaker 2001).

Older individuals usually have more income available than younger people on average (U.S. Census Bureau 2016a). Among the middle and upper classes, once children have left home and they are done helping with the college costs, there is more discretionary money to spend. With their homes paid for and the extra time available, shopping is a leisurely pursuit for many. Nazareth (2007) in her book, *The Leisure Economy*, writes convincingly of a generation of Baby Boomers flooding the market with time on their hands. Additionally, she adds, Generation X, a cohort that values work less and leisure more than the Baby Boomers, will soon follow. They were also raised on restaurant food, designer jeans, and the like, and will insist on an even more goods-and-services-based economy and lifestyle. Thus as these younger generations age, they will likely strive for continuity with what they have always done and will carry these behaviors, norms, and values of consumerism into later life as well (Nazareth 2007). Amid all this consumption, however, are the beginnings of a realization that this purchasing is tied into larger issues of waste, carbon footprints, and climate change (Danziger 2011, Nazareth 2007, Schor 2010). Simultaneously, the amount of excess spending money is dwindling in most families (Porter 2012). Slowly, countercultures are emerging that are steeped in buying and eating local, avid recycling, and making rather than buying products (Schor 2010). It remains to be seen what will carry into later life for these families.

The Other Side

Of course, not everyone will have a life of leisure and shopping in their later years. Socioeconomic factors between men and women, married versus not married, and among underrepresented minorities will make a difference. People with pensions and ample savings will have a very different experience than those hoping to live on Social Security. Having a secure income in later life translates to better health on average and more opportunity for activities. Without such income, activities closer to home such as internet surfing, watching TV, and visiting friends will be more common. For older women with few means, a lifestyle of shopping as an activity may not be realistic; however, taking care of grandchildren is more likely.

Travel and Adult Education Programs

One change in activity in later life is an interest in pursuits outside of work and childrearing. With increased time and money comes increased ability to travel among the middle and upper classes. The travel industry has seen an increase in travel expenses and experiences over time (Nazareth 2011). One program directed toward older adults is Road Scholar (formerly Elderhostel). The program began in the United States in 1975 to provide travel and lifelong learning experiences to those over fifty-five years of age (http://www.roadscholar.org). One of the original ideals behind the organization was to promote active learning later in life. This program is geared toward adventures in learning: it is a not-for-profit program that allows older adults to travel with affordable lodging. It now ventures to over 150 countries, and also offers "day of discovery" programs and experiential learning trips—which connect participants with locals on short trips—to those living in retirement communities. Similar programs abound in churches, community centers, and libraries across the country. OLLI (Osher Lifelong Learning Institute) is another learning program aimed at older adults and is active in many universities across the country. Seniors can travel together, volunteer, learn about travel, take college courses in an area of interest, or learn a new skill. As future generations have higher levels of education and more experience with travel, it is predicted that programs like Road Scholar will continue to grow.

Grandparenting

In the context of continuity theory, parenting is an ongoing activity that lasts many years while a child is growing up, and one that most would agree never ends. Thus it follows that a natural progression in continuing this activity is grandparenting. Thinking about selective optimization with compensation theory, since parenting full-time is a tough job, most grandparents do not take care of grandchildren full-time. Rather they choose what they will do, but leave the full-time, 24-hour care to parents. Even so, grandparenting has become a major activity for many in later life.

Longer lives mean more years available to be a grandparent. When one thinks about his or her own grandparents, many different visions come to mind. Many older people did not know their grandparents, as they likely died at earlier ages. Uhlenberg (2009:493) estimates that among ten-year-olds, only 23 percent knew all their grandparents in 1960, whereas by 2020, almost half would have all grandparents alive. As grandparents live longer, children know them for a longer period of time. Grandparents provide many functions to a family, including support, sharing family stories, and engaging in leisure activities with grandchildren. For some grandparents, grandparenting is more than leisure. Some regularly help their adult children with childcare, housework, meals, and driving their grandchildren where they need to go. Other grandparents have taken over raising their grandchildren—leading to a second run on parenting. Let us turn to these roles in grandparenting.

Extended Time Grandparenting—Quality, and Quantity

Most people become grandparents while they still work themselves (Harrington Meyer 2014). They often must decide what level of involvement they want in their grandchildren's lives. The process is ongoing, and changes are based on factors such as geographical proximity, help needed by adult children, availability of grandparents, health of grandparents, interest, and so on. Being a grandparent can involve a multitude of activities, including leisure and fun, playing with young grandchildren, taking them on excursions, and babysitting. Grandparents also often provide financial support to their children, grandchildren, and even great-grandchildren, both in terms of finances and in in-kind support such as buying school uniforms and books for their grandchildren. While rare, it is possible to become a grandparent as early as one's late thirties (if one had a teenage pregnancy and so did their child); however, it is more likely to happen later. About half of the population become grandparents by age 50, and the average age to become a grandparent is forty-eight years old (Newman 2009). Younger grandparents are more likely to work themselves and have less time available for their grandchildren. However, they also have more physical ability to engage in some of the physical work of caring for small children. Older grandparents, especially if a grandchild is born when they are closer to eighty years old (for example, if one has a child at forty years of age and then their child has a baby when they are near forty as well), likely have much more free time but less physical strength and stamina to keep up with diapering a baby or running after toddlers. In the future, we will likely continue to see fewer very young grandparents, but will see more people becoming first-time grandparents at older ages.

Many women are facing grandparent responsibilities while they are still working. Unlike most grandfathers in this generation, these women juggle care and paid work. Just as motherhood has become more intense, with greater expectations of what is required to keep children active and competitive (Hays 1996), being a grandmother too has become more involved as they are

Younger grandparents are generally able to take care of small children without much trouble. However, for older grandparents, the physical demands of taking care of children can be exhausting. iStock/ DessieDavidova

expected to help their working children with childcare, increased homework expectations, and increased levels of extracurricular activities. Thus it appears that intensive parenting and the phenomena of overscheduling children and setting up play dates will trickle down to grandparents as well. In her research, Harrington Meyer (2014) interviewed women who spoke of being exhausted by the work of caring for grandchildren, often juggling their own jobs and aging parents' needs. They also spoke of the joy of being a grandparent. What was clear was that they were not just there for the fun parts of raising children; they were also bathing, feeding, driving, and taking care of children overnight. They took time off from work to help with their grandchildren and all except four of the forty-eight interviewed said they provided more care than their grandparents had provided (Harrington Meyer 2014:22). Thus, she concludes, expectations have increased for how much care they should provide. One interesting finding from this research is how these women actively made themselves unavailable at times so that they didn't have to provide assistance. They felt so much pressure to be there for their own children that they came up with legitimate excuses when they needed a break (for instance, they would work longer hours so they were not available to babysit). The grandmothers all loved their grandchildren and caring for them; however, they also admitted that at times it was a lot of work. Although there have been changes in gender roles, she notes in her book (Harrington Meyer 2014) that grandparenting is primarily a "woman's job" and that few spoke of the work their husbands did in helping with the babysitting.

With smaller families also come fewer grandchildren per grandparent. As such, it is estimated that only 20 percent of grandparents will have more than two sets of grandchildren by 2020 (because these grandparents only had two children themselves) (Uhlenberg 2009). Grandchildren will also have fewer sets of cousins competing for attention, which will allow grandparents to allocate more financial and time resources to fewer children, enabling them to have potentially more quantity and quality relationships with their grandchildren. It could also bode well toward enhanced expectations of caring for the few grandchildren one has. While today it is still common to see obituaries where one was a grandmother of thirteen, this type of family structure will be much less common in the future—especially among middle and higher socioeconomic status individuals.

What clearly is becoming more common is the beanpole family structure, a term coined by Bengtson (2001) to describe more vertical generations of family compared to horizontal generations. Put differently, there are fewer members of family in each generation, but more generations alive at the same time, allowing for more multigenerational bonds (Bengtson 2001; Connidis 2010; Silverstein and Giarrusso 2010). This trend should continue in the future and will allow for more collective history among generations as the old can pass more down to the young in terms of stories and lessons learned from their lives (Williams, Woodby, and Drentea 2010).

Grandparenting as an Identity

The research on age identity and grandparenting peaked in 2003 (Kaufman and Elder 2003). Little more has been written on the subject, as presumably the concept has not changed much over the years. In life, each of us juggles multiple roles. One may be a paid worker, parent, spouse, brother or sister, daughter or son, and so on. The importance or salience of each role shifts based on the current situation. For instance, when one's child is sick, the parent role is the most salient. However, when one has to give a presentation to a group of sales representatives, the role of paid worker may surge ahead. Role salience for grandparenting predicts how active one will be in this role. According to a study by Reitzes and Mutran (2004), there is a gender difference in which role salience appears to matter more for grandfathers than grandmothers. They found that how grandfathers view their grandparent role is most important in what type of grandparent they become. This is because, as men of these generations, they are not necessarily expected to be active in children's lives, thus the role of grandparent is more by choice and voluntary for men. This is especially the case for grandparents of today who were born during a transitional time when many men were less involved in childrearing on average, and women were beginning to work outside of the home more.

The researchers posit that salience is not as central to the grandmother role because contact with grandchildren is simply expected for women. Indeed, much of the work of grandparents is shouldered by grandmothers (Harrington Meyer 2014).

Styles of Grandparenting

Since the 1980s, scholars have tried to pinpoint different grandparenting styles (Cherlin and Furstenberg 1985). In order to do this, researchers typically interview a large group of grandparents and ask them about all aspects of their grandparent-grandchild relationships. One such study took place in Iowa, with a focus on rural grandparents, and is considered a classic in the field (Mueller, Wilhelm, and Elder 2002). Researchers conducted phone interviews with up to four grandparents of the high school seniors (897 grandparents) in their sample. They asked about face-to-face contact, activities done together, intimacy, helping, assistance, and authority/discipline. Based on these measures or dimensions, they created a typology of five distinct styles of grandparenting. These included *influential, supportive, passive, authority-oriented*, and *detached*. Since high school seniors are quite independent and no longer require the parenting type of help that younger grandchildren require, this typology is more geared toward grandparent-grandchildren relationships that have matured beyond childhood. Table 6.1 summarizes the five types of grandparenting styles.

TABLE 6.1   Types of Grandparenting Styles

Type	Percent of Sample	Traits
Influential	17	Score high on all of the dimensions Most active in grandchild's daily life
Supportive	25	Very similar to influential grandparents, except on one dimension—authority Active, close ties to their grandchildren, but do not become primary authority figure
Passive	19	Moderately involved in grandchild's life Fairly frequent visitation, don't engage in providing discipline or instrumental assistance
Authority-oriented	13	Moderately engaged in grandchild's life Primary role is being an authority figure; giving advice and "being a voice of wisdom"
Detached	28	Least involved in the grandchild's life, often geographically distant

Source: Table derived from Mueller, Wilhelm, and Elder (2002:360–88).
Note: Based on five dimensions: face-to-face contact, activities done together, intimacy, helping, assistance, and authority/discipline.

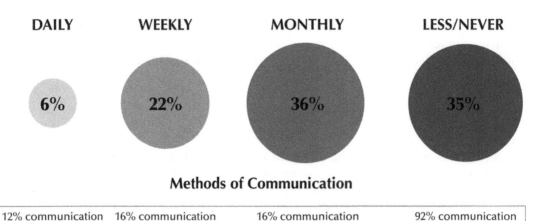

DAILY	WEEKLY	MONTHLY	LESS/NEVER
6%	22%	36%	35%

Methods of Communication

12% communication via letter or email	16% communication via social media	16% communication via text	92% communication via phone

FIGURE 6.3 How Often Do Adults Keep in Touch with Grandparents?
Source: Adapted from Pew Research Center Survey. October 27–December 18, 2014

Another factor in understanding levels of attachment is proximity, that is, how close the grandparent lives to the grandchild. Grandparents who live farther away from their grandchildren will most likely have a more detached or passive style of grandparenting (Mueller, Wilhelm, and Elder 2002). Discipline would be near impossible to impose. Affection and instrumental help such as driving or monitoring a sick child are also not possible. However, there are many ways for grandparents, grandchildren, and adult parents to communicate. In a study done by the Pew Research Organization (Anderson 2015), researchers found that adult children communicate with their parents via letters and email (12 percent), social media (16 percent), texting (16 percent), and of course via phone (92 percent).

Being in contact with grandparents is important to most adult children. That said, 35 percent of adults reported being in contact with grandparents less than monthly or never. In comparison, 6 percent report being in touch daily. Most respondents reported weekly (22 percent), and monthly (36 percent) (Anderson 2015) (see figure 6.3). One type of grandparenting has even greater proximity—when the grandparent and grandchild co-reside.

Parenting as a Grandparent

While most of the above discussion treats grandparenting as a discretionary activity in which grandparents choose when and how they will spend time with grandchildren, some bear the main responsibility for raising their grandchildren. About 7.8 million children under the age of eighteen are living in homes in which grandparents or other relatives are the householder (AARP 2015). The parents may sometimes live with the grandparents as well (co-residence), and may revolve in and out of the household. This can be due to a number of reasons, but usually involves problems such as drug use, mental illness, divorce, young age of the mother, financial need, or incarceration among the parent(s) (Scommegna 2012). It is more common among those who are socially disadvantaged; however, it affects all SES strata. Thus, the grandparents are frequently involved in, and are possibly mourning, the situation of their own children while also taking care of their children's children (skipped generation) (Hayslip and Kaminsky 2005). As would be expected, much of the work falls on the shoulders of grandmothers.

Another group currently experiencing this family structure is children with active-duty parents in the military. As parents are deployed, more children are left behind with a civilian parent, or with a grandparent or guardian. About one million military personnel are parents (Casey 2009).

An Example of Custodial Grandparenting

Siblings Chad and Jolene lived in Kansas. They experienced a lot of hardship, both economically and emotionally, before they moved in with their grandparents. Their mother was in no position to take care of her children; she was addicted to drugs and was in and out of jail. She was not reliable in their childhood. The kids would live with her until she disappeared and then they were shuttled off to their paternal grandparents, friends, other family, foster homes . . . whoever would take them. For most of their young childhood, they lived with their father, who was a trucker for an oil rig company and was gone for weeks at a time. Their paternal grandparents took care of them off and on until their father died.

Chad and Jolene's parents were divorced. Their father either committed suicide (the official story and what is on his death certificate) or he was killed by his fiancée (which is what the family actually thinks happened). As soon as their father died, the children officially moved in with their grandparents, who were in their fifties at the time. Chad was 13, and Jolene was 12. Their world changed dramatically. The grandfather had retired from the military, and their grandmother taught science at a middle school and later taught home economics at a high school. The children also received a monthly stipend from Social Security after their father died so they were boosted into the middle class.

The grandparents experienced two major tragedies: both of their sons died unexpectedly. They explained that the same year that Chad and Jolene's father was murdered, his brother (the grandmother's only other son and the children's uncle) died in a car accident. The grandmother maintains that if Chad and Jolene hadn't moved in when they did, she would never have made it through such a difficult time. The children had filled the void that was left when both of her sons died. Thus the newly reconstituted family changed even more as they adjusted to their new permanent family. They also had to adjust to the lingering sadness that permeated their lives.

The children's lives changed in a third way as well—they now had discipline and structure. Growing up, Chad remembers not having any rules. Once he moved in with his rather strict grandparents, he remembered, "suddenly, there was strict discipline, a strong work ethic, and respect was demanded." Chad and his sister were held to a much higher standard and were far more accountable for their behavior and their actions than they had been while living with either of their parents.

As difficult as his childhood seems, Chad, now in his early thirties, maintains that the most difficult things he went through are unique to him, and others have more difficulties or a different set of difficulties. He said there's no reason for him to dwell on the negatives of his past because it will only bring him down. He also said that he "can't use his life experiences as excuses"—there's no reason why he can't be a great father and husband because of a unique childhood. His youth isn't an excuse—it's an empowerment to him. He joined the military and is currently a drill sergeant, is married, has children, and reports that he is doing well.

TABLE 6.2   Grandchild Characteristics Living with a Grandparent Householder (N=922,208)

Characteristics of Grandchildren	(Percentage)
Age	
Under 6 years	23.50
6–11	35.50
12–17	41.00
Race/Ethnicity	
White	56.80
Black or African American	29.10
American Indian and Alaska Native	2.30
Asian	1.10
Native Hawaiian and Other Pacific Islander	.02
Some other race	3.50
Two or more races	7.00
Hispanic or Latino origin (of any race)	16.70
Mean Family Income	$36,351
Public Assistance in the past 12 months[a]	43.60

Source: Table created by author using 2010–2014 American Community Survey 5-year estimates with American Fact Finder. Retrieved on January 8, 2016, from query https://factfinder.census.gov/faces/tableservices/jsf/pages/product-view.xhtml?pid=ACS_14_5YR_S1001&prodType=table.
Note: Children are under eighteen years of age. Grandparent is the adult responsible for the grandchild or grandchildren with no parent present in the household.
[a] Includes SSI, cash public assistance income, food stamps/SNAP benefits.

Grandparents become involved with childrearing in military families when one of the grandchildren's parents is stationed or deployed. Sometimes, when a mother or father is stationed away from home, the spouse or partner left behind will move in with a grandparent to help share in childcare and childrearing, thus the household structure includes a grandparent(s), children, and a parent. However, sometimes in dual-military marriages, both parents are sent overseas and the grandparent(s) become main guardians. In any case, the effects on the children and families of those in the military include issues of stress and anxiety as families wrestle with multiple moves, family separations, school disruptions, and the reality that a family member may be harmed or killed (Casey 2009; Lester et al. 2010).

There are two main types of family arrangements in this situation: **coparenting** families, in which the three generations (grandparent, grandchild, and parent) live together, or the **custodial** or skipped-generation household, in which the grandparent raises the child without the parent present (Scommegna 2012).

On average, grandparents raising grandchildren have lower incomes than grandparents who do not take care of their grandchildren (Scommegna

2012). They also experience more health problems, in part due to their lower socioeconomic status and additional stressors. Research is clear that when children are raised in a socially disadvantaged household, there are fewer resources that the grandparents have to share (such as money, time, and education (Uhlenberg 2009).When custodial grandparents' have psychological distress, or when their marital relationships are strained, the children have a harder time adjusting (Smith and Hancock 2010). Table 6.2 shows grandchildren in the situation of living with a grandparent as the householder with no parents present. Clearly, this group of almost a million children under the age of eighteen shows signs of being disadvantaged. Most of the children are adolescents between the ages of twelve and seventeen, with whites having the highest rate of such living arrangements at almost 57 percent. It is notable that about 29 percent of the children are African American. The average income is $36,351 and almost 44 percent of these grandchildren receive some form of public assistance.

Divorce, Reconstituted Families, and Grandparents

One major change that has affected many grandparents directly over the past fifty years or so is a significant increase in the divorce rate. To understand the consequences, take, for instance, a first marriage in which the couple has two children. Both sets of grandparents live nearby and dote on the children. Then the couple divorces and, as is usually the case, the children live with the mother. The ties to the maternal grandparents stay strong. As time passes, the father moves away and remarries. He is quite distant with his own first-family children. The paternal grandparents, however, still live nearby and still work to maintain connections to their grandchildren. The mother eventually remarries as well, and now the grandparents have to negotiate with a new stepfather to their grandchildren in order to gain regular access to them. These types of scenarios, with multiple outcomes, occur frequently in the United States. Maternal grandparents tend to have more contact than paternal grandparents (Stewart 2007). At times, it is with great sorrow that the paternal grandparents struggle and lose contact with children through divorces and remarriages (Doyle, O'Dywer, and Timonen 2010).

Stepgrandparents also adopt a new role, and must negotiate their new relationships with their new stepgrandchildren (Stewart 2007). All of these changes to grandparenting in the twentieth and twenty-first centuries continue to occur. With a better understanding of grandparenting and stepfamilies, families may be able to create better plans for the biological grandparents to maintain the level of association they wish to have with their grandchildren. When parents have good relationships with their parents, the negative grandparent/grandchild relationship is not inevitable (King 2003), and both grandparents can still arrange to be active in the child's life if they wish.

There is one more type of divorce to consider, and that is when the *grandparents* get divorced in later life. This is often called gray divorce. Gray divorce is when older adults divorce after many years of marriage, and it is also on the rise (Brown and Lin 2012). Research (King 2003) finds that there is a negative effect on the ties between grandchildren and grandparents when the grandparents are divorced. After a divorce, grandfathers are frequently not as good at keeping connected to their grandchildren. Traditionally, they may have left all planning, gift shopping, and social contact to their wife (that is, the grandmother). Without that connection, they must try harder to make connections with the grandchildren. In addition, the ties often erode for paternal grandparents, often due to distance.

In sum, grandparenting is one of the major roles and activities that take place in later life. Many social factors affect grandparenting. These include such dimensions as closeness of family ties, amount of free time, ideology and salience of the role, situations in which parents need help, and proximity to family, to name a few. Many families, however, do not live near their children, which is often due to their jobs. In the next section, moving is explored. Sometimes the moves in later life are to be closer to grandchildren and children—and sometimes farther. Bringing in activity and continuity theories again, we recognize how people re-create their lives later in life.

Moving, Activities, and Families in Later Life

Most older people consider aging in place the ideal (Bookman and Kimbrel 2011). People want to be in their own homes, with the comfort of their neighborhoods, and within reach of their social networks. Familiarity helps with comfort, socializing, and also with social support. Moving, on the other hand, is stressful—even when it is desired. Moving disrupts everything and can be especially challenging for the very elderly or those in early stages of dementia. In addition, moving often involves downsizing, which means getting rid of a lifetime of acquired things. However, older people do often move later in life for different reasons—to live in more favorable climates, to pursue a more active lifestyle, to downsize from larger homes, or to be near family. Moving for health reasons occurs when homes are no longer suitable, for instance, if a home becomes too large to maintain or has a second story and steep stairs.

Those researchers at the forefront of understanding migration patterns in the context of family and aging believe there are four distinct times of migration for families (Plane and Jurjevich 2009). Building off the classic work of Litwak and Longino (1987), Plane and Jurjevich (2009) examine how each stage in the life course affects the propensity to move as well as the type and size of city (or rural area) to which one will move. The first two move phases are in early adulthood—first, when young adults launch into their first job, the military, or a place of higher education, and second, when young families have children and seek more space and affordable housing. The latter two phases in later adulthood are described below (Plane and Jurjevich 2009).

Later life moves are divided into two general phases. The first involves young empty-nesters, aged 55–64, who may be in a preretirement stage but may also be seeking to move for career advancement. Either way, they are liberated by no longer being worried about school districts and the continuity of their children's education. Once their children are gone, they may no longer wish to live in child-centered suburbs. They are young and healthy enough to move and are seeking new experiences. Additionally, they may still be free from the responsibility of taking care of their own aged parents. They can now pursue the activities they enjoy; this time is sometimes called encore adulthood (Moen 2016)—a second new adulthood in which people can pursue new interests and lifestyles. Using the three theories outlined at the beginning of the chapter, they may continue to engage in activities they enjoy, seeking out similar but new experiences in new locales.

The second phase is the golden-aged mover (eighty years old and older) who often moves back to larger or midsized cities to be near to one of their adult children. This is sometimes precipitated by the death of a spouse or partner. Thus, this second movement disproportionately affects women, as men typically die earlier than women. These women may be leaving a retirement community or a second vacation home, which may be in a more remote location, and coming back to a larger city. Sometimes there is a final move when failing health precipitates the need for nursing-home or assisted-living care (Plane and Jurjevich 2009).

With the aging of the population, there is an increased need for housing for older adults. Many types of housing opportunities exist and there has been a rise in the number and variety of possibilities; among these are assisted living, memory care, naturally occurring retirement communities (norcs), vouchers (formerly section 8 housing), religious-based subsidized housing, and so on (Schnure and Venkatesh 2015).

A major draw to housing beyond single-home housing is the provision of structured and leisure activities, and the availability of some monitoring of older adults. Most of these types of communities are affluent and geared toward upper-middle-class Americans with ample financial resources (McHugh and Larson-Keagy 2005; Schnure and Venkatesh 2015). They are rather homogenous and at times intolerant of diversity, including age diversity. Many of the communities are age-restricted (McHugh and Larson-Keagy 2005) and do not allow young families to even visit for an extended period of time.

Some older Americans enjoy time with their families but relocate when the weather is either too cold or too hot. They are nicknamed **snowbirds** and **sunbirds**. Snowbirds are those who migrate from cold climates in the winter and live in the south, predominantly in Florida and Arizona. Sunbirds are those who have already migrated to the south, but then visit family up north for a month or more during the hot summer months. Usually they are from places like Florida (Smith and House 2006). Smith and House (2006) estimate that upward of 12 percent of Florida's permanent residents aged 55 or older spent more than thirty days somewhere other than their place of usual residence in the previous year in 2005. Many of these sunbirds visit family back in their original hometowns. They also offer families a warm place to visit during the cold months of winter.

Thus there is some movement among the older population. Much of it is related to families in that it involves changes when parents launch children, and then as a means to maintain family ties. Movement into nursing homes and assisted-living facilities, which is related to health, will be discussed in another chapter. With smaller families, more freedom, and fewer family obligations, we expect to see more transience in the future.

Technology

Connectivity and Social Media

Digital technologies are affecting all modes of communication. Computers, mobile devices, and smartphones have all changed communication across the world. Texting, FaceTime, Skype, and Google Chat, to name a few, are changing interactions and communications, and changing how we think about social relationships. E-readers have changed how print media is delivered. Social media sites such as Instagram, Facebook, Twitter, and LinkedIn are ways older adults interact with others, and maintain social relationships, both new and old. Thus a major activity in people's lives today is consuming electronic media and spending time online on the internet. Scholarly research on the topic tries to assess under which conditions increased connectedness to others helps to avoid social isolation and loneliness for the elderly later in life.

Older adults are increasingly becoming active on the internet and have cell phones; however, they lag behind middle-aged adults and young people. A recent study reports 59 percent of U.S. adults over age 65 go on the internet (as compared to 86 percent of all adults ages 18+) (Smith 2015). Thirty-seven percent of those 65 and older use social media, compared to only 11 percent in 2010 (Perrin 2015). Similarly, 77 percent of older adults (65 and over) have cell phones, as compared to 91 percent of all adults ages 18 and over (Smith 2015). It is difficult to track internet usage because it is rising so quickly among this older age group, but there is a considerable increase from just five to ten years ago (Fox 2004).

However, there is still a **digital divide** between who has access to good computing resources such as fast internet connections. Clearly, a digital divide exists between rich versus poor, low versus high education, urban versus rural, old versus young (Hale, Cotten, Drentea, and Goldner 2010). The previous racial divide we saw appears to have abated (Hale, Cotten, Drentea, and Goldner 2010; Perrin 2015). Similarly, the gender difference in internet usage also reached parity over a decade ago (Fox 2004). There is still a divide between young and old. Older people are less likely to use the internet. The usage drops precipitously in the oldest age range, with only 37 percent of those over age 80 on the internet (Smith 2015). The divide then creates a system of those who have access to the internet and stay connected to others, and those who do not. So many activities and resources have gone online (banking, shopping, e-government, or schoolwork). Companies, universities, and banks assume everyone has access to computers and the internet, completely leaving some older adults out of the internet transformation.

One in-depth study examined reasons for going online and found that a major reason older adults over fifty do so is for fun (Nimrod 2011). In her research examining six top senior websites in the United States, the United Kingdom, and Canada over the course of a year, she found that most of the 50,000 or so posts were fun or joking around. It was not that the individuals discussed fun, rather they engaged in games such as cognitive games, trivia posts, associative games (where each post builds on the previous one), and creative games such as rhyming sentences. The main topics in the activities included sex, gender differences, aging, grandparenting, faith, politics, and alcohol. This type of online gaming and conversation offers older adults a place for interaction and cognitive stimulation. Thus a primary reason older people use communication technology is for interaction.

Among older adults, women are more likely to be motivated to keep in touch with family online and female parents search more for health information than nonparent men or women (Cotten, Anderson, and McCullough 2013; Stern, Cotten, and Drentea 2012; Yost et al. 2016). One major trend is the increase of older people using social media to keep in touch with family (Nef et al. 2013; Yost et al. 2016). For many older women, getting on Facebook keeps them in contact with their families (Yost et al. 2016). In one project in Alabama, researchers went into assisted and independent living communities and trained residents for eight weeks. They found that while many were either too frail or simply not willing to try, those who did go through the training enjoyed connecting to their family and friends, as well

iStock/Rawpixel

as with other residents. Thus these older adults reported less depression and loneliness (Winstead et al. 2013). Moreover, most did not want the training to end when the classes were completed. Research shows that for retired older people, internet use was associated with lower levels of depression, especially for those living alone (Cotten, Ford, Ford, and Hale 2014).

Of course, current generations of older Americans were not raised with computers; future generations will be much more technologically savvy. As each successive cohort of older adults replaces the next, adults will enter old age having used these technologies. As those who were born with this technology (digital natives) age, they can maintain a level of continuity by using social media and the internet in their activities across the life course. Selective optimization with compensation is a useful theory here; as older adults experience vision or hearing declines, they may adjust to larger devices or computer modifications for activities they could have done on their phones when they were younger.

Summary

This chapter began by examining activity, continuity, and selective optimization with compensation theories and a general discussion of activities. We reviewed the major family-related activities of the older population and speculated how they will change and grow. We predicted how there will be growth in leisure activities such as shopping and travel. Grandparenting was discussed in detail, with attention to how it is currently experienced, and how it may change over time with more stepfamilies. We examined when grandparents become primary caregivers for their grandchildren. Other activities, such as the use of technology, were also discussed. The current status of older adults' online presence was discussed, noting how they are using the internet for leisure and social connections. With an eye toward activity and continuity theories, we predict that individuals will continue to be active in later life, depending on their physical, psychological, and cognitive abilities.

Critical Thinking Questions

1. How would you describe the differences among continuity theory, activity theory, and selective optimization with compensation theory? Are they still useful today? Why do some consider them outdated?

2. Apply the three theories to the work and activity of being a cabinetmaker, a marathon runner, and an accountant earlier in the life course. How would each theory predict changes over time?

3. Consider how you use social media today. Which platforms do you use? Which do you think will be still in use when you are in your seventies? Can you think of social media that would be especially useful for older adults?

Chapter 7

Health and Caregiving

CHAPTER OBJECTIVES

1. Be able to explain cumulative advantage and disadvantage and how they affect health.
2. Understand the difference between the failure of success versus the compression of mortality views.
3. Understand the effects of socioeconomic status on health and mental health and the types of health outcomes it affects.
4. Relate how low versus high socioeconomic status will affect families and health in later life.
5. Consider all aspects of caregiving.

Loretta Pettway (born 1942) has gained a reputation throughout the United States as an exceptional quiltmaker, even though the poverty and location of rural Gee's Bend, Alabama, limit contact outside the area. In the book *Gee's Bend: The Women and Their Quilts* (Beardsley et al. 2002), Ms. Pettway remembers her childhood, one in which she moved many times from uncles to aunts to grandparents. She said:

> I never had a child life. My mother left when I was 'round about seven or eight . . . We were farming and I would go in the field from Monday til Saturday, twelve o'clock . . . I get to go to school a little bit, in October and November and December. Then we get ready to knock cotton stalks and break up the land for start the farming over . . . I had an abusive husband. He was a drinker, he was a gambler, he was a smoker. He had a lot of habits. My husband was real jealous; beat me up if he sees me talking to a man. I had seven children . . . [and we farmed]. I had to take children into the fields. They would sit in the wagon under the tree while we was out in the field working. . . . [from 5 AM to dark] . . . [we would sell blackberries, and my grandmother would carry them on her head in a pail or tub]. I always suffer with bad headaches and could never tote nothing on my head. (Beardsley et al. 2002:80)

In this passage, Loretta Pettway describes a life of hard work, of emotional, physical, and psychological disadvantage. The narrator of the documentary *Quiltmakers of Gee's Bend* (Alabama Public Television 2005) states that everyone has had a hard life, but that Loretta's life was much harder than others'. As a result, she suffers from many problems in her older age, including what appears to be serious depression. Despite these issues, she has produced quilts among the best in the United States. When she began, she put together quilts from the only fabric she had—old jeans legs from a life of field work. As a resident of Alabama, I can imagine the heat and sun in the fields in Alabama, the boredom of seven children in a wagon all day, or trying to break up clay soil by hand. This hard work, combined with the psychological trauma from an abusive marriage, has rendered her with serious problems in later life. In the documentary, she is filmed refusing to get on the bus tour for the quilt artists in which they visit museums displaying their quilts. She could not enjoy participating in these events (Alabama Public Television 2005); rather, she preferred to stay at home, rather isolated, while her fellow quiltmakers traveled the United States.

Robert and Belinda, a married couple, are really enjoying their later years. Born in 1950 and 1953, respectively, both worked most of their adult lives. Robert was an engineer-manager and retired at age 61, and Belinda was an elementary school principal who retired at age 55. Between them, they have multiple college degrees. Here is a sample from a recent Christmas letter:

> Wow! Another year has just flashed by . . . traveling, biking, reading, taking classes, going to concerts and the theatre, meeting friends for coffee. It's true: time flies when you're having fun. If that sounds familiar it should. It's what we wrote last year. And we're very pleased to report it applies just as well to this year. . . . This year we visited the Grand Canyon and Death Valley, CA, on our way to an Elderhostel in Colorado. We then returned for Robert's mother's 93rd birthday, and then in July we went to Toronto, Canada. In August, we did the big one: Europe . . . Back in Wisconsin in September where we participated in an Elderhostel in Duluth, Minnesota, for bird watching.

Both Robert and Belinda have had a lifelong love of learning, and many trips throughout their lives have been educational. They spent time biking and birding and just being outdoors. In middle age, they were avid cross-country skiers. Both had generous vacation times; Belinda had 6–8 weeks off each summer. When I asked how they had kept up this active lifestyle, Belinda stated that they always had good health coverage from their employers, including dental insurance and lots of preventive services such as routine checkups, annual immunizations, and weekly visits to a wellness center. She also pointed out that they have friends who are equally active, who encourage them and support their efforts.

This chapter examines health and caregiving. We are living longer and generally healthier lives; experiences and circumstances accumulate over the years, and we experience either a cumulative advantage or cumulative disadvantage in health in later life. For Loretta, who was born and raised in the Black Belt of Alabama (named for its soil, but it also has a mostly Black or African American population and is an area of persistent poverty) (Wharton and Church 2009), her experiences and environment have come together to create a lifetime of disadvantage—even in the wake of being discovered for her remarkable artistic talent. For Belinda and Robert, a lifetime of financial and health advantages has led to a wonderful and healthy early retirement. Through these two vignettes, two different ways our lives can change over time are shown.

This chapter begins with two vignettes, one from rural Alabama and the other from Wisconsin, depicting very different life experiences. Both vignettes exemplify the theory of cumulative advantage and disadvantage, and their effects on healthy living and health overall. The Alabamian has endured a great deal of poverty and hardship, and has later-life health issues. The Wisconsinites are experiencing a later life filled with activities and fun. The chapter provides an explanation of the expansion versus the compression of morbidity, and then examines socioeconomic status and health. Next, the effects of social support are discussed, as well as the level of assistance (such as help from caregivers) required later in life. Finally, it ends with a discussion of living arrangements and adaptations to the home as our health declines. In each case, the family is typically drawn in to assist with decisions, and we conclude with the health needs of older adults and how the family is involved.

Theory—Cumulative Advantage and Disadvantage

The theory of cumulative advantage and disadvantage (CAD) is related to life course theory. The theory examines how cohorts of individuals end up doing well—or not—over time: much of it is related to social inequality. Advantage and disadvantage begin to accumulate in childhood with parents' socioeconomic status and schooling experiences that then affect the type of job and income one receives later (Dannefer 2003; Lynch 2003; O'Rand 2003; Wickrama, Conger, and Abraham 2005). More education is also associated with better social networks and social support (Cutler and Lleras-Muney 2006), which ultimately affects health and well-being (Thoits 2011). The main idea is that the accumulation of advantages such as higher education, income, strong family support, and a healthy lifestyle (including having good health care and health insurance—in effect, the rich get richer) conferred upon individuals is exemplified by better health in later life. Those with higher socioeconomic status and greater advantages tend to adopt healthier lifestyles (Cockerham 2013). In contrast, the accumulation of disadvantages such as lower levels of education and poor health care (especially in childhood), poor family ties and support, and unhealthy lifestyle practices also accumulate over time (thus, the poor get poorer). One's location in the social hierarchy affects resources, which can be used as capital that ultimately affects mental and physical health (Dannefer 2003; Ferraro and Shippee 2009; Shippee, Wilkinson, and Ferraro 2012; Thoits 2011; Wickrama, Conger, and Abraham 2005), and mortality (Olshansky et al. 2012). Women are more likely to experience economic hardship, especially if they are single mothers raising children. Over time, the cumulative financial hardship affects their health (Shippee, Wilkinson, and Ferraro 2012).

iStock/fstop123

Among older adults, we see a diversification of the outcomes in later life, especially pertaining to health, in which most young people have good health, but as we age, there is greater variation in the experience of health. A life of advantage generally leads to better health and a longer life, whereas a life of disadvantage has worsening effects on the individual over time (Braveman et al. 2010; Smith 2007; Taylor 2010).

The inequalities in earlier life also lead to unequal experiences in later life for underrepresented minorities (Olshansky et al. 2012; Spence, Adkins, and Dupre 2011; Williams, Priest, and Anderson 2016) as well as for women who have experienced disadvantage (Perry, Harp, and Oser 2013). Thus, as we see above in the life story of Ms. Pettway, an African American woman from a very rural and poor part of Alabama, a life experience of poverty, abuse, and disadvantage understandably has led to health and mental health problems in later life. Robert and Belinda have experienced an advantaged lifestyle, high levels of education, and income and preventive health care and services. Therefore, they enjoy a full life in old age.

Improved Health Overall, Vitality, and Aging Well

Health

Borrowing from the WHO (World Health Organization) definition, "Health is a state of complete physical, mental, and social well-being and not merely the absence of disease or infirmity" (WHO 2017). In this chapter I discuss physical health and well-being. Many think about health in older age as the ability to still live independently—that is, to live in one's own home or to live with minimal assistance during the day. A growing movement wants to consider aging well and with vitality, forestalling the natural health declines that occur in later life as long as possible. As people live longer, there is more emphasis on maintaining a higher quality of life in old age.

The health of our loved ones as they age is intricately and intimately tied to our families and ourselves. We worry for those who are older and having health problems; we also often take care of family members. As health declines overall, multiple systems to provide care and treatment are needed. When there is a health crisis, social, governmental, medical, and family systems may all be activated. All of these changes in health occur more frequently in old age. One of the main ways to describe these health declines is by understanding their impact on the activities of daily living.

Activities of Daily Living

Activities of daily living (ADLs) are one way to measure how healthy (or unhealthy) individuals are as they age. Sometimes these are also called functional limitations. ADLs are the things we must do every day to take care of ourselves and to function well. They tap into the basics of self-care and mobility. Many different scales are used to measure ADLs to assess varying levels of functional impairment and independence. The most basic set of ADLs usually includes the following (Katz et al. 1963):

- Bathing
- Dressing
- Transferring from bed or chair
- Walking
- Eating
- Toilet use

Some distinguish between BADLs (that is, the basic ADLs listed above) and IADLs (instrumental ADLs). IADLs (Powell and Brody 1969) have more to do with one's interaction with the environment. These include:

- Doing laundry
- Housekeeping
- Preparing food
- Using the telephone
- Managing transportation
- Keeping track of medicines
- Handling finances
- Shopping

Once practitioners such as nurses and occupational and physical therapists can score patients on ADLs, appropriate therapy and assistance can be recommended to them and their families. A person's range of ability can vary greatly with each life skill and some forms of assistance are much more difficult than others to give. Help with grooming, such as brushing hair or shaving, is fairly easy to provide to a loved one, whereas help with toileting is much more difficult both physically and psychologically (Twigg et al. 2010). Sociologists, psychologists, social workers, and those with jobs in patient health care and medicine all use ADL scales to understand health status and health needs. Using ADL scales, we can measure and evaluate health declines in later life.

Figures 7.1 and 7.2 show difficulty with self-care in bathing and dressing by sex and age, based on the American Community Survey. From these pie charts, we see that in the younger age group of those 65–74, about the same percentage of women and men have trouble bathing or dressing (though women have a little more at 4.9 percent, compared to men's 4.2 percent). However, once we examine the older age group of those 75 and over, the percent of men has more than doubled to 11.1 percent, but women have more than tripled at 15.9 percent. Thus, while percentages are not high per se in either population, there is a gender difference.

Percent with self-care difficulty, age 65 to 74

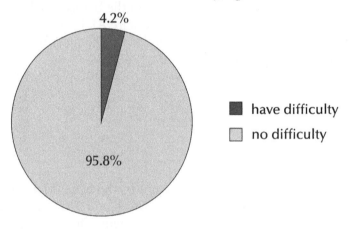

Percent with self-care difficulty, age 75 and over

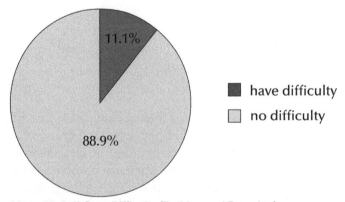

FIGURE 7.1   Men with Self-Care Difficulty (Bathing and Dressing)
Source: American Fact Finder. American Community Survey data 2010–2014. 5-Year Estimates. Retrieved January 15, 2016

Percent with self-care difficulty, age 65 to 74

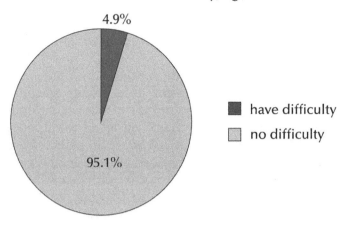

Percent with self-care difficulty, age 75 and over

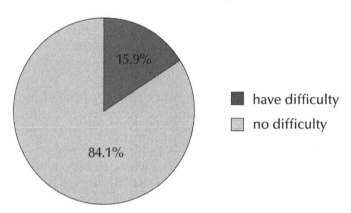

FIGURE 7.2   Women with Self-Care Difficulty (Bathing and Dressing)
Source: American Fact Finder. American Community Survey data 2010–2014. 5-Year Estimates. Retrieved January 15, 2016

Expansion versus Compression of Morbidity

A debate in the area of health is that of the expansion versus the compression of morbidity. Over time, some older adults have an increase in disabilities and functional impairments that limit their health and mobility. The final years of one's life usually entail at least one health condition that must be treated. Many people who live a very long time, the so-called oldest old who live beyond age 85, generally have several health issues with which to contend. That said, problems with BADLs are not that common. In the 65–74 age range, only about 3 percent have three or more BADLs, and in the 85 and over age group, about 10 percent have trouble with three or more BADLs (CDC 2009). However, researchers who study the final years debate whether old age is fraught with long-term morbidity—that is, being ill or having sickness. As we saw in chapter 1, increasing numbers of older adults are living longer lives, with relatively good health. The debate then is whether there is an expansion of the time that we live feeling unwell with multiple health problems (an expansion of morbidity) or whether, because we are living healthier lives, it is only the very final years of life that are problematic (a compression of morbidity).

On the one hand, as a population, we are becoming healthier in later life, which may lead to a **compression of morbidity** wherein only the final years will be affected by disability for most (Fries 1980). Modifiable lifestyle factors such as staying active, walking, eating a healthy diet, not smoking, and avoiding obesity (Jacob et al. 2016) are all associated with increased health in old age. Advances in medicine have also enabled us to live longer. Higher levels of education have a protective effect as well (Freedman 2007; Olshansky et al. 2012). In this view, only in the last months to years of their lives do people experience a health decline. Evidence from research supports this view: among those who live an exceptionally long life, there is a compression of morbidity (Ismail et al. 2016).

On the other hand, researchers argue, there is an **expansion of morbidity**. That is, medical advances allow those who are chronically ill to live longer, even though this frequently leads to more health complications in advanced old age (Gruenberg 2005). For instance, individuals who would have died earlier in the past currently live longer with proper insulin treatment for diabetes, but they may suffer more complications like blindness and amputations later in life. This is also called the failure of success or increasing misery hypothesis (Gruenberg 2005). In this view, disability is becoming unavoidable because individuals do not die of infectious disease or other causes earlier in their lives. There has been a rise in the need for caregiving over time (Ankuda and Levine 2016; NFCA 2015), and people are encouraged to create living wills to make multiple decisions about how they want to live should they become disabled. There has also been a trend of increased caregiving being received in the home from family and paid caregivers (Ankuda and Levine 2016).

Evidence for each side exists (Ismail et al. 2016; Geyer 2016; Steensma, Loukine, and Choi 2017). What is important to understand is that to some extent both are true. An expansion of morbidity can drain family resources. Living a long time in sickness is often expensive for families who may have to pay for medicines, home adjustments, doctor visits, and other treatments. Expansion of morbidity means more people may have to move into assisted-living facilities and long-term care when their loved ones can no longer take care of them, or if there are no family or friends to take care of them. This is costly (Brick et al. 2017; Faes 2016). Also, the amount spent in the final months to days of life can be astounding. The decision to move someone to a skilled nursing facility is usually a hard one for family members to make but at some point they may realize that they can no longer care for their loved one at home. In the future, there will likely be more expansion, as we live longer and have more medical options for treatment. However, when the final years of life are full of pain, suffering, and worry, families are stressed to the limits.

Alternatively, it is also important for families to expect a compression of morbidity. In later life, we may not be as likely to run a marathon (though some do); however, we can expect to exercise daily and to keep an active social calendar. More people will live longer and maintain good health, and families will generally have older members who experience many years of high quality of life. Individuals can usually expect to live active lives, with plans for how to spend the second half of their lives, as well as end-of-life plans for how they want their death and dying to be handled.

Socioeconomic Status and Health

There is a robust relationship between socioeconomic status and well-being. Overall, those who have higher levels of socioeconomic status have better mental and physical health, and those with low socioeconomic status have poorer health on average (Braveman et al. 2010; Cockerham 2006; House, Lantz, and Herd 2005; Matthews, Gallo, and Taylor 2010; Lahelma et al. 2006; Mirowsky and Ross 2003a; Smith 2007). Differences in income, wealth, poverty, and economic hardship all affect health (Kahn and Pearlin 2006; Drentea and Reynolds 2012; 2015).

The pattern is also termed the socioeconomic gradient or social gradient in health (Braveman et al. 2010). As SES increases, so does health, until middle and later life. House, Lantz, and Herd (2005) found that most people are born in relatively good health; however, as we age, there are more differences between those with the highest versus the lowest levels of socioeconomic status. In other words, the variation in health grows by socioeconomic status in middle life. It is only at the end of life that we see the widening differences closing again. This is because once people reach age 90 or so, many are in relatively poor health and socioeconomic status does not matter as much. The upper limits of life spans are around 100, thus everyone converges at the end of the age spectrum because that is the extent of a human life. As such, the widening gap of SES during middle life is associated with cumulative advantage and disadvantage. The rewards and penalties of SES get "under our skin" and show in widened health disparities. However, later in life, as among the oldest age groups, the health disparities may not matter *as* much because everyone who is still living is going to experience death in the next ten years or so (thus providing support for the compression of morbidity thesis).

Much of the research on socioeconomic status and well-being has focused on the strong relationship between education and well-being (Miech, Pampel, Kim, and Rogers 2011; Mirowsky and Ross 2003a; 2003b; 2008; 2015; Smith 2007). Education is associated with better physical health. Higher education correlates with less functional impairment and healthier behaviors including more exercise, better food choices, and fewer negative behaviors such as smoking, excessive drinking, and living a sedentary

iStock/AlexRaths   iStock/diego_cervo

lifestyle (Freedman et al. 2007; Taylor 2010; Mirowsky and Ross 2003b; 2015). Greater education is also associated with better mental health such as less depression and anxiety, feeling more joyful and enthusiastic, and having a greater sense of control (Mirowsky and Ross 2003b; 2015).

Mirowsky and Ross (2003b) write about structural amplification with regard to the benefit of education on health. That is, an individual's resources, and especially level of education, allow them to avoid or escape bad situations, or to alleviate an uncomfortable or inevitable situation. The ability to call upon one's personal resource of education, and all the other benefits it affords, demonstrates how cumulative advantage occurs. This resource gives access to other resources that may help, such as higher income and better support networks. Similarly, low education makes matters worse, and leads a bad situation to become worse. People with lower levels of education may not be able to rely as much on their knowledge, resources (especially income and good health insurance), networks, or neighborhood and community resources for help (Miech et al. 2011; Mirowsky and Ross 2003b; Olshansky et al. 2012).

Table 7.1 shows some of the ways in which higher education leads to better physical and mental health. When thinking about what it is that really allows higher education to translate into better health, several possibilities come to mind. Here are a few to consider, and you could likely add some more of your own.

In modern families, levels of education are rising. Thus, the protective effects of education, which have not always been available to the cohort of older people, will likely be more prevalent in the future. In fifty years, the number of older adults who complete high school and earn college degrees will rise significantly compared to the seniors of today. As a result, we can expect better social support, coping skills, problem-solving abilities, and so on for them. It is expected that this will alleviate some stress, as higher education brings about better mental and physical health.

However, there is other evidence that we may not witness this antici-pated upturn in older adults' health and well-being. While education has

TABLE 7.1   **Possible Ways That Higher Education Leads to Improved Health**

More social support	Articulation of thoughts and ideas
Practice of social skills	Thinner/healthier networks of people
More choices	Empowered to think critically
Self-discipline	Courage to take risks
Skills/knowledge	Awareness of selfhood
Learning of actual health behaviors at school	Ability to self-advocate
Cultural capital via personal presentation	Cognitive flexibility
Independence	Own "own" ideas
Efficacious social networks	Higher income
Problem-solving skills	Better rapport with doctors

increased, other negative trends have occurred in the past fifty years or so, including reduced physical activity, increased obesity, increased reliance on prescription medicine, and increased consumption of manufactured food. In his articles, Mirowsky (2010; Mirowsky and Ross 2015) outlines these changes in behavior, and shows how each of these trends leads to lower cognitive function in later life. He discusses this "default American lifestyle" as one with more reliance on cars, as well as sedentary work and leisure. It also includes more prepared meals, restaurant food, and processed food. We do not expend energy collecting and making our food, and we eat food with more chemicals in it. We have also reduced the number of fruits and vegetables in our diet. Mirowsky then describes our increased reliance on prescription medicine, in part due to higher blood pressure, triglycerides, and cholesterol levels that are caused by higher body mass. These accumulate in our bodies over time, further hampering cognitive function (Mirowsky 2010; Mirowsky and Ross 2015). Thus he paints a picture of countervailing trends in later life health. While we do live longer and are less likely to smoke, we have adopted unhealthy lifestyles that could harm us in old age.

Caregiving

Caregiving involves providing assistance and support to those who need help with aspects of daily life. Of the estimated 43.5 million caregivers for adults in the United States (NFCA 2015), most are family members who informally provide the overwhelming majority of long-term care services in the country. Caregiving is a complex and difficult job, often balanced with employment and caring for one's own family. It is known to be stressful, and is associated with depression for both the caregiver and care recipient (Ejem, Drentea, and Clay 2015).

Caring for others generally takes on three forms: instrumental, emotional, and informational. Instrumental help includes activities such as shopping for someone who is disabled or cleaning for an older parent. Caregiving also involves a great deal of emotional support, which may include listening, counseling, and offering companionship. Finally, part of caring for others may be informational in nature, such as learning how to alter the living environment of someone in the first stages of dementia (Drentea 2016).

As people age, they often become more limited in their mobility. They may have trouble driving or they may start limiting how far they venture from their homes or even their bedrooms. Researchers call this **life space,** which is simply the distance one ventures from their own bed, conceptualized in the form of a series of concentric circles that outline one's physical space (O'Connor et al. 2010; Baker, Bodnar, and Allman 2003). It can range from one's bedroom to the entire country or world. As life space decreases, often it is in conjunction with mental and physical decline (O'Connor et al. 2010; Baker, Bodnar, and Allman 2003). It then corresponds with the need for more caregiving, as more needs to be brought to the person.

Caregiving Measures

Caregiving is measured by ascertaining what type of care is provided and how many hours are spent caring for others over a typical day, week, month, or year. The stressors and resources that caregivers have are important to consider when examining if there is burden on the caregiver. For instance, stressors such as a job (especially when the caregiver is working a lot of hours), physical impairment, or young children in the home can be hard on caregivers who must juggle their lives with the needs of others in their care. Resources such as education, good income, and a broad support system help the caregiver. Sex, race or ethnicity, and age of both caregiver and care recipient are also important to consider.

Some research highlights positive aspects of caregiving, in which caregivers have reported the meaning and fulfillment that caring for someone has brought to their lives (Sanchez-Ayendez 1998). Frequently, those caring for parents say that caring for a parent is a privilege and that "since they took care of me, now it's my turn to take care of them." It can provide a sense of meaning for the caregiver, especially when caring for a parent, spouse, or adult child. In many Asian American families, taking care of one's parents is considered obligatory due to filial piety, that is, the belief that one must be completely respectful and obey their parents, and later take care of them. At the same time, while people may want to take care of their loved ones, most of the research examines the stresses surrounding caregiving.

Research usually evaluates caregiver burden and the level of stress and burnout associated with caregiving. One well-known way of conceptualizing this is to divide caregiving into objective burden (such as time spent helping someone to eat) and subjective burden (such as feeling embarrassment about helping your parent use the toilet) (Montgomery, Gonyea, and Hooyman 1985).

Researchers also try to assess the context in which the caregiving relationship takes place, and many have designed interventions to support the caregivers (for example, Drentea, Clay, Roth, and Mittelman 2006). **Respite care**, often provided by for-profit businesses, allows caregivers to have a break while someone else cares for their loved one on a short-term basis. This provides the caretaker respite in order for them to take care of their own needs—which may be as simple as going grocery shopping or getting their hair cut. Another way to cope with caregiver burden is to use adult daycare services that provide structured time and activities for seniors. Many working women use this option. The adult daycare center provides stimulation, such as crafts, and supervision to an older person while the main caretaker works during the day.

As previously stated, most caregiving is done in the home. This saves our health care system and government a lot of money. In fact, one estimate of the economic value of informal caregiving for the nation is $470 billion per year (Reinhard, Feinberg, Choula, and Houser 2015). Studies show that one is more likely to be admitted into nursing home care if they are white. This is due to socioeconomic status but also factors such as strong kinship beliefs and mistrust of medical establishments by African Americans, Hispanics, and Asian Americans (Goldner and Drentea 2009). Having a family member take care of you increases your likelihood of staying out of a nursing home, and for those with no family members, or in some cases having your adult child take care of you, increases the chance of nursing home placement (Buys et al. 2013; Goldner and Drentea 2009). Those with a drop in ADL functioning, and those with Alzheimer's disease are more difficult to take care of and are more likely to need professional care (Buhr, Kuchibhatla, and Clipp 2006). Once a family member has many comorbidities such as heart disease and diabetes, their patient care can become quite complex, and often is too much for family members to manage. Families need assistance with the multiple treatments and medical regimens that must be followed. In addition, some behaviors are very difficult to handle, such as incontinence or belligerent behavior associated with Alzheimer's disease. When the medical or psychological problems become too much, families consider home health care options and skilled nursing facilities, which are discussed later in this chapter.

More sociologists and those who work in the area of work and carework have begun to use the term *carework* instead of *caregiving*. Carework shows that caring for family members is a duty that is not always voluntary. There are several reasons caregiving is not a free choice. First, cultural expectations in most countries dictate that it is typically women who are expected to provide care and often the duty goes to the youngest daughter in a family. Thus it is not that women freely choose to give care, but that they have a constrained choice that society expects them to follow (Bird and Rieker 2008). Second, with the high cost of formal caregiving and nursing home options, only those with greater financial resources have the option to decline in-home caregiving, thus further showing the inequality of who cares for whom (Bookman and Kimbrel 2011). Consider, for instance, that in some countries the welfare state offers so much assistance that caregiving at home is not as necessary. Conversely, in poor countries, families must do all of the caring, as there is little if any state-level assistance. As such, the welfare state is not always stable and dependent, showing that there are contextual and geopolitical differences in who chooses to provide care (Harrington Meyer et al. 2000). Thus sociologists have chosen the word carework to highlight the inequality in who generally cares for others (Drentea 2016).

The typical family caregiver is a forty-eight-year-old woman caring for a relative (usually her mother). She is married, employed, and has children. Approximately 66 percent of family caregivers are women (NFCA 2009), and even though most women are employed now, compared to years ago, they are as likely to provide care (Pavalko and Wolfe 2016). Women on average live longer than men and it is common that the wife takes care of the husband as they age. If the wife dies first, then care of her husband is usually done by other women, usually a daughter or daughter-in-law. Since much of caregiving involves personal attention, most women are more comfortable with women taking care of them. Also, due to social norms, men are used to women doing the more affective tasks involving emotional support.

The **principle of substitution** states that there is an order of preference for who is asked to provide care for a sick or disabled relative (Cantor 1979). Similarly, the **hierarchical-compensatory model** suggests that there is a hierarchy of desired caretakers based on the primacy of the relationship (Cantor 1979). This corresponds with the principle of substitution model, which described the hierarchy of preference of who will be called upon to provide care (Shanas 1979). The order of preference begins with the spouse, next come the children, and finally other kin. The preferred order also usually calls upon women first. Thus the principle of substitution calls upon spouses, daughters, daughters-in-law, and then sons. The next rung of care would go to neighbors, friends, and formal care services. However, in the case of a daughter or daughter-in-law helping a father in intimate care, there are considerable uncomfortable feelings for most. So even though this arrangement is fairly common, it is generally not ideal for either party and can cause shame and embarrassment (Sanchez-Ayendez 1998). In the case of a father–daughter caretaking relationship, it is not uncommon for an available male family member or a hired caretaker to take over the intimate care duties so that the dignity of the care recipient is maintained. Given the major family trends of the last fifty years, including divorce, fewer children, and childlessness, fewer spouses and children will be available to provide care. Also, with the transience of American culture, many are far from their families.

Men's Caregiving—Increase in Male Caregiving

The percentage of men providing care is increasing (Ribeiro and Paul 2008; Russell 2007; Kramer 2005). This increase in male caregiving is due to various reasons, including an aging population and greater need. Men who are married to women who need help are usually the first in line to provide some care (Kramer 2005).

Men's growth in caregiving also reflects current society's changing gender roles that allow men to care for their family members. Currently, the masculine repertoire allows for a slightly greater range of emotion, caring, and caretaking. Finally, the changing demographics of families are part of the cause as well; as we experience lower fertility rates, it is often the case that aging parents do not have many children to help them. One may only have one child—a son—who is available to provide care.

Men generally benefit from having female caregivers, whereas women are not as likely to benefit. For instance, in a study of the declining activity of daily living, men received more care for their declining health than women. As soon as women get better, men decrease the amount of care provided (Noël-Miller 2010). However, men are increasingly being called upon to take care of others.

When men provide care, usually for their wives, they need to do the same jobs that women would do in the same situation. This may include cooking, feeding, bathing, and help with intimate care such as going to the bathroom. Studies show that when men provide care, they too experience a mixture of emotions including pride, love, and honor, but also more commonly caregiver burden (Calasanti and King 2007; Ribeiro and Paul 2008). Men have not traditionally been socialized to be caregivers, and they may draw upon more masculine repertoires of coping. For instance, in a study of male caregivers by Calasanti and King (2007), the authors interviewed twenty-two men to understand how they provide care. The men drew from work experiences to reconcile and cope with providing care to their wives. They drew upon several repertoires, such as blocking emotion, self-medication, and use of force at times. One example comes from a particularly difficult situation in which health providers told the husband he must make sure his wife with dementia practices regular hygiene by showering. He said he had used force to accomplish the task—that is, he made sure it happened. Thus while force is not ideal, he did it to keep his wife at home and care for her—that is, as an act of love. In situations of caring for others, individual choices and decisions must be made daily by the caregiver. Similarly, Russell (2007) found men to be more successful in making the transition to caregiver when they use a combination of management skills and nurturing skills.

When men do care for others, it often is to provide more informational and formal assistance such as help with keeping up the house or helping with finances (Drentea and Goldner 2006). Men can and do engage in more physical aspects of care as well. However, in a rare glimpse into the more personal aspects of caring for someone, a *New York Times* writer described the intimate and rather surreal experience of caring for a mother with cognitive impairment. The article was about Peter Nicholson. While he was in his fifties, his mother suffered a series of strokes. In order to take care of her, Peter quit his job and moved in with her. He lost 45 pounds and developed anemia, in part because of stress. He said that she doesn't know who he is sometimes.

Providing care is very isolating for him, he rarely gets out, and he also cannot lament with other men, as they do not usually have similar experiences. Leland (2008) quotes Peter:

> The journey has been surreal, but especially at bath time. [Though he is not squeamish about it, he said.] The weirdness permeates our relationship. She doesn't know if I'm her husband or her boyfriend or her neighbor. She knows she trusts me. . . . sometimes she says things like, "I adore you" . . . it's my mom, for Christ sakes.

Clearly, the experience of caring for another adult body can be uncomfortable for many—especially when it goes against the cultural norms of a son caring for his mother. However, caring for others can also be rewarding, while also very stressful, as Peter described:

> This is a very revealing journey about who I am to me and my family, and what's important to me.

Intimate care of bodies is known as body work in sociology. Body work involves all labor associated with the physical care of the body. When individuals are unable to take care of all of their body needs, others must step in to do it. Body work examines how caregivers and family members then must do the work of the body. It can be frustrating, time-consuming, and distasteful. Body work literature examines the characteristics that this type of work involves, such as intimacy, respect, and dignity, and the physicality of caring for the impaired body (England and Dyck 2011; Twigg et al. 2010).

We will see a growth in caregiving around the world as age structures become more top-heavy with older people living longer. The needs in places like the United States and Europe will continue to grow as life expectancy increases. As most women are now in the workforce, fewer people are at home to take care of those needing care. Thus caregiving may employ more people trading off-care duties. It is plausible that there will be more gender equity in caregiving as both men and women will share the responsibilities—perhaps based less on gender roles and more on who has time or flexibility to take care of a loved one. There is some evidence for this already, with the rise in male caregivers. However, these changes will occur rather slowly and it will still be the case that women will primarily provide care.

Need for Social Support

Social support is the exchange of help that we give to and receive from others. It helps us deal with problems, gain emotional strength, maintain resilience, and face hardships. Actual social support, and even just the *perception* that one has social support, is associated with greater physical and mental health (Thoits 2011). There are different types of social support: for instance, having someone to talk to in times of need is invaluable. Other times, the support we need is physical in nature, that is, we need someone to drive us to the doctor or help with grocery shopping.

Social support helps us cope with disability and disease; it also helps us cope with life changes and transitions. As families age, many transitions occur that affect our quality of life. Social support helps individuals cope and know they are not alone. In this way, we see that social support bolsters our life experiences.

Social support is not distributed evenly. Women are much more likely to give and receive social support and use it as a form of coping. While men benefit from social support when they are married, women typically benefit from it whether they are single, married, divorced, or widowed. This is because women are better at seeking other women for friendship, regardless of marital status. They are also much more active in helping others. This is in large part because current gender norms are structured so that women are socialized to be caring (Rosenfield and Mouzon 2013).

Families typically use social support in different ways over the life course. In the early years, a new couple may call upon their parents for advice on where to live and what type of home to buy. Or, a single mother may want assistance with childcare. Later in life, adult children provide care and support for their aging parents. Thus much social support is intergenerational, that is, parents help children and children help parents. Social support can go in both directions at the same time as well (Ejem, Drentea, and Clay 2015; Lin and Wu 2014). For instance, one can receive financial assistance and babysitting help from their parents for their child, then take their aging parents to doctors' appointments when needed.

There are many ways of thinking about social support. Sometimes we measure it by examining the size of one's social network and the frequency of contact with others. But usually we think about it in terms of emotional social support—such as having someone to turn to in times of need, someone in whom we can confide, and someone to lean on. Instrumental support is actual physical help such as driving someone somewhere, cleaning the house, helping someone with bathing, or providing financial support. Sometimes we also talk about informational support, which is having someone to turn to for help understanding things. For instance, when a person is newly diagnosed with a disease, it can be helpful if someone who has the condition provides them with information about it. Online support groups are common as well. Occasionally we discuss social support as tangible versus intangible, in which tangible support is material aid, money, and help with the house whereas intangible support is affective in nature, such as love, affection, esteem, and empathy.

One model used in the study of social support examines how it is given and received in the aging family context. As people age, their social networks typically become smaller. Socioemotional selectivity theory states that as people get older, they realize that time matters more and they search more for meaning. As such, they become more selective in how and who they invest in emotionally, and they become better at emotional regulation (Carstensen et al. 2011; Löckenhoff and Carstensen 2004).

Social support and social networks are known to influence health lifestyles. As shown in the work of Christakis and his colleagues (Smith and Christakis 2008), people interact with other people in their social network and provide social support to one another. They also influence one another in the course of their socializing and, as such, there are great similarities in health lifestyle behaviors (such as eating, obesity, exercising, smoking, drinking, and so on). Acceptance by group members of certain behaviors and circumstances is important; one of the reasons that Robert and Belinda (discussed at the beginning of the chapter) remain in shape is that their social network is supportive of staying active—an interesting concept, and one to consider when choosing friends and spouses. Certainly their level of affluence and high socioeconomic status also is predictive of their higher health lifestyle.

Social support is also useful with the opposite problem of being over-weight—that is, when older adults become frail and lose weight. Studies have shown that simply spending the time to eat with an older person increases their caloric intake. For many older adults, being place-bound and isolated results in being at greater nutritional risk. This was more common among women, who frequently were not married and didn't drive (Locher et al. 2005). These women no longer had to cook for someone and thus they did not cook for themselves either. In their paper examining one thousand community-dwelling older adults 65 and over, Locher et al. (2005) found that African Americans were more socially isolated, with women at greater nutritional risk. Correspondingly, those with low income were also associated with nutritional risk. Social support mattered a great deal; research found that having someone sit with them while eating increased their daily caloric intake by 114 calories. That could equal about a pound a month. This is clinically important because if a 100-pound woman lost a pound per month, she would lose more than 5 percent of her body weight in six months (Locher et al. 2005). Thus, the social support of simply eating with someone can make a big difference over time.

Alzheimer's Disease—A Special Case in Caregiving and Social Support

There are many different types of dementias. Alzheimer's disease (AD) is the most common. AD is a progressive disease that affects the part of the brain that impairs memory and at least one other thinking function (for example, language, perception of reality, etc.). An estimated 5 million people have AD, with predictions for that number to reach either 14 million (Alzheimer's Disease 2010; ADEAR 2010) or about 13 million by 2050 (Grochowski 2014).

The highest risk factor for Alzheimer's disease *is* increased age. The likelihood of developing Alzheimer's disease doubles every 5.5 years from age 65 to age 85. Whereas only 1–2 percent of individuals aged 70 have Alzheimer's disease, some studies found that around 40 percent of individuals aged 85 have Alzheimer's disease (Alzheimer's Disease 2010; ADEAR 2010). Thus with the aging population, there will be an increase in people with AD (nonetheless, at least half of people who live past age 95 do not have Alzheimer's disease). Obviously, AD is a growing concern for families as people age.

It is especially difficult to take care of someone with AD because of the psychological elements for the caregiver. At some point, the person afflicted with AD may not recognize their loved ones. They may also engage in strange behaviors that are upsetting to family members, such as nudity, wandering, incontinence, and hostility. The average time from discovery of the disease to death is 6–8 years. During these years, the disease progresses, and there are increasing restrictions of activities. AD is also the leading reason for persons requiring care outside of general old age (NFCA 2009).

As described by former first lady Nancy Reagan, who was married to president Ronald Reagan, one of the hardest parts of taking care of someone with Alzheimer's is that they never get better. She noted how you enter your golden years thinking you will share your memories, but you cannot do that with someone with Alzheimer's.

Warning Signs of Alzheimer's Disease

iStock/Rawpixel

- Memory loss
- Difficulty performing familiar tasks
- Problems with language
- Disorientation with regard to time and place
- Poor and decreased judgment
- Problems with abstract thinking

- Misplacing things
- Changes in mood and behavior
- Changes in personality
- Loss of initiative

Source: https://www.medicinenet.com/alzheimers_disease/ article.htm, downloaded January 14, 2010

Many people worry they are getting AD or that their loved ones have it based on forgetfulness. Memory loss does occur with age, but AD is a progressive disease that starts slowly and may go undetected for some time. Sometimes, the person starts having trouble with daily functions such as paying bills or with reading comprehension. As the disease progresses, the behavior becomes more marked. The box above lists 10 warning signs of AD.

Families who have a loved one with AD struggle with the need to be around the person all the time. In my own research, we examined how a counseling intervention enhanced social support for those caring for someone with AD (Drentea, Clay, Roth, and Mittelman 2006). The intervention had a treatment and control group of two hundred spouse caregivers from the New York area. The spouse caregivers were quite old and very homebound, as they did not want to leave their loved one with someone else. The treatment group received individual and family counseling. We examined what type of help they needed (for example, financial, physical, advice, socializing, emotional support) and found that those who received the counseling intervention reported higher levels of social support over time. Seeing people in person and having close network members, as well as emotional support, all led to higher perceptions of social support. Interestingly, in this study, phone calls didn't matter. In the context of caring for someone with AD, people needed emotional support and people visiting them. They were isolated in their homes and felt supported by the psychological respite of someone visiting them.

Living Arrangements

As we age, there may be reasons to change our living arrangements. Many people voluntarily downsize their homes after their children have grown and left the home. Others want to be closer to family. Some have to move to assisted-living facilities for help with ADLs. Still others simply want to live somewhere new or somewhere with more recreation and/or services. Once children have moved out of the house, some people may not want to deal with the upkeep of a large home, multiple levels, and a yard. The reasons are many. Here we concentrate on those types of moves that are related to health and the aging family.

Many people move to be closer to grandchildren after they have retired (Plane and Jurjevich 2009). They may downsize and move closer to at least one son or daughter once they are free from jobs and children. This enables a two-way exchange of support and interaction. Grandparents stay in touch and provide care for their sons, daughters, and grandchildren. In exchange, the younger generation helps the older generation with occasional household needs, provides support, and company. Ultimately, they may also provide care if health falters.

In most cases, people prefer to live in their own homes throughout their lives, though they may need to make changes to them. Sometimes people move to a retirement community (as discussed in chapter 6) in which more services are provided, such as caring for the home and grounds. Those with larger homes or upstairs bedrooms may move into one-story homes or apartments. The need to relocate often corresponds with some common problems that arise in old age—arthritis, heart disease, lung disease, and cancer—which can all affect the ability to move around. One way to lengthen the time spent in a home is through assistive technology.

Assistive Technology

Assistive technology consists of using home modification products for the adaptation of equipment and residences for older adults to allow families and individuals to continue to live in their own residences and do things for themselves. Physical and occupational therapists can determine what type of device may help an individual, and sometimes individuals or their families discover the need themselves. For instance, if one cannot read their clock in the morning because the numbers are too small, they can get a clock that projects the time in large numbers on the ceiling. Another common adaptation is to install a new higher toilet and handrails in the bathroom for safety. These changes and added safety features help to keep people in their homes, allowing them to "age in place."

As people age in place, there is a push for even more sophisticated and useful assistive technology to help us stay in our own homes. Homeowners and their families make many of these changes to assist in independent living. Some of the general adjustments are listed in figures 7.3–7.5 (adapted from Miskelly 2001; Hoenig et al. 2003; Levine et al. 2003; Mann et al. 1999).

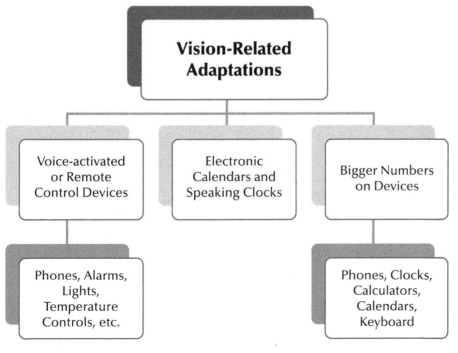

FIGURE 7.3

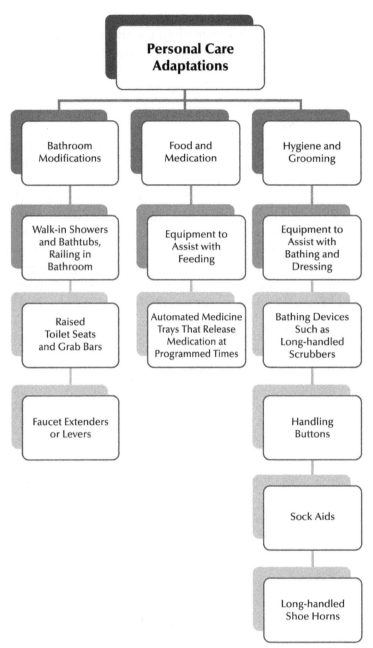

FIGURE 7.4

These figures show the many ways in which we can make adjustments to the home. As one can see, many of the adjustments needed could address multiple issues such as vision and mobility disabilities at the same time. Families, with the guidance of professionals, can help adapt homes to the special needs of those requiring assistance.

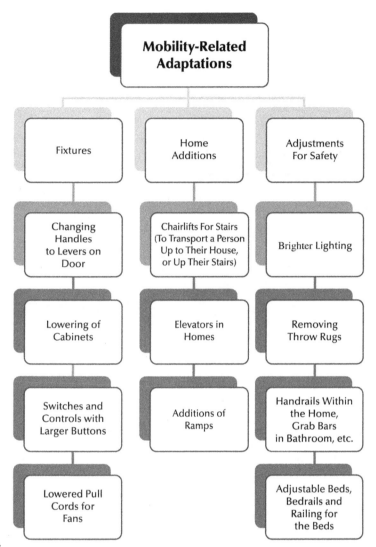

FIGURE 7.5

Assisted Care, Advanced Care Planning, and End-of-Life Decisions

At some point, it may be necessary to move beyond basic home adaptation and get more help. Families use assisted care such as home health aides, long-term care facilities, and SNFs (skilled nursing facilities) when needed. Families call in home health care workers when some of the health procedures needed become too difficult, or when there is no one to help, as in the case of an older woman living alone or a man who no longer has a spouse to care for him. Women are more likely to be allowed to move back out of long-term care facilities after their health improves because they usually have more family ties and support systems available (Mudrazija, Thomeer, and Angel 2015). Men, on the other hand, once admitted, are more likely to stay because they likely do not have close family members who will take care of them (Mudrazija, Thomeer, and Angel 2015).

ZUMA Press Inc./Alamy Stock Photo

Home health care workers can bridge the gap between home and assisted care. They can, for instance, take and record vital health signs, administer an IV drip if needed, and monitor medicines. By employing home health care, the person still can live in the home but can get medical treatment when needed. This type of care can also alleviate some of the burden placed on primary caretakers, usually women, especially as medical treatment becomes more invasive, personal, or frequent. Medicare will cover ten hours a week of home care only if skilled nursing care is required (Bookman and Kimbrel 2011). Medicaid, which is available to those who have limited income that is below the poverty line and few assets, also covers some nursing care and SNFs. However, eligibility varies by state. Often people must spend down their assets over time (usually on health care costs) before they become Medicaid eligible (Bookman and Kimbrel 2011).

Home health care cannot bridge all gaps. When the needs become too great for family and home health care to handle, those who need additional help sometimes move into long-term care facilities such as assisted-living communities, which are usually graded by the level of independence one enjoys, or to SNFs, which are generally round-the-clock and provide more nursing care. An estimated 1.5 million people (mostly female, white, and 65 and over) live in nursing homes (Jones et al. 2009). Put differently, it is estimated that about 3.6 percent of the population aged 65 and over lives in institutional settings, such as nursing homes. Among the oldest old, those 85 and over, this number rises to approximately 11 percent (USDHHS 2012). Medicare will cover a stay in an SNF only if daily nursing or rehab services are needed (Bookman and Kimbrel 2011). Ideally, families, social workers, caretakers, and those in the medical field come together and discuss the needs of the person, and then decide the best options when one needs a skilled-nursing facility. The move into an assisted-living facility or SNF is usually disruptive and difficult for family members. In particular, for the older adults who are moved, they feel a great reduction in their sense of autonomy (Johnson and Bibbo 2014). At the same time, after adjusting, the ability to socialize, the lack of responsibility for a household, and the freedom from cooking can be a relief.

Advanced care planning (ACP) is the process of families communicating their wishes for end-of-life care and final arrangements, which may involve legal documents such as advance directives (AD) which spell out these specifics for health care providers. These conversations are difficult for most families to have, but are very useful to both families and health care providers if the time comes when decisions of care must be made. Research shows planning is eased by a supportive environment in the family, with limited criticism (Boerner, Carr, and Moorman 2013). Families and spouses can feel guilty and lonely when they ultimately make a decision to admit their husband or wife to a facility. Getting end-of-life care and handling the death of a loved one, in any institution, is sad and distressing, and families often feel a lack of control as well, since they no longer are the caretakers (Drentea, Williams, Burgio, and Bailey 2016).

The United States has seen a rise in palliative care units across the country. These help individuals to be comfortable, once they have illnesses that render them terminally ill. In fact, the number of hospitals with palliative care units has increased from around one-quarter of those in a state in 2000 to almost 75 percent in 2010 (Hughes and Smith 2014). The growth is still occurring, and it does vary by state. Similarly, hospice, which includes comfort measures in one's home, has been growing, and has become a much-used service by families to help their loved ones in their last days to months of life (Hughes and Smith 2014). Ultimately, with end-of-life decisions, families must decide how to handle increasing health decline among loved ones.

Summary

This chapter examined some of the health issues related to aging, and how families are expected to be involved. Living longer is associated with more health issues. Chronic illnesses such as heart disease, hypertension, cancer, arthritis, and diabetes are quite common with older adults. Those of higher socioeconomic status generally enjoy better health than those of lower socioeconomic status. With improvements in medicine, and a generational increase in education, we may see even more healthy aging, with a compression of morbidity only in the final years of life. Many issues affect families in aging. Families should think through potential living arrangements and assisted living, social support, and caregiving before these become issues in their lives. Moreover, families should think about how to change their own homes, and those of their loved ones, as functional limitations and needs increase. The theory of cumulative advantage and disadvantage shows how a life of high socioeconomic status often transitions one to a privileged old age, whereas cumulative disadvantage leads to fewer choices due to economics and more struggles in old age. In both cases, families can help older loved ones as they experience health decline.

Critical Thinking Questions

1. Consider an example of cumulative advantage and cumulative disadvantage among people you know or from a movie. In what ways could the progressive snowballing of the effects of SES on health have been stopped or turned around in each case?

2. Will men and women ever reach parity in caregiving and carework? Why or why not?

3. With increased longevity, and the greater number of adults in society today, what small changes can we make to increase the mobility of older adults in homes and in public places?

Chapter 8

Conclusion

CHAPTER OBJECTIVES

1. Consider how all changes addressed in the book will affect older adults and their families.

2. Review the proposed six dominant social changes.

3. Familiarize yourself with elder mistreatment.

Later adulthood is a time of many changes. All families' and individuals' lives change over time, as children grow up and leave the household, unions dissolve through divorce or separation, or health declines. Inevitably if a union is intact at the end of life, one partner will die first, leaving the other partner to adjust to life without their loved one. Work lives change as well, and many people slow down, change jobs, and ultimately end their paid work lives. Leisure time increases. Some people experience an extended amount of free time, which can be enjoyable for many but can also be very challenging if declining health becomes more of an issue. The family experiences loss of loved ones and friends as we age and many in our social network die. Some have mental health challenges as they move through these changes and losses. Depression is not uncommon in old age (FIFARS 2016).

This chapter reviews major issues that will greatly affect families and aging. In addition, ideas will be offered regarding the trends of the future. It is very difficult to try to predict beyond fifty years or so when examining social trends, so the predictions offered here are for the next ten to fifty years at best. Many of the current trends have been ongoing, others are abrupt. We will examine the difference between slow versus fast changes in society. We will also examine another area that has not yet been discussed in this book—that of elder mistreatment. Often when discussing families, we focus on the functional and normative experience of families doing their best to get along, despite circumstances and hardship. Elder mistreatment or abuse requires examination of dysfunction in the family. Much of the section will examine elder mistreatment in the family context. However, there are two other types of elder mistreatment. First is that perpetrated by paid caregivers. Second is the concept of self-mistreatment, characterized by being mentally or physically challenged to the point of neglecting one's own health and well-being (Anetzberger 2012), which will be discussed in more depth later in the chapter.

Societal Changes

This book examines a multitude of social changes that are currently affecting families. It examines how these changes ultimately impact the experience of aging in families. Social changes can be relatively slow, causing gradual changes in social life. Alternatively, social change can be swift and have a major impact on society. An example of a social change that is occurring somewhat slowly is the general increase in levels of education over the past one hundred years. Each successive cohort has been more likely to go past eighth grade at a minimum and also to graduate high school. In 1947, only 33 percent of Americans finished high school. Now many more people go to college, and among those over the age of twenty-five, about 33 percent now receive a college degree, and 89 percent finish high school (U.S. Census Bureau 2017). More traditionally underrepresented minorities are going to college as well—among African Americans the rate has doubled since the early 1990s, from around 11 percent to 23 percent completing four-year college (U.S. Census Bureau 2017). Increases have also been noted among Hispanics, currently at 16 percent (historical data are not available) (U.S. Census Bureau 2017). These changes in education correspond with changes in the workplace from farming and manufacturing to a more professional and service-oriented economy. Increased education will also be interrelated with increased life expectancy (Lynch 2003; Miech et al. 2011; Mirowsky and Ross 2008), since education is associated with better health on average.

Social change can also occur quickly, such as when a new law is put in place and adjustments need to be made in order to implement and enforce it. The faster the social change, the more likely there will be a cultural lag as it takes time for societal norms to catch up to new conventions. Many changes discussed in this book are rather sudden from a historical perspective, such as the change in the divorce rate, the number of children living in single-parent homes, and the rise of the internet with all their ensuing opportunities and challenges. A good example of a dramatic change that has occurred is the number of Baby Boomers reaching retirement age. It is unprecedented to have such a large number of people reaching the same milestones at the same time. Baby Boomers changed the educational landscape when swells of children reached school age at the same time. Now they are affecting the workplace and Social Security as they leave the workplace. Another example is the legalization of gay marriage. The Supreme Court mandate in 2015 allowing gay marriage overturned previous laws. Courthouses quickly had to change procedures, and even their forms, to allow gay marriage. In addition, many gay couples are now marrying and will age together, and they now have legal status and documentation that will be important at the end of their lives. For younger people as well, greater openness with regard to sexual orientation and sexual identity is affecting how adolescents come of age. Greater awareness will lead to more openness and flexibility late in life (Institute of Medicine 2011).

Modern history has seen several major social changes that affect both families and aging. This book's purpose is to explore the many circumstances and changes in society and address how they will affect families later in life. Longer life expectancy affects the outcomes expected in almost every case. Additionally, an increase in the number of older adults affects the impact these social changes will have on society.

Chapter 1 reviewed many general demographic patterns. With increased life expectancy, many co-occurring changes were discussed, such as a greater need for caregiving, later-life health, and an increase of centenarians in the population. As a society, we need to constantly consider how increased life expectancy will affect our development, interactions, and social institutions. Chapter 2 showed the diversity of families and American society. Now there is more openness and cultural acceptance for a variety of lifestyles. Certainly with more freedom of possibilities comes an increase in the numbers of people experiencing life beyond the nuclear and extended family structure. It reviewed current divorce trends, single-parenting, and childlessness, to name a few trends. Social change is not always peaceful and easy, but society will continue to adapt (Coontz 2016). Modern versus traditional views of family social change were introduced. Readers will need to decide for themselves how they feel about the various changes and, more importantly, given the complexity of family studies, under which conditions one favors or opposes them. Chapter 3 covered changing gender roles; men's and women's roles have become less rigid, and women are more likely to actively pursue work and leisure. Dating and sexuality were discussed, as well as changing norms of intimacy. In addition, it examined how gendered roles are associated with mental health outcomes. Future predictions indicate there will be more freedom in sexuality and intimacy, and more latitude in gender expression. Chapter 4 reviewed both delayed parenthood (when people start families later in life) and also the experiences of families once children are gone from the home. Central to this chapter was how scientific discovery has affected and led to more instances of delayed childbirth. Intergenerational linkages were considered in a time of fewer children and siblings in one's immediate family. In the future, delayed childrearing will continue, with the average parental age at the birth of their first child incrementally edging up as well. Chapter 5 covered work and retirement, examining the older worker, financial considerations, and ultimate exit from work. It showed how people move toward retirement, and how savings, health, and family status all play a role in the ability to quit work. Again, more opportunities for reduced hours but continued work would be beneficial to many older adults. Chapter 6 examined activities in later life, as people move from obligatory activities such as work to discretionary activities in leisure. Grandparenting was central to this chapter, and communication and changing technology was addressed. Many more years of leisure time leaves many untapped opportunities for activity in later life. It will be wise to consider what one wants to do in later life. We will likely have a lot of free time before reaching a point of infirmity. In chapter 7 we reviewed health from multiple perspectives regarding issues such as health and mortality to caregiving and dementia. This chapter also considered how changes in assistive technology could play a role in aging. There are a lot of issues that are raised when a large proportion of the population has failing health. Social institutions will need to address these changes in society. More people alive at any one time will have some form of dementia, and society and families will need to adjust to these changes.

Dominant Social Changes: Future Directions for Society

Considering all the changes we have discussed throughout the book, this chapter presents six major social changes that will affect aging families. Future directions and consequences of the changes are suggested. We discuss technology, globalization, multiple family changes, and changing roles for older adults.

Technology and Communication

Fast-changing technology, social media, smart phones, and mobile devices have altered the speed and distance with which we communicate. Due to

iStock/Rawpixel

these changes, telecommuting from home is common, family group texts keep extended families up-to-date within seconds anywhere, and Skype and Google Chat allow us to talk face-to-face. Older adults who are not well versed in these technologies can be taught to use email or Facebook and how to text. However, training older people on technology requires slower and repeated lessons. One-on-one training is also useful (Winstead et al. 2013; Yost et al. 2016).

Globalization and Families

Globalization is changing the way families experience aging. The interconnections among transportation, technology, communications, and economies are fast-paced. Globalization has taken place at an exceedingly fast rate. The United States has experienced a large inflow of immigrants, and it is now common to fly all over the world. One estimate by the United Nations states that 1.2 billion people took an international flight in 2015 (Visa 2017). To understand the scale of this, consider that the world currently has about 7 billion people, so that means that one in seven people took an international flight. Of course, many people take repeated flights, so it is not 1.2 billion different people. Older travelers are considered one of the fastest-growing markets, with the number of travelers 65 and over expected to double by 2025 (Visa 2017). Families now fly regularly to see their relatives and they vacation in new locales. These cultural changes have strong impacts on finding a mate and family formation. The global village of today offers interaction for its inhabitants. The social ramifications of such high levels of travel and globalization include increasing awareness of and opportunities to meet others from around the world.

Intercultural Marriage and Increasing Heterogeneity of Families

Intercultural marriage is the union of two people from two different cultures. They may be from different countries, religions, faiths, or cultural backgrounds. In order to understand intercultural marriage, first we will review three basic definitions that are relevant. **Propinquity** is the state of being geographically close to someone. In the past, propinquity often predicted one's intimate partner choices. People married those who were geographically close to them. **Homophily** is the trait in which people tend to be attracted to those who are similar to themselves. **Heterophily** is when individuals who are different from one another are attracted to one another. Most evidence shows that we have both less propinquity and homophily in marriage and unions, and increased heterophily with intermarriage among those of different races, ethnicities, cultures, religions, and geographic locations, including different continents (Daneshpour and Fathi 2016). Many aging families will need to have increased cultural awareness and more understanding of multiculturalism in order to get along with many different types of people in their families (Boswell 2015; Silverstein and Giarrusso 2010). As such, families are increasingly finding themselves in situations in which one of their children becomes intimately involved with someone from a different culture, with a different background, family customs, faith, and religion. This increased heterophily in marriage will be seen in families over time, and indeed, mate selection has demonstrated greater heterophily over the years except in terms of education (Skopek, Schulz, and Blossfeld 2011). Interfaith marriages are on the increase in the United States, and many families must forge new customs in how to go through the marriage celebration, as well as how to raise children and honor religious holidays.

Among the older generations, family members are sometimes surprised by and not happy about these unions. In the aging family, when care is needed later in life, these same daughters-in-law or sons-in-law or adult children's partners will be the ones to provide care, and they may have extremely different belief systems and cultures. In the future, as these families become more common, couples (and their relatives) will need to negotiate cultural expectations with regard to raising children and religious, birth, marital, and burial customs. Thus, drawing upon Cherlin's 1978 classic work on remarriage as an incomplete institution, intermarriage of those from vastly different cultures and religions might also be considered as an incomplete institution in which ceremonies, holidays, births, deaths, and weddings all must be negotiated to satisfy each person's background and beliefs. The added constant negotiations of important rites of passage will possibly put strain on these couples and their families. Preparing counselors, clergy, and mental health professionals to help families seek solutions will be beneficial (Maynigo 2017).

Families adopt the traditions of their local culture, like this Hispanic family in California enjoying turkey on Thanksgiving, but also Mexican deviled eggs. Marmaduke St. John/Alamy Stock Photo

However, modern life in families has already become more about voluntary reciprocity rather than obligation (Connidis 2010). The reader may recall the latent kin matrix, in which family members enact family ties, or family-of-choice ties, when needed or desired. Many who remain single may not be steeped in strong family networks. They may not have children or siblings, and thus will have extra challenges. With few automatic choices in who to turn to as they age, they will need to be more active in creating their own social support networks.

Increased Distance from Families and Smaller Families

As families mature, they may also have to contend with being very far from one another, during a time when health and/or psychological health after losing loved ones requires more frequent visits with family. Adaptations may be required, for example, when a mother needs to get on an overseas plane flight to visit her family. There are no easy solutions. Older people often require care in later life, and desire to be around family. At the same time, moving a loved one around the world in old age, especially when they have never lived elsewhere, is not always possible or desirable either. Thus in the future, in these long-distance families, one's adult children may not be very useful for day-to-day hands-on help in older age—when they live across the county, let alone on another continent. Smaller families also mean less likelihood of having immediate family members nearby. Paid caregivers, often female labor from other countries, may be hired to assist in caregiving, thus creating a global exchange and economy of caregivers (Ehrenreich and Hochschild 2002). The trend of a growing number of international caregivers seems unlikely to reverse, and families should consider whether they will employ these workers and, if so, how to humanely help these younger workers (mostly women) to get back to their home countries to visit *their* aging parents and often their own children (Ehrenreich and Hochschild 2002).

Increased Choices for Living Arrangements

Another trend that is likely to grow is the need for many different types of living arrangements in old age. Options include living independently with some adaptive strategies (such as one-story houses and rails in bathroom showers) to living with family to living with nonfamily members. The many different family forms discussed in chapter 2, such as staying single, being childfree, and living a DINKS lifestyle, all have implications for later-life living. Some people with health problems may live in assisted-living facilities. Group living has different variations as well, such as a group of people who are united through family or friendship networks, or those who are formally put together by an assisted-living community. In some cases, each person has their own room, and then shares common spaces such as the kitchen and living room. In other cases, each person may have their own room with meals taken in a cafeteria. There will be an increase in all types of senior housing. Many people will take their aging parents into their homes; however, a growing number of people will not have children they can depend upon for care. Creatively solving these challenges is an area for growth in the economy. Intergenerational linkages could also be useful, for example, pairing an older person with a college-age student. The older person may have the home, available space, and cheap rent—and can share these resources in exchange for the assistance and companionship of the younger individual. While these arrangements have existed for years, this seems a prime area for growth—especially considering the rise in college-student debt (Houle and Warner 2017). Recent research shows that Millennials, that is, those born between about 1982 and 2004, make up about one-quarter of all family caregivers (National Alliance of Caregiving 2015). Those in this group, however, are less likely to be college graduates and more likely to have a high school degree with some college courses. They earn less on average than their non-caregiving counterparts (National Alliance of Caregiving 2015).

More Social Roles for Later Life

As life expectancy increases, there will be an increased need for more social roles that people can occupy for an extended amount of time. More part-time jobs, or phased retirement options, will be useful for those who wish—or must—continue to work. This allows people to spend some hours working but not at full-time status. For many older workers, a 40-hour work week is no longer feasible due to health concerns. Even when in good health, fatigue can set in. Moreover, for those who are financially stable, other interests may be more enticing. Many older adults also help their adult children, often helping to take care of grandchildren. Temporary jobs may also be attractive to an older age group who may want to earn money but do not want to tie themselves permanently to any one job. One does not usually consider temporary work agencies for older adults; however, their skills may match some of these jobs. Accommodations might be needed, such as being allowed to sit rather than stand, or having an additional break. Having some income may be helpful to the individual and potentially to their family. Also, engaging in productive activity is rewarding (Matz-Costa et al. 2014). Conducting work by telecommuting from home is a good option. It allows some income, but does not require travel, driving, or walking a lot, and some caregiving and/or care receiving could still occur.

More volunteering opportunities would be useful as well to provide older adults a sense of purpose and meaning, without the stressors of paid work. Volunteering that can be done at home may appeal to some. Others might prefer to go somewhere and perform volunteer work at a place of business or other venue. In order to reap the social benefits of volunteering, it is usually best to meet with the same group of people repeatedly. For instance, singing in a church choir once a week will require weekly practice sessions and open the door to a sense of community. Similarly, sorting used items at a women's shelter once a month with the same group allows acquaintances to check in with one another periodically during the year. Conversely, handing out water at a marathon for a 4-hour shift may be fun for some, but is an opportunity that will not become available again until the next marathon. Thus, when choosing volunteer work, the goals of the individual are important. When organizing volunteer work, the needs of older workers should be kept in mind, allowing chances for them to sit down, take breaks, or be driven by younger volunteers—especially at night. Grandparenting is another meaningful role that many older adults spend time doing. Families may become involved in their older parents' activities, and feel a sense of relief and appreciation that their parents are continuing productive activities in later life.

Elder Mistreatment

Elder abuse, also termed **elder mistreatment**, involves having unpleasant, unwanted, and sometimes criminal actions committed against an older person. The victim is usually over age 60 or 65, depending on the parameters of the

verbal—abuse involving yelling, insults, put-downs

emotional—similar to above, may be more manipulative, can involve withholding of love or affection

financial—controlling someone's money, stealing money, convincing older adult to spend

social—withholding social relationships from older adult, isolating them, not allowing phone contact

physical—punching, pushing, hitting, slapping, not cleaning body if needed, withholding food, water, medicine

sexual—unwanted sexual conduct, unwanted sexually suggestive conversations

self—not caring for oneself, resisting needed medicine, hurting oneself, not performing regular hygiene

FIGURE 8.1 Types of Elder Mistreatment

study. Elder abuse can be classified into verbal and emotional abuse, financial abuse, social abuse, physical abuse, and sexual abuse. It is difficult to define because issues of frequency, severity, and cultural context are all considered when trying to name elder mistreatment (Anetzberger 2012). Physical and sexual abuse can become legal issues, as can financial abuse. Figure 8.1 shows the different types of elder abuse.

All types of elder mistreatment can be hard to detect because they usually involve a private relationship between a family member and an older adult, often in one's personal residence or in an assisted-living situation (Halphen and Burnett 2014). It is vastly underreported, with one study estimating that only one in fourteen cases is reported (Rosen 2014). The older adult may depend upon the family member for help, finances, food, and support. The older adult who is physically challenged and less mobile is at a greater disadvantage. He or she may not be able to reach out to other family members for help, due to social isolation, or because no other family exists. In addition, they may have cognitive decline that limits their ability to reach out and tell others, or they may not fully understand what they are experiencing. Moreover, they might be embarrassed or frightened, and thus will not seek help. Thus elder abuse is especially hard to detect because the victims are not always able to speak for themselves, may have limited mobility, and may not be cognitively aware of the situation. In addition, isolated older adults can be invisible to a neighborhood. Unlike children, who are expected to go to school, or might be seen playing or coming in and out of a home, it is not uncommon for frail older adults to live in a home and never leave the house. Thus, neighbors and others may not even know that someone lives there.

Some also consider **self-abuse** under the umbrella term of elder mistreatment. Self-abuse is the inability to care for oneself because of cognitive, psychological, and/or physical problems that then lead to unhealthy situations that affect one's body, mind, social situations, and/or finances (Halphen and Burnett 2014). Often, these situations are discovered once the situation has deteriorated. For instance, in one very graphic example from research on end of life (Drentea, Williams, Burgio, and Bailey 2016), a daughter describes the scene in which she found her father. She writes:

> [My brother] called 911 and the cops and the firemen came in an ambulance . . . they had to bust the door to get in there . . . the stench was so bad. He was just in his golf shirt and his underwear, because he was trying to get back and forth to the bathroom, and a lot of times he didn't make it 'cause he either had loose stool or something. There was dung on the carpet, on the couch, on the chair, all in the bathroom, floor, commode. . . . He was disoriented and dehydrated.

Self-abuse requires help in the same way that elder abuse requires help. The person needs to get out of the situation, and they are unable to do so alone.

Research has found that the most prevalent mistreatment of older adults is verbal abuse (Waite and Das 2010). Similarly, the "National

Elder Mistreatment Study," an examination of adults aged 60 and over, showed a one-year prevalence of 4.6 percent for emotional abuse (Acierno et al. 2010). Acierno et al. (2010) also found a one-year prevalence of 1.6 percent for physical abuse, 5.1 percent for potential neglect, and 5.2 percent for current financial abuse. One in ten respondents reported *some* type of abuse in the past year (Acierno et al. 2010). These findings are comparable to Waite and Das's (2010) work, in which they found 15 percent of respondents (12 percent men, 18 percent women) reported experiencing being put down or enduring insults. They also found that 6 percent (no sex differences) experienced financial abuse in which people reported having money or belongings taken away or having someone withhold something from them. Finally, they only found 1 percent reporting physical abuse (Waite and Das 2010).

There is very little information on sexual abuse, though in the "National Elder Mistreatment Study," less than 1 percent reported sexual abuse (Acierno et al. 2010). In another review, researchers were able to conclude from six articles on elder sexual abuse that it does occur in nursing homes, and that both older women and men are victims. Both staff and other residents (mostly men) are the perpetrators (Malmedal, Iversen, and Kilvik 2015). However, these authors also cite the lack of information on the problem. We do know that, overall, elder mistreatment is underreported. Older at-risk people will likely always be vulnerable to abuse, and the reality of their isolation makes it difficult to detect. Those who are victims of their own family members may be located and isolated in a home, with little to no contact with the outside world. Perpetrators of abuse may be family, caregivers (paid or unpaid), financial advisors, housekeepers, or other workers present in the home. Those who are victims in assisted-living facilities may be hurt by their own families or they may be hurt by visitors, employees, or other residents. Finally, in a self-neglect situation, a person may be unable to understand, or unwilling to tell others, that they are unable to take care of themselves. Suggestions for ameliorating the situation include training health care professionals such as doctors, nurses, dentists, physical therapists, and others to recognize signs of abuse. Sometimes pharmacists may notice that an older adult is getting painkillers, especially given the opioid problem in the United States. Keeping the problem in the news will remind well-intentioned family members to look for signs of abuse. Finally, nursing home staff should be monitored, with thorough background checks of workers. More social support for families from agencies, families, and government policies could help alleviate caregiver stress, potentially minimizing some of the mistreatment. In sum, while all of these may help, it is a hard situation to uncover. Older vulnerable adults are isolated. With an increase in number of older adults in the population as Baby Boomers get older, there will likely be a rise in elder mistreatment.

Summary

This book addressed major current changes in families, and how they will affect families in later life. Those who were born after the 1950s came of age after the sweeping reforms of Civil Rights, the Women's Rights Movement, and the sexual revolution. They witnessed delayed first marriage and widespread availability of birth control. They saw changes in living arrangements—mainly an increase in cohabitation, stepfamilies, and a peak in the divorce rate in the early 1980s. Furthermore, they witnessed the legalization of same-sex unions. Many have seen changes in their own families. People have fewer children on average, and a growing percentage of women will be childless. Having fewer children will ultimately lead to fewer siblings and fewer siblings mean fewer problem-solvers and caregivers when mom or dad get old. Other older adults engage in a living arrangement called LAT—living apart together. For various reasons, sometimes financial, sometimes due to their adult children, these older adults have a significant other but decide to live in their own homes and not marry. Many children were raised for at least some time in a single-parent home, or are currently being raised by a single parent. While remarriage is desired by some, it will not be by everyone, and this book addressed how this may play out in old age. Those students reading this book might not have children at all, or they may not begin their families until they are well into their thirties. Having children as an older parent has rewards and challenges—both of which were addressed in the book. We are living longer, may be divorced or separated, and may seek new love in old age. While we may have fewer children or siblings, we will have more generations alive at the same time. Our families will continue to adapt as society changes, and we will still have family issues such as love, respect, and growth, as well as frustration and disappointment—as has been the case for centuries upon centuries.

Critical Thinking Questions

1. What are some medical advances that were discussed in this book that might affect families in later life?
2. What are some ways government can assist families in later life? How can community organizations help older adults and their families?
3. Consider three major trends from this book. How will the aging family experience be different for Millennials when they reach age 65 with regard to these trends?

Glossary

age bias The stereotyping of people's work skills and abilities based on their age rather than personal experience.

assistive technology Consists of using home modification products for the adaptation of equipment and residences for older adults.

autonomy The ability to do what one wants to do, when one wants to do it.

Baby Boomers A large cohort in the population of the United States who were born after World War II, between 1946 and 1964.

caregiving The provision of assistance and support to someone in need, usually helping with aspects of daily life and/or providing emotional support.

cohabitation Living arrangement in which two unmarried individuals, either of same or opposite sex, live together in an intimate relationship.

committed activities Productive roles such as paid work, housework, house and yard maintenance, and shopping.

compression of morbidity The view that, with healthy lifestyles and healthy aging, we are well most of our lives, and only in the final years of life will we experience extended sickness and disability. In other words, our healthy life expectancy has expanded, and the unhealthy time is shortened to the final years or months of life.

coparenting family Three generations (grandparent, grandchild, and parent) live together in the same household.

custodial family When the grandparent raises the child without the parent present.

dependency ratio Ratio of nonworking (dependents) to those of working age. Working age range is usually about 19–64 years old in developed nations.

digital divide The social inequality that exists between those with access to fast computers, internet, cell phones, and so on, compared to those without. The digital divide exists between rich and poor, low versus high education, urban versus rural, old versus young, and minorities versus non-minorities, and leads to social inequality in other areas as well.

discretionary activities Free-time pursuits such as socializing, entertainment, hobbies, and general leisure.

dispossession The movement of property away from the older generation, often given to the younger generation or to charity.

double jeopardy When one considers two lower-level statuses at a time, for instance, being female and poor.

elder mistreatment Involves having unpleasant, unwanted, and sometimes criminal actions committed against an older person.

expansion of morbidity The view that medical advancement allows the chronically ill to live longer, even though this leads to more health complications in advanced old age.

family of choice Creating one's own family with those they want to be with, regardless of blood or marriage.

family of origin The family into which we are born or adopted.

fictive kin Those who are not considered traditional family but who serve the function of family by supplying social/emotional and/or instrumental support.

gender flexible Being more flexible in terms of gendered norms and behaviors, and/or with regard to gender identity. Not conforming to a strict binary of masculine and feminine behavior and identity.

health disparities Preventable differences in health outcomes of different subsets of the population, usually due to racial bias, geographical limitation, or socioeconomic status.

heterophily Seeking others or being with others with different traits, such as those who practice different religions, come from different regions of world, or have different levels of education.

hierarchical-compensatory model When choosing caregivers, there is a hierarchy of desired caretakers based on the primacy of the relationship. Typically it begins with spouse and then moves down the family tree, with a preference for female caretakers.

homophily Seeking others based on traits in common, such as similar levels of education, religious beliefs, or age.

incomplete institution Concept based on Cherlin's 1978 work that, unlike marriage, remarriage and stepfamilies are an incomplete institution because they lack the norms implicit in a first-married family.

intergenerational linkages The social relationships or social ties among the different generations in family life.

latent kin matrix Available family relations that may be called upon by family members for support. Family members are called upon by choice rather than obligation or need.

LGBTQ This acronym stands for lesbian, gay, bisexual, transgender, and queer. In this book, it is used inclusively to apply to those of other gender identities and sexualities as well. Occasionally, the term **LGB** is utilized when referencing a study which covered only those identities.

life space The distance one ventures from their own bed, conceptualized as concentric circles of distance.

living apart together (LAT) A living arrangement in which a couple of same or opposite sex maintains an intimate relationship but continues to keep separate homes. They may spend most hours together, but still have the comfort of their own solitary homes.

obligatory activities Activities that are required in daily life, such as sleeping, eating, and personal care or grooming.

phased retirement Gradual retirement in which workers reduce their work hours and/or responsibilities before they completely retire.

principle of substitution The order of preference for who is asked to provide care for a sick or disabled relative.

propinquity Being geographically close to someone. Traditionally in the marriage market, propinquity played an important role because those with whom we were geographically close were those we tended to marry.

respite care Break for caregivers that gives them time to rest, take a break, and/or take care of their own needs while someone else cares for their loved one on a short-term basis.

sandwich generation Family situation in which a parent needs to take care of both children and older parents or in-laws at the same time. Usually refers to women and the stress of being sandwiched between generations.

selection bias or effect When a group of people select themselves into a category, yielding a nonrandom or biased effect.

self-abuse A type of elder mistreatment. The inability to care for oneself because of cognitive, psychological, and/or physical problems. Ultimately leads to an unhealthy lifestyle.

snowbirds Those who migrate from cold climates in the winter and live in the south, predominantly in Florida and Arizona.

structural lag A lag between time and the social structure when a society does not have the infrastructure, norms, rules, and/or laws to adapt to the cultural shift.

sunbirds Those who have already migrated to the south but visit family up north for one month or more during the hot summer months. Usually they are from places like Florida.

transfers Involve a shifting of resources from one source to another among generations.

triple jeopardy When one considers three lower statuses at a time (such as being female, African American, and older).

References

AARP (American Association of Retired Persons). 2015. "GrandFacts: State Fact Sheets for Grandparents and Other Relatives Raising Grandchildren." Retrieved January 7, 2015 (http://www.aarp.org/content/dam/aarp/relationships/friends-family/grandfacts/grand-facts-national.pdf).

Abma, Joyce C., and Gladys M. Martinez. 2006. "Childlessness among Older Women in the United States: Trends and Profiles." *Journal of Marriage and Family* 68(4):1045–56.

Acierno, Ron, Melba A. Hernandez, Ananda B. Amstadter, Heidi S. Resnick, Kenneth Steve, Wendy Muzzy, and Dean G. Kilpatrick. 2010. "Prevalence and Correlates of Emotional, Physical, Sexual, and Financial Abuse and Potential Neglect in the United States: The National Elder Mistreatment Study." *American Journal of Public Health* 100(2):292–97.

Adams, Kathryn Betts, Sylvia Leibbrandt, and Heehyul Moon. 2011. "A Critical Review of the Literature on Social and Leisure Activity and Wellbeing in Later Life." *Ageing and Society* 31(4):693–712.

ADEAR (Alzheimer's and Related Dementias Education and Referral Center). 2010. Retrieved June 2, 2010 (http://www.nia.nih.gov/Alzheimers).

Alabama Public Television. 2005. *The Quiltmakers of Gee's Bend*. Director Celia Carey.

Alley, Dawn E., Norella M. Putney, Melissa Rice, and Vern L. Bengtson. 2010. "The Increasing Use of Theory in Social Gerontology: 1990–2004." *Journal of Gerontology: Social Sciences* 65B(5):583–90.

Alzheimer's Disease. 2010. Retrieved June 2, 2010 (http://www.medicinenet.com/alzheimers_disease/article.htm).

American Community Survey (ACS). 2014. "Technical Documentation." Retrieved May 8, 2014 (https://www.census.gov/programs-surveys/acs/technical-documentation.html).

Anderson, Monica. 2015. "On Grandparents Day, Will You Call, Text, or Write?" Retrieved March 29, 2017 (http://www.pewresearch.org/fact-tank/2015/09/11/on-grandparents-day-will-you-call-text-or-write/).

Anetzberger, Georgia J. 2012. "An Update on the Nature and Scope of Elder Abuse." *Generations* 36(3):12–20.

Angel, Jacqueline, and Fernando Torres-Gil. 2010. "Hispanic Aging and Social Policy." Pp. 1–19 in *Aging in America,* edited by J. C. Cavanaugh and C. K. Cavanaugh. Santa Barbara, CA: Praeger.

Ankuda, Claire, and Deborah Levine. 2016. "Trends in Caregiving Assistance for Home-Dwelling, Functionally Impaired Older Adults in the United States, 1998–2012." *JAMA* 316(2):218–20.

Ardelt, Monika. 2000. "Still Stable after All These Years? Personality Stability Theory Revisited." *Social Psychology Quarterly* 63(4):392–405.

Arnett, Jeffrey Jensen. 2015. *Emerging Adulthood: The Winding Road from the Late Teens through the Twenties.* Oxford: Oxford University Press.

Atchley, Robert C. 1989a. "A Continuity Theory of Normal Aging." *Gerontologist* 29:183–90.

Atchley, Robert C. 1989b. "Continuity Theory and the Evolution of Activity in Later Adulthood." Pp. 5–16 in *Activity and Aging: Staying Involved in Later Life,* edited by J. Kelly. Newbury Park, CA: Sage.

Atchley, Robert C. 1999. *Continuity and Adaptation in Aging.* Baltimore: Johns Hopkins University Press.

Avison, William R., Jennifer Ali, and David Walters. 2007. "Family Structure, Stress, and Psychological Distress: A Demonstration of the Impact of Differential Exposure." *Journal of Health and Social Behavior* 48:301–17.

Baker, Patricia Sawyer, Erik Bodner, and Richard Allman. 2003. "Measuring Life-Space Mobility in Community-Dwelling Older Adults." *Journal of the American Geriatrics Society* 51:1610–14.

Baltes, Paul B. 1987. "Theoretical Propositions of Life-Span Developmental Psychology: On the Dynamics between Growth and Decline." *Developmental Psychology* 23(5):611–26.

Baltes, Paul B., and Margret M. Baltes. 1990. "Psychological Perspectives on Successful Aging: The Model of Selective Optimization with Compensation." Pp. 1–34 in *Successful Aging Perspectives from the Behavioral Sciences,* edited by P. B. Baltes and M. M. Baltes. Cambridge: Cambridge University Press.

Bancroft, John H. J. 2007. "Sex and Aging." *New England Journal of Medicine* 357(8):820–22.

Bareket-Bojmel, Liad, Simone Moran, and Golan Shahar. 2016. "Strategic Self-presentation on Facebook." *Computers in Human Behavior* 55:788–95.

Barrett, Anne E., and Cheryl Robbins. 2008. "The Multiple Sources of Women's Aging Anxiety and Their Relationship with Psychological Distress." *Journal of Aging and Health* 20(1):32–65.

Bauman, Zygmunt. 2007. *Work, Consumerism, and the New Poor*. Maidenhead, UK: Open University Press.

Baxter, Janeen, Belinda Hewitt, and Michele Haynes. 2008. "Life Course Transitions and Housework: Marriage, Parenthood, and Time on Housework." *Journal of Marriage and Family* 70(2):259–72.

Beardsley, John, Jane Livingston, Alvia Wardlaw, and William Arnett. 2002. *Gee's Bend: The Women and Their Quilts*. Atlanta: Tinwood Books.

Bengtson, Vern L. 2001. "Beyond the Nuclear Family: The Increasing Importance of Intergenerational Bonds." *Journal of Marriage and Family* 63(1):1–16.

Bengtson, Vern L., and Marguerite DeLiema. 2016. "Theories of Aging and Social Gerontology: Explaining How Social Factors Influence Well-Being in Later Life." Pp. 25–56 in *Gerontology: Changes, Challenges, and Solutions*, edited by Madonna Harrington Meyer and Elizabeth A. Daniele.

Bengtson, Vern L., Elisabeth O. Burgess, and Tonya M. Parrott. 1997. "Theory, Explanation, and a Third Generation of Theoretical Development in Social Gerontology." *Journal of Gerontology: Social Sciences* 52B(2):S72–S88.

Best, Steven, and Douglas Kellner. 1991. *Postmodern Theory: Critical Interrogations*. New York: Guilford Press.

Billari, Francisco C., Alice Goisis, Aart C. Liefbroer, Richard A. Settersten, Arnstein Aassve, Gunhild Hagestad, and Zsolt Spéder. 2011. "Social Age Deadlines for the Childbearing of Women and Men." *Psychology and Counseling* 26(3):616–22.

Bird, Chloe E., and Patricia P. Rieker. 2008. *Gender and Health: The Effects of Constrained Choices and Social Policies*. New York: Cambridge University Press.

Boerner, Kathrin, Deborah Carr, and Sara Moorman. 2013. "Family Relationships and Advance Care Planning: Do Supportive and Critical Relations Encourage or Hinder Planning?" *The Journals of Gerontology: Series B* 68(2):246–56.

Bookman, Ann, and Delia Kimbrel. 2011. "Families and Elder Care in the Twenty-First Century." *The Future of Children* 21(2): 117–40.

Boswell, Gracie. 2015. "Cultural Diversity and Aging in the United States." In *The Wiley Blackwell Encyclopedia of Race, Ethnicity, and Nationalism*. Wiley Online Library: John Wiley & Sons.

Braveman, Paula A., Catherine Cubbin, Susan Egerter, David Williams, and Elsie Pamuk. 2010. "Socioeconomic Disparities in Health in the United States: What the Pattern Tells Us." *American Journal of Public Health* 100(S1):S186–96.

Brick, Aoife, Samantha Smith, Charles Normand, Sinéad O'Hara, Elsa Droog, Ella Tyrrell, Nathan Cunningham, and Bridget Johnston. 2017. "Costs of Formal and Informal Care in the Last Year of Life for Patients in Receipt of Specialist Palliative Care." *Palliative Medicine* 31(4):356–68.

Brown, Susan, and I-Fen Lin. 2012. "The Gray Divorce Revolution: Rising Divorce among Middle-Aged and Older Adults, 1990–2010." *The Journals of Gerontology: Series B* 67(6): 731–41.

Brown, Susan, Jennifer Bulanda, and Gary Lee. 2005. "The Significance of Nonmarital Cohabitation: Marital Status and Mental Health Benefits among Middle-Aged and Older Adults." *The Journals of Gerontology: Series B* 60(1):S21–S29.

Brown, Susan, Gary Lee, and Jennifer Bulanda. 2006. "Cohabitation among Older Adults: A National Portrait." *The Journals of Gerontology: Series B* 61(2):S71–S79.

Brown, Susan L., and Sayaka K. Shinohara. 2013. "Dating Relationships in Older Adulthood: A National Portrait." *Journal of Marriage and Family* 75(5):1194–202.

Buettner, Dan. 2009. *The Blue Zones: Lessons for Living Longer from People Who've Lived the Longest*. Washington, DC: National Geographic Society.

Buhr, Gwendolen T., Maragatha Kuchibhatla, and Elizabeth C. Clipp. 2006. "Caregivers' Reasons for Nursing Home Placement: Clues for Improving Discussions with Families Prior to Transition." *Gerontologist* 46(1):52–61.

Bures, Regina M., Tanya Koropeckyj-Cox, and Michael Loree. 2009. "Childlessness, Parenthood, and Depressive Symptoms among

Middle-Aged and Older Adults." *Journal of Family Issues* 30(5):670–87.

Buys, David, Casey Borch, Patricia Drentea, Mark LaGory, Patricia Sawyer, Richard Allman, Richard Kennedy, and Julie Locher. 2013. "Physical Impairment Is Associated with Nursing Home Admission for Older Adults in Disadvantaged But Not Other Neighborhoods: Results from the UAB Study of Aging." *Gerontologist* 53(4):641–53.

Cacioppo, John T., Mary Elizabeth Hughes, Linda J. Waite, Louise C. Hawkley, and Ronald A. Thisted. 2006. "Loneliness as a Specific Risk Factor for Depressive Symptoms: Cross-Sectional and Longitudinal Analyses." *Psychology and Aging* 21(1):140–51.

Calasanti, Toni, and Neal King. 2007. "Taking 'Women's Work' 'Like a Man': Husbands' Experiences of Care Work." *Gerontologist* 47(4):516–27.

Calasanti, Toni, and Kathleen Slevin. 2001. *Gender, Social Inequalities, and Aging.* Walnut Creek, CA: AltaMira Press.

Camia, Catalina. 2013. "Obama Presses for Gay Marriage in Inaugural Speech." *USA Today,* January 21. Retrieved February 8, 2013 (http://www.usatoday.com/story/news/politics/2013/01/21/obama-inauguration-speech-gay-marriage-stonewall/1851999/).

Cantor, Marjorie H. 1979. "Neighbors and Friends: An Overlooked Resource in the Informal Support System." *Research on Aging* 1(4):434–63.

CAPC (Center to Advance Palliative Care). 2012. "Growth in Palliative Care in U.S. Hospitals: 2012 Snapshot." Retrieved March 19, 2012 (https://media.capc.org/filer_public/e1/c9/e1c93c86-7fad-4aa6-b5e0-7757ef313da0/capc-growth-analysis-snapshot-2011.pdf).

Carr, Deborah. 2004. "The Desire to Date and Remarry among Older Widows and Widowers." *Journal of Marriage and Family* 66(4):1054–68.

Carr, Deborah, and Kathrin Boerner. 2013. "Dating after Late-Life Spousal Loss: Does It Compromise Relationships with Adult Children?" *Journal of Aging Studies* 27(4):487–98.

Carstensen, Laura L. 1992. "Social and Emotional Patterns in Adulthood: Support for Socioemotional Selectivity Theory." *Psychology and Aging* 7(3):331–38.

Carstensen, Laura L., Bulent Turan, Susanne Scheibe, Nilam Ram, Hal Ersner-Hershfield, Gregory R. Samanez-Larkin, Kathryn P. Brooks, and John R. Nesselroade. 2011. "Emotional Experience Improves With Age: Evidence Based on Over 10 Years of Experience Sampling." *Psychology and Aging* 26(1):21–33.

Casey, Judi. 2009. "Work-Family Information on: Military Families." *Effective Workplace Series, Sloan Work and Family Research Network* 14:1. Retrieved January 5, 2011 (http://wfnetwork.bc.edu/pdfs/EWS14_militaryfamilies.pdf).

Centers for Disease Control and Prevention (CDC). 2006. "Leading Causes of Death 1900–1998." Retrieved October 4, 2006 (https://www.cdc.gov/nchs/data/dvs/lead1900_98.pdf).

Centers for Disease Control and Prevention (CDC). 2009. "Limitations in Activities of Daily Living and Instrumental Activities of Daily Living, 2003–2007." Retrieved October 31, 2012 (https://www.cdc.gov/nchs/health_policy/adl_tables.htm).

Centers for Disease Control and Prevention (CDC). 2013. "Leading Causes of Death." Retrieved April 23, 2015 (https://www.cdc.gov/nchs/fastats/leading-causes-of-death.htm).

Centers for Disease Control and Prevention (CDC). 2018. "Assisted Reproductive Technology (ART)." Downloaded July 15, 2018 (https://www.cdc.gov/art/index.html).

Chang, Po-Ju, Linda Wray, and Yeqiang Lin. 2014. "Social Relationships, Leisure Activity, and Health in Older Adults." *Health Psychology* 33(6):516–23.

Cherlin, Andrew J. 1978. "Remarriage as an Incomplete Institution." *American Journal of Sociology* 84(3):634–50.

Cherlin, Andrew J. 1992. *Marriage, Divorce, Remarriage.* Cambridge, MA: Harvard University Press.

Cherlin, Andrew. 2010a. "Demographic Trends in the United States: A Review of the Research in the 2000s." *Journal of Marriage and Family* 72(3):403–19.

Cherlin, Andrew. 2010b. *The Marriage-Go-Round: The State of Marriage and the Family in America Today.* New York: Knopf Doubleday.

Cherlin, Andrew. 2013. "Health, Marriage, and Same-Sex Partnerships." *Journal of Marriage and the Family* 54(1):64–66.

Cherlin, Andrew J., and Frank F. Furstenberg, Jr. 1985. "Styles and Strategies of Grandparenting." Pp. 97–116 in *Grandparenthood,* edited by V. L. Bengston and J. F. Robertson. Beverly Hills: Sage.

Childfree-by-Choice Pages. Retrieved October 13, 2016 (http://www.childfree.net/).

Christakis, Nicholas A., and James H. Fowler. 2007. "The Spread of Obesity in a Large Social Network Over 32 Years." *New England Journal of Medicine* 4(357):370–79.

Clouston, Sean, and Nicole Denier. 2017. "Mental Retirement and Health Selection: Analyses from the U.S. Health and Retirement Study." *Social Science and Medicine* 178:78–86.

Cockerham, William. 2006. *Sociology of Mental Disorder*. 7th edition. Upper Saddle River, NJ: Pearson.

Cockerham, William. 2013. *Social Causes of Health and Disease*. 2nd edition. Hoboken, NJ: Wiley.

Colby, Sandra L., and Jennifer M. Ortman, 2014. "Projections of the Size and Composition of the U.S. Population: 2014 to 2060, Current Population Reports, P25-1143." U.S. Census Bureau, Washington, DC. Retrieved July 13, 2018 (https://www.census.gov/content/dam/Census/library/publications/2015/demo/p25-1143.pdf).

Coltrane, Scott, Ross D. Parke, Thomas Schofield, Tshua J. Shigeru, Michael Chavez, and Shoon Lio. 2008. "Mexican American Families and Poverty." Pp. 162–73 in *Handbook of Families of Poverty*, edited by D. R. Crane and T. B. Heaton. Thousand Oaks, CA: Sage.

Connidis, Ingrid Arnet. 2010. *Family Ties and Aging*. 2nd edition. Los Angeles: Pine Forge Press.

Coontz, Stephanie. 2016. *The Way We Never Were: American Families and the Nostalgia Trap*. New York: Basic Books.

Cornwell, Erin, and Linda Waite. 2009. "Social Disconnectedness, Perceived Isolation, and Health among Older Adults." *Journal of Health and Social Behavior* 50(1):31–48.

Costa, Paul T., Jr., and Robert R. McCrae. 1980. "Still Stable After All These Years: Personality as a Key to Some Issues in Adulthood and Old Age." Pp. 65–102 in *Life-Span Development and Behavior*, edited by P. B. Baltes. New York: Academic Press.

Cotten, Shelia R., William A. Anderson, and Brandi McCullough. 2013. "Impact of Internet Use on Loneliness and Contact with Others among Older Adults: Cross-Sectional Analysis." *Journal of Medical Internet Research* 15(2):e39.

Cotten, Shelia R., George Ford, Sherry Ford, and Timothy Hale. 2014. "Internet Use and Depression among Retired Older Adults in the United States: A Longitudinal Analysis." *The Journals of Gerontology: Series B* 69(5):763–71.

Council of State Governments. 2005. *Trends in America: Charting the Course Ahead*. Lexington, KY.

Cruz, Taylor M. 2014. "Assessing Access to Care for Transgender and Gender Nonconforming People: A Consideration of Diversity in Combating Discrimination." *Social Science and Medicine* 110:65–73.

Curtin, Sally C., Joyce C. Abma, and Kathryn Kost. 2015. "2010 Pregnancy Rates among U.S. Women." National Center for Health Statistics. Retrieved July 15, 2018 (https://www.cdc.gov/nchs/data/hestat/pregnancy/2010_pregnancy_rates.htm).

Curtis, Glade, and Judith Schuler. 2013. *Your Pregnancy after 35*. 3rd edition. Cambridge, MA: Perseus.

Cutler, David M., and Adriana Lleras-Muney, 2006. "Education and Health: Evaluating Theories and Evidence." NBER Working Papers 12352, National Bureau of Economic Research. Retrieved April 5, 2017 (https://ideas.repec.org/p/nbr/nberwo/12352.html).

Cutler, Stephen J., John Hendricks, and Amy Guyer. 2003. "Age Differences in Home Computer Availability and Use." *The Journals of Gerontology: Series B* 58(5):271–80.

Daneshpour, Manijeh, and Elham Fathi. 2016. "Muslim Marriages in the Western World: A Decade Review." *Journal of Muslim Mental Health* 10(1).

Dannefer, Dale. 2003 "Cumulative Advantage/Disadvantage and the Life Course: Cross-Fertilizing Age and the Social Science Theory." *The Journals of Gerontology: Series B* 58(6):S327–S337.

Dannefer, David, and Peter Uhlenberg. 1999. "Paths of the Life Course: A Typology." Pp. 306–26 in *Handbook of Theories of Aging*, edited by V. Bengtson and P. Uhlenberg. New York: Springer.

Danziger, Pamela N. 2011. *Putting the Luxe Back in Luxury*. Rochester, NY: Paramount.

De Jong Gierveld, J. 2004. "Remarriage, Unmarried Cohabitation, Living Apart Together: Partner Relationships Following Bereavement or Divorce." *Journal of Marriage and Family* 66(1):236–43.

De Jong Gierveld, J., and Anna Peeters. 2003. "The Interweaving of Repartnered Older Adults' Lives with Their Children and Siblings." *Ageing and Society* 23:187–205.

DeKlyen, Michelle, Jeanne Brooks-Gunn, Sarah McLanahan, and Jean Knab. 2006. "The Mental Health of Married, Cohabiting, and Non-Coresident Parents with Infants." *American Journal of Public Health* 96(10):1836–41.

DeLamater, John. 2012. "Sexual Expression in Later Life: A Review and Synthesis." *Journal of Sex Research* 49(2–3):125–41.

Dilworth-Anderson, Peggye, and Monique Cohen. 2009. "Theorizing Across Cultures." Pp. 487–97 in *Handbook of Theories of Aging*, edited by V. Bengtson, D. Gans, N. Putney, and M. Silverstein. New York: Springer.

Dilworth-Anderson, Peggye, and Tandrea Hilliard. 2013. "Social Networks and Minority Elders." Pp. 405–16 in *Handbook on Minority Aging*, edited by K. E. Whitfield and T. A. Baker. New York: Springer.

Dobriansky, Paula J., Richard M. Suzman, and Richard J. Hodes. 2007. "Why Population Aging Matters: A Global Perspective." National Institute on Aging. National Institutes of Health. Washington, DC: U.S. Department of Health and Human Services. Retrieved January 18, 2016 (https://www.nia.nih.gov/sites/default/files/2017-06/WPAM.pdf).

Doyle, Martha, Ciara O'Dywer, and Virpi Timonen. 2010. "'How Can You Just Cut Off a Whole Side of the Family and Say Move On?' The Reshaping of Paternal Grandparent-Grandchild Relationships Following Divorce or Separation in the Middle Generation." *Family Relations* 59(5):587–98.

Drentea, Patricia. 2000. "Age, Debt, and Anxiety." *Journal of Health and Social Behavior* 41(4):437–50.

Drentea, Patricia. 2002. "Retirement and Mental Health." *Journal of Aging and Health* 14(2):167–94.

Drentea, Patricia. 2005. "Work and Activity Characteristics Across the Life Course." *Structure of the Life Course: Advances in Life Course Research* 9:305–331.

Drentea, Patricia. 2016. "Caregiving." In *The Blackwell Encyclopedia of Sociology*, 2nd edition, edited by George Ritzer. Malden, MA: Blackwell.

Drentea, Patricia, Olivio Clay, David Roth, and Mary Mittelman. 2006. "Predictors of Improvement in Social Support: Five-Year Effects of a Structured Intervention for Caregivers of Spouses with Alzheimer's Disease." *Social Science and Medicine* 63(4):957–67.

Drentea, Patricia, and Melinda Goldner. 2006. "Caregiving Outside the Home: The Effects of Race on Depression." *Ethnicity and Health* 11(1):41–47.

Drentea, Patricia, and John R. Reynolds. 2012. "Neither a Borrower Nor a Lender Be: The Relative Importance of Debt and SES for Mental Health among Older Adults." *Journal of Aging and Health* 24(4):668–90.

Drentea, Patricia, and John R. Reynolds. 2015. "Where Does Debt Fit in the Stress Process Model?" *Society and Mental Health* 51(1):16–32.

Drentea, Patricia, Beverly R. Williams, Kathryn L. Burgio, and F. Amos Bailey. 2016. "'He's on His Dying Bed': Next-of-Kin's Experiences of the Dying Body." *Death Studies* 40(1):1–10.

Eardley, Ian, Craig Donatucci, Jackie Corbin, Amr El-Meliegy, Konstantinos Hatzimouratidis, Kevin McVary, Ricardo Munarriz, and Sung Won Lee. 2010. "Pharmacotherapy for Erectile Dysfunction." *Journal of Sexual Medicine* 1(2):524–40.

Earl, Catherine, Philip Taylor, and Christopher McLoughlin. 2015. "Recruitment and Selection of Older Workers." *Encyclopedia of Geropsychology* 13(1):2–8.

Edin, Kathryn. 2000. "What Do Low-Income Single Mothers Say about Marriage?" *Social Problems* 47(1):112–33.

EEOC. 2017. "Age Discrimination." Retrieved April 9, 2017 (https://www.eeoc.gov/eeoc/publications/age.cfm).

Ehrenreich, Barbara, and Arlie Russell Hochschild. 2002. *Global Women: Nannies, Maids, and Sex Workers in the New Economy*. New York: Henry Holt.

Ejem, Deborah, Patricia Drentea, and Olivio Clay. 2015. "The Effects of Caregiver Emotional Stress on the Depressive Symptomatology of the Care Recipient." *Aging and Mental Health* 19(1):55–62. https://doi.org/10.1080/13607863.2014.915919.

Ekerdt, David J. 1986. "The Busy Ethic: Moral Continuity between Work and Retirement." *Gerontologist* 26(3):239–44.

Ekerdt, David J. 2009. "Dispossession: The Tenacity of Things." Pp. 63–78 in *Consumption and Generational Change: The Rise of Consumer Lifestyles*, edited by I. R. Jones et al. New Brunswick, NJ: Transaction.

Ekerdt, David J., and L. Baker. 2014. "The Material Convoy after Age 50." *The Journals of Gerontology: Series B* 69(3):442–50.

Elder, Glen H., Jr., Monica Kirkpatrick Johnson, and Robert Crosnoe. 2003. "The Emergence and Development of Life Course Theory." Pp. 3–19 in *Handbook of the Life Course*, edited by J. T. Mortimer and M. J. Shanahan. New York: Kluwer Academic.

Ellison, Christopher G., Scott Schieman, and Matt Bradshaw. 2014. "The Association between

Religiousness and Psychological Well-Being among Older Adults: Is There an Educational Gradient? Pp. 263–88 in *Religion and Inequality in America*, edited by Lisa A. Keister and Darren E. Sherkat. New York: Cambridge University Press.

Elwert, Felix, and Nicholas A. Christakis. 2006. "Widowhood and Race." *American Sociological Review* 71(1):16–41.

Elwert, Felix, and Nicholas A. Christakis. 2008. "The Effect of Widowhood on Mortality by the Causes of Death of Both Spouses." *American Journal of Public Health* 98(11):2092–98.

England, Kim, and Isabel Dyck. 2011. "Managing the Body Work of Home Care." *Sociology of Health and Illness* 33(2):206–19.

Ephron, Nora. 2006. *I Feel Bad about My Neck: And Other Thoughts on Being a Woman.* New York: Vintage Books.

Erikson, Erik. 1964. *Childhood and Society.* New York: Norton.

Eskildsen, Manuel, and Thomas Price. 2009. "Nursing Home Care in the USA." *Geriatrics and Gerontology International* 9(1):1–6.

Estes, Carroll L., Simon Biggs, and Chris Phillipson. 2009. *Social Theory, Social Policy and Ageing: A Critical Introduction.* Berkshire, UK: Open University Press.

Evenson, Ranae J., and Robin W. Simon. 2005. "Clarifying the Relationship between Parenthood and Depression." *Journal of Health and Social Behavior* 46(4):341–58.

Faes, Kristof, Veerle De Frène, Joachim Cohen, and Lieven Annemans. 2016. "Resource Use and Health Care Costs of COPD Patients at the End of Life: A Systematic Review." *Journal of Pain and Symptom Management* 52(4):588–99.

Ferraro, Kenneth F., and Tetyana Pylypiv Shippee. 2009. "Aging and Cumulative Inequality: How Does Inequality Get Under the Skin?" *Gerontologist* 49(3):333–43.

FIFARS (Federal Interagency Forum on Aging-Related Statistics). 2016. *Older Americans 2016: Key Indicators of Well-Being.* Washington, DC: U.S. Government Printing Office. Retrieved July 13, 2018 (https://agingstats.gov/docs/LatestReport/Older-Americans-2016-Key-Indicators-of-WellBeing.pdf).

Flippen, Chenoa, and Marta Tienda. 2000. "Pathways to Retirement: Patterns of Labor Force Participation and Labor Market Exit among the Pre-Retirement Population by Race, Hispanic Origin, and Sex." *The Journals of Gerontology: Series B* 55B(1):S14–S27.

Fox, Susannah. 2001. *Wired Seniors: A Fervent Few, Inspired by Family Ties.* Pew Internet and American Life Project.

Fox, Susannah. 2004. *Older Americans and the Internet.* Pew Internet and American Life Project.

Fox, Susannah. 2010. *Four in Ten Seniors Go Online.* Pew Internet and American Life Project.

Fredriksen-Goldsen, Karen I., and Hyun-Jun Kim. 2017. "The Science of Conducting Research with LGBT Older Adults—An Introduction to Aging with Pride: National Health, Aging, and Sexuality/Gender Study." *Gerontologist* 57(1):S1–S14.

Fredriksen-Goldsen, Karen I., Hyun-Jun Kim, Charles A. Emlet, Anna Muraco, Elena A. Erosheva, Charles P. Hoy-Ellis, Jayn Goldsen, and Heidi Petry. 2011. "The Aging and Health Report: Disparities and Resilience among Lesbian, Gay, Bisexual, and Transgender Older Adults." National LGBT Health and Aging Center. Seattle: Institute for Multigenerational Health, University of Washington. Retrieved March 10, 2012 (https://depts.washington.edu/agepride/wordpress/wp-content/uploads/2012/10/fact-sheet-keyfindings10-25-12.pdf).

Fredriksen-Goldsen, Karen I., and Anna Muraco. 2010. "Aging and Sexual Orientation: A 25-Year Review of the Literature." *Research on Aging* 32(3):372–413.

Freedman, Vicki A., Robert F. Schoeni, Linda G. Martin, and J. C. Cornman. 2007. "The Role of Education in Explaining and Forecasting Trends in Functional Limitations among Older Americans." *Demography* 44(3):459–78.

Fries, James E. 1980. "Aging, Natural Death, and the Compression of Morbidity." *New England Journal of Medicine* 303(3):130–5.

Fry, Richard, and Jeffrey S. Passel. 2014. "In Post-Recession Era, Young Adults Drive Continuing Rise in Multi-Generational Living." Pew Research Center. Retrieved July 16, 2018 (http://www.pewsocialtrends.org/2014/07/17/in-post-recession-era-young-adults-drive-continuing-rise-in-multi-generational-living/).

Galinsky, Adena, Martha McClintock, and Linda Waite. 2014. "Sexuality and Physical Contact in National Social Life, Health, and Aging Project Wave 2." *The Journals of Gerontology, Series B* 69(8):S83–S98.

Galinsky, Ellen, Kerstin Aumann, and James T. Bond. 2009. *Times Are Changing: Gender and Generation at Work and at Home.* New York: Families and Work Institute.

Garrison, Marsha, and Elizabeth S. Scott. 2012. *Marriage at the Crossroads: Law, Policy, and the Brave New World of Twenty-First-Century Families.* New York: Cambridge University Press.

Gassoumis, Zachary D., Kathleen H. Wilber, and Fernando Torres-Gil. 2008. "Latino Baby Boomers: A Hidden Population." UCLA Center for Policy Research on Aging. Policy Brief 3. Retrieved February 6, 2015 (http://www.academia.edu/300742/Latino_Baby_Boomers_A_Hidden_Population).

Gates, Gary J. 2013. "Demographics and LGBT Health." *Journal of Health and Social Behavior* 54(1):72–74.

Gauthier, Anne H., and Timothy M. Smeeding. 2003. "Time Use at Older Ages: Cross-National Differences." *Research on Aging* 25(3):247–74.

Gay Marriage. 2015. Retrieved August 25, 2015 (http://gaymarriage.procon.org/view.resource.php?resourceID=004857).

Gerson, Kathleen. 2010. *The Unfinished Revolution: How a New Generation Is Reshaping Family, Work, and Gender in America.* New York: Oxford.

Geyer, Siegfried. 2016. "Morbidity Compression: A Promising and Well-established Concept?" *International Journal of Public Health* 61(7):727–28.

Gilleard, Chris, and Paul Higgs. 2009. "The Third Age: Field, Habitus, or Identity?" Pp. 23–36 in *Consumption and Generational Change: The Rise of Consumer Lifestyles,* edited by I. R. Jones et al. New Brunswick, NJ: Transaction.

Ginsburg, Kenneth R., the Committee on Communications, and the Committee on Psychosocial Aspects of Child and Family Health. 2007. "The Importance of Play in Promoting Healthy Child Development and Maintaining Strong Parent-Child Bonds." *Pediatrics* 119(1):182–91.

Goldner, Melinda, and Patricia Drentea. 2009. "Caring for the Disabled: Applying Different Theoretical Perspectives to Understand Racial and Ethnic Variations among Families." *Marriage and Family Review: Special Issue: The Family and Disability* 45(5):499–518.

Goldscheider, Frances K. 2000. "Men, Children and the Future of the Family in the Third Millennium." *Futures* 32(6):525–38.

Goodman, Christopher J., and Steven M. Mance. 2011. "Employment Loss and the 2007–09 Recession: An Overview." *Monthly Labor Review* 134:3–12.

Gott, Merryn. 2006. "Sexual Health and the New Ageing." *Age and Ageing* 35(2):106–7.

Gott, Merryn, and Sharron Hinchliff. (2003). "Barriers to Seeking Treatment for Sexual Problems in Primary Care: A Qualitative Study with Older People." *Family Practice* 20(6):690–95.

Grieco, Elizabeth M., Yesenia D. Acosta, G. Patricia de la Cruz, Christine Gambino, Thomas Gryn, Luke J. Larsen, Edward N. Trevelyan, and Nathan P. Walters. 2012. "The Foreign-Born Population in the United States: 2010." American Community Survey Reports. ACS 19. U.S. Census Bureau. Retrieved February 8, 2013 (http://www.census.gov/prod/2012pubs/acs-19.pdf).

Grochowski, Janet R. 2014. *Families and Health.* Thousand Oaks, CA: Sage.

Grollman, Eric. 2014. "Multiple Disadvantaged Statuses and Health: The Role of Multiple Forms of Discrimination." *Journal of Health and Social Behavior* 55(1):3–19.

Gruenberg, E. M. 1977. "The Failure of Success." *Milbank Memorial Fund Quarterly* 55:3–24.

Gruenberg, Ernest M. 2005. "The Failure of Success." *Milbank Memorial Fund Quarterly* 83(4):779–800.

Gustman, Alan L., Thomas L. Steinmeier, and Nahid Tabatabai. 2011. "How Did the Recession of 2007–2009 Affect the Wealth and Retirement of the Near Retirement Age Population in the Health and Retirement Study?" MRRC Working Paper WP 2011-253. Ann Arbor: University of Michigan Retirement Research Center.

Ha, Jung-Hwa. 2005. "The Effect of Parent-Child Geographic Proximity on Widowed Parents' Psychological Adjustment and Social Integration." *Research on Aging* 27(5):578–610.

Hale, Timothy M., Shelia Cotten, Patricia Drentea, and Melinda Goldner. 2010. "Rural-Urban Differences in General and Health-Related Internet Usage." *American Behavioral Scientist* 53(9):1304–25.

Halphen, John M., and Jason Burnett. 2014. "Elder Abuse and Neglect: Appearances Can Be Deceptive." *Psychiatric Times* 1–5.

Hamilton, Brady E., and Stephanie J. Ventura. 2012. "Birth Rates for U.S. Teenagers Reach Historic Lows for All Age and Ethnic Groups." NCHS Data Brief, No. 89. Hyattsville, MD: National Center for Health Statistics. Retrieved May 11, 2012 (http://www.cdc.gov/nchs/data/databriefs/db89.pdf).

Harrington Meyer, Madonna. 2014. *Grandmothers at Work: Juggling Families and Jobs.* New York: New York University Press.

Harrington Meyer, M., and Pamela Herd. 2007. *Market Friendly or Family Friendly? The State and Gender Inequality in Old Age.* New York: Russell Sage Foundation.

Harrington Meyer, M., Pamela Herd, and Sonya Michel. 2000. "Introduction: The Right to—or Not to—Care." Pp. 1–4 in *Care Work: Gender, Class, and the Welfare State,* edited by M. H. Meyer. New York: Routledge.

Harrington Meyer, Madonna, Douglas Wolf, and Christine Himes. 2006. "Declining Eligibility for Social Security Spouse and Widow Benefits in the United States?" *Research on Aging* 28(2):240–60.

Harris, Kathleen Mullan, and Thomas W. McDade. 2018. "The Biosocial Approach to Human Development, Behavior, and Health Across the Life Course." *Russell Sage Foundation Journal of the Social Sciences* 4(4):2–26.

Hash, Kristina M., and Mariann Mankowski. 2017. "Caregiving in the LGBT Community." *Annual Review of Gerontology and Geriatrics* 37(1):77–87.

Havighurst, Robert J. 1963. "Successful Aging." Pp. 299–320 in *Processes of Aging*, edited by R. Williams, C. Tibbitts, and W. Donahue. New York: Atherton.

Hays, Sharon. 1996. *The Cultural Contradictions of Motherhood.* New Haven, CT: Yale University Press.

Hayslip, Bert, and Patricia L. Kaminski. 2005. "Grandparents Raising Their Grandchildren: A Review of the Literature and Suggestions for Practice." *Gerontologist* 45(2):262–69.

Hayward, Mark D., Eileen M. Crimmins, Toni P. Miles, and Yu Yang. 2000. "The Significance of Socioeconomic Status in Explaining the Racial Gap in Chronic Health Conditions." *American Sociological Review* 65(6):910–30.

Hill Collins, Patricia. 2000. *Black Feminist Thought: Knowledge, Consciousness, and the Politics of Empowerment.* New York: Routledge.

Hoenig, Helen, D. H. Taylor, and F. A. Sloan. 2003. "Does Assistive Technology Substitute for Personal Assistance among the Disabled Elderly?" *American Journal of Public Health* 93(2):330–37.

Hoeymans, Nancy, Albert Wong, Coen H. van Gool, Dorly J. H. Deeg, Wilma J. Nusselder, Mirjam M. Y. de Klerk, Martin P. J. van Boxtel, and H. Susan J. Picavet. 2012. "The Disabling Effect of Diseases: A Study on Trends in Diseases, Activity Limitations, and Their Interrelationships." *American Journal of Public Health* 102(1):163–70.

Hofferth, Sandra L., and Frances K. Goldscheider. 2010. "Family Structure and the Transition to Early Parenthood." *Demography* 47(2):415–37.

Hollingshead, August B., and Frederick C. Redlich. 1958. *Social Class and Mental Illness: A Community Study.* New York: John Wiley.

Holtfreter, Kristi, Michael Reisig, and Jillian Turanovic. 2016. "Self-Rated Poor Health and Loneliness in Late Adulthood: Testing the Moderating Roles of Familial Ties." *Advances in Life Course Research* 27:61–68.

Holt-Lunstad, Julianne, Timothy B. Smith, and J. B. Layton. 2010. "Social Relationships and Mortality Risk: A Meta-Analytic Review." *PLoS Medicine*. Retrieved January 12, 2016 (http://journals.plos.org/plosmedicine/article?id=10.1371/journal.pmed.1000316).

Houle, Jason N., and Cody Warner. 2017. "Into the Red and Back to the Nest? Student Debt, College Completion, and Returning to the Parental Home among Young Adults." *Sociology of Education* 90(1):89–108.

House, James S., Paula M. Lantz, and Pamela Herd. 2005. "Continuity and Change in the Social Stratification of Aging and Health Over the Life Course: Evidence from a Nationally Representative Longitudinal Study from 1986 to 2001/2002 (Americans' Changing Lives Study)." *The Journals of Gerontology: Series B* 60(2):S15–S26.

Hu, Yuanreng, and Noreen Goldman. 1990. "Mortality Differentials by Marital Status: An International Comparison." *Demography* 27(2):233–50.

Hughes, Mark T., and Thomas J. Smith. 2014. "The Growth of Palliative Care in the United States." *Annual Review of Public Health* 35:459–75.

Hurd Clarke, Laura. 2011. *Facing Age: Women Growing Older in Anti-Aging Culture.* Plymouth, UK: Rowman & Littlefield.

Hyde, Martin, Paul Higgs, Chris Gilleard, Christina Victor, Richard D. Wiggins, and Ian Rees Jones. 2009. "Ageing, Cohorts, and Consumption: The British Experience 1968–2005." Pp. 93–125 in *Consumption and Generational Change: The Rise of Consumer Lifestyles,* edited by I. R. Jones et al. New Brunswick, NJ: Transaction.

Imparato, Tresa, and Debra Sanders. 2012. "STD Prevalence Demands Clinical Awareness." *Aging Well* 5(1):14.

Institute of Medicine Committee on Lesbian, Gay, Bisexual, and Transgender Health Issues and Research Gaps and Opportunities. 2011. *The Health of Lesbian, Gay, Bisexual, and Transgender People: Building a Foundation for Better Understanding.* Washington, DC: National Academies Press. Retrieved May 8, 2015 (https://www.ncbi.nlm.nih.gov/books/NBK64808/).

International Data Base. 2014. "International Programs." IDB 1950–2050. Retrieved February 3, 2014 (https://www.census.gov/programs-surveys/international-programs/about/idb.html).

IOM (Institute of Medicine) and NRC (National Research Council). 2014. *Financing Long-Term Services and Supports for Individuals with Disabilities and Older Adults: Workshop Summary.* Washington, DC: National Academies Press.

IPUMS USA (Integrated Public Use Microdata Series). 2014. Retrieved May 9, 2014 (https://usa.ipums.org/usa/).

Ismail, Khadija, Lisa Nussbaum, Paola Sebastiani, Stacy Andersen, Thomas Perls, Nir Barzilai, and Sofiya Milman. 2016. "Compression of Morbidity Is Observed across Cohorts with Exceptional Longevity." *Journal of the American Geriatrics Society* 64(8):1583–91.

Jackson, George, Hunter C. Gillies, and Ian H. Osterloh. 2005. "Past, Present, and Future: A 7-Year Update of Viagra® (sildenafil citrate)." *International Journal of Clinical Practice* 59(6):680–91.

Jacob, Mini E., Laura M. Yee, Paula H. Diehr, Alice M. Arnold, Stephen M. Thielke, Paulo H. M. Chaves, Liana Del Gobbo, Calvin Hirsch, David Siscovick, and Anne B. Newman. 2016. "Can a Healthy Lifestyle Compress the Disabled Period in Older Adults?" *Journal of the American Geriatrics Society* 64(10):1952–61.

Janeway, Elizabeth. 1975. "On the Power of the Weak." *Signs* 1(1):103–9.

Johnson, Kimberly J., and Jan E. Mutchler. 2014. "The Emergence of a Positive Gerontology: From Disengagement to Social Involvement." *Gerontologist* 54(1):93–100.

Johnson, Rebecca, and Jessica Bibbo. 2014. "Relocation Decisions and Constructing the Meaning of Home: A Phenomenological Study of the Transition into a Nursing Home." *Journal of Aging Studies* 30:56–63.

Johnson, Richard W. 2011. "Phased Retirement and Workplace Flexibility for Older Adults: Opportunities and Challenges." *Annals of the American Academy of Political and Social Science* 638(1):68–85.

Johnson, Richard W., and Barbara A. Butrica. 2012. "Age Disparities in Unemployment and Reemployment during the Great Recession and Recovery." Brief 3. Retrieved April 1, 2017 (http://webarchive.urban.org/UploadedPDF/412574-Age-Disparities-in-Unemployment-and-Reemployment-During-the-Great-Recession-and-Recovery.pdf).

Johnson, Richard W., and Corina Mommaerts. 2009. "Unemployment Rate Hits All-Time High for Adults Age 65 and Older." *Urban Institute.* Retrieved December 30, 2009 (https://www.urban.org/publications/411846.html).

Jones A. L., L. L. Dwyer, A. R. Bercovitz, and G. W. Strahan. 2009. "The National Nursing Home Survey: 2004 Overview." National Center for Health Statistics. *Vital Health Statistics* 13:1–167.

Jones, Nicholas, and Jungmiwha Bullock. 2012. *The Two or More Races Population: 2010.* 2010 Census Briefs. Washington, DC: U.S. Census Bureau. Retrieved March 30, 2014 (http://www.census.gov/prod/cen2010/briefs/c2010br-13.pdf).

Kahn, Joan R., and Leonard I. Pearlin. 2006. "Financial Strain over the Life Course and Health among Older Adults." *Journal of Health and Social Behavior* 47(1):17–31.

Kalousova, Lucie, and Sarah A. Burgard. 2013. "Debt and Foregone Medical Care." *Journal of Health and Social Behavior* 54(2):204–20.

Karraker, Amelia, John DeLamater, and Christine R. Schwartz. 2011. "Sexual Frequency Decline from Midlife to Later Life." *The Journals of Gerontology: Series B* 66B(4):502–12.

Katz, Sidney, Amasa B. Ford, Roland W. Moskowitz, Beverly A. Jackson, and Marjorie W. Jaffe. 1963. "Studies of Illness in the Aged: The Index of ADL: A Standardized Measure of Biological and Psychosocial Function." *JAMA* 185(12):914–19.

Katz, Stephen, and Toni Calasanti. 2015. "Critical Perspectives on Successful Aging: Does It 'Appeal More Than It Illuminates'?" *Gerontologist* 55:26–33.

Kaufman, Gayle, and Glenn Elder Jr. 2003. "Grandparenting and Age Identity." *Journal of Aging Studies* 17(3):269–82.

Keister, Lisa. 2007. "Upward Wealth Mobility: Exploring the Catholic Advantage." *Social Forces* 85(3):1195–1226.

Kelly-Moore, Jessica, and Kenneth Ferraro. 2005. "A 3-D Model of Health Decline: Disease,

Disability, and Depression among Black and White Older Adults." *Journal of Health and Social Behavior* 46(4):376–91.

Kennedy, Sheela, and Bumpass, Larry. 2008. "Cohabitation and Children's Living Arrangements: New Estimates from the United States." *Demographic Research* 19:1663–92.

Kenworthy, Lane. 2010. "Rising Inequality, Public Policy, and America's Poor." *Challenge* 53(6):93–109.

King, Valarie. 2003. "The Legacy of a Grandparent's Divorce: Consequences for Ties between Grandparents and Grandchildren." *Journal of Marriage and the Family* 65(1):170–83.

King, Valarie, and Mindy Scott. 2005. "A Comparison of Cohabiting Relationships among Older and Younger Adults." *Journal of Marriage and Family* 67(2):271–85.

Kizer, Jennifer Graham. 2009. "Becoming a Mom Over 40: What It's Really Like." *Health* 23(10):120.

Kochhar, Rakesh. 2004. "The Wealth of Hispanic Households: 1996–2002." Pew Hispanic Center Report. Retrieved September 18, 2006 (http://pewhispanic.org/files/reports/34.pdf).

Kohn, Melvin L., and Carmi Schooler. 1983. *Work and Personality*. Norwood, NJ: Ablex.

Koropeckyj-Cox, Tanya. 1998. "Loneliness and Depression in Middle and Old Age: Are the Childless More Vulnerable?" *Journal of Gerontology: Social Sciences* 53B(6):S303–S312.

Koropeckyj-Cox, Tanya, and Vaughn R. A. Call. 2007. "Cross-National Comparisons Characteristics of Older Childless Persons and Parents." *Journal of Family Issues* 28(10):1362–1414.

Kramer, Betty J. 2005. "Men Caregivers: An Overview." Pp. 3–19 in *Men as Caregivers*, edited by B. J. Kramer and E. H. Thompson Jr. New York: Prometheus Books.

Krause, Neal, and R. David Hayward. 2014. "Religion, Finding Interests in Life, and Change in Self-Esteem during Late Life." *Research on Aging* 36(3):364–81.

Kübler-Ross, Elisabeth. 1969. *On Death and Dying*. New York: Routledge.

Lahelma, Eero, Mikko Laaksonen, Pekka Martikainen, Ossi Rahkonen, and Sirpa Sarlio-Lähteenkorva. 2006. "Multiple Measures of Socioeconomic Circumstances and Common Mental Disorders." *Social Science and Medicine* 63(5):1383–99.

Lavelle, Bridget, and Pamela J. Smock. 2012. "Divorce and Women's Risk of Health Insurance Loss." *Journal of Health and Social Behavior* 53(4):413–21.

Lawton, M. Powell, and Elaine M. Brody. 1969. "Assessment of Older People: Self-Maintaining and Instrumental Activities of Daily Living." *Gerontologist* 9(3):179–86.

Leavengood, Lee Bird. 2001. "Older People and Internet Use." *Generations* 25(3):69–71.

LeBlanc, Allen J., David M. Frost, and Kayla Bowen. 2018. "Legal Marriage, Unequal Recognition, and Mental Health among Same-Sex Couples." *Journal of Marriage and Family* 80(2):397–408.

Lehman, Dawn. 2012. "Supporting Caregivers of All Cultural Backgrounds." Orange Paper from MatherLifeways. Retrieved January 2, 2016 (https://docplayer.net/27121743-Supporting-caregivers-of-all-cultural-backgrounds.html).

Leicht, Kevin T., and Scott T. Fitzgerald. 2014. "The Real Reason 60 Is the New 30: Consumer Debt and Income Insecurity in Late Middle Age." *The Sociological Quarterly* 55:236–260.

Leland, John. 2008. "More Men Take the Lead Role in Caring for Elderly Parents." *New York Times*, November 28.

Lester, Patricia, Kris Peterson, James Reeves, Larry Knauss, Dorie Glover, Catherine Mogil, Naihua Duan, William Saltzman, Robert Pynoos, Katherine Wilt, and William Beardslee. 2010. "The Long War and Parental Combat Deployment: Effects on Military Children and At-Home Spouses." *Journal of the American Academy of Child and Adolescent Psychiatry* 49(4):310–20.

Levine, Sharon, Jeremy Boal, and Peter Boling. 2003. "Home Care." *Journal of the American Medical Association* 290(9):1203–07.

Lewin, Alisa C. 2017. "Health and Relationship Quality Later in Life: A Comparison of Living Apart Together (LAT), First Marriages, Remarriages, and Cohabitation." *Journal of Family Issues* 38(12):1754–74.

Lin, I-Fen, and Hsueh-Sheng Wu. 2014. "Patterns of Coping among Family Caregivers of Frail Older Adults." *Research on Aging* 36(5):603–24.

Lin, I-Fen, Susan L. Brown, and Cassandra Jean Cupka. 2017. "A National Portrait of Stepfamilies in Later Life." *The Journals of Gerontology: Series B*:gbx150.

Lin, I-Fen, Susan L. Brown, Matthew R. Wright, and Anna M. Hammersmith. 2016. "Antecedents of Gray Divorce: A Life Course Perspective." *The Journals of Gerontology: Series B*:00:1–10.

Litwak, E., and Charles F. Longino Jr. 1987. "Migration Patterns among the Elderly: A Developmental Perspective." *Gerontologist* 27:266–72.

Liu, Hui, Corinne Reczek, and Dustin Brown. 2013. "Are Same-Sex Cohabitors Less Healthy Than People in Other Union Statuses?" JHSB Policy Brief. *Journal of Health and Social Behavior* 54(1):24.

Locher, Julie L., Christine S. Ritchie, David L. Roth, Patricia Sawyer Baker, Eric V. Bodner, and Richard M. Allman. 2004. "Social Isolation, Support, and Capital and Nutritional Risk in an Older Sample: Ethnic and Gender Differences." *Social Sciences and Medicine* 60(4):747–61.

Locher, Julie. L., Caroline O. Robinson, F. Amos Bailey, William R. Carroll, Douglas C. Heimburger, M. Wasif Saif, W. Gabriel Tajeu, and Christine S. Ritchie. 2010. "Disruptions in the Organization of Meal Preparation and Consumption among Older Cancer Patients and Their Family Caregivers." *Psycho-Oncology* 19(9):967–74.

Locher, Julie L., Caroline O. Robinson, David L. Roth, Christine S. Ritchie, and Kathryn L. Burgio. 2005. "The Effect of the Presence of Others on Caloric Intake in Homebound Older Adults." *The Journals of Gerontology: Series A* 60(11):1475–78.

Löckenhoff, Corinna, and Laura Carstensen. 2005. "Socioemotional Selectivity Theory, Aging, and Health: The Increasingly Delicate Balance between Regulating Emotions and Making Tough Choices." *Journal of Personality* 72:1395–424.

Lodge, Amy C., and Debra Umberson. 2012. "All Shook Up: Sexuality of Mid- to Later Life Married Couples." *Journal of Marriage and the Family* 74(3):428–43.

Longino, Charles F., Jr. 1996. "An Aging Population May Not Be Harmful to America." Pp. 25–31 in *An Aging Population: Opposing Viewpoints*, edited by C. Cozic. San Diego: Greenhaven.

Loue, Sana, and Martha Sajatovic, eds. 2008. *Encyclopedia of Aging and Public Health.* New York: Springer.

Luppa, Melanie, Tobias Luck, Siegfried Weyerer, Hans-Helmut König, Elmar Brähler, and Steffi G. Riedel-Heller. 2010. "Prediction of Institutionalization in the Elderly: A Systematic Review." *Age and Ageing* 39(1):31–38.

Lynch, Scott M. 2003. "Cohort and the Life-Course Patterns in the Relationship between Education and Health: A Hierarchical Approach." *Demography* 40(2):309–31.

Malach Pines, Ayala, Margaret B. Neal, Leslie B. Hammer, and Tamar Icekson. 2011. "Job Burnout and Couple Burnout in Dual-Earner Couples in the Sandwiched Generation." *Social Psychology Quarterly* 74(4):361–86.

Malmedal, Wenche, Maria Helen Iversen, and Astrid Kilvik. 2015. "Sexual Abuse of Older Nursing Home Residents: A Literature Review." *Nursing Research and Practice* (http://dx.doi.org/10.1155/2015/902515).

Mann, William, Kenneth Ottenbacher, Linda Fraas, Machiko Tomita, and Carl Granger. 1999. "Effectiveness of Assistive Technology and Environmental Interventions in Maintaining Independence and Reducing Home Care Costs for the Frail Elderly." *Archives of Family Medicine* 8:210–17.

Marmot, Michael. 2001. "Inequalities and Health." *New England Journal of Medicine* 345(2):134–6.

Marsh, Kris, William A. Darity Jr., Philip N. Cohen, Lynne M. Casper, and Danielle Salters. 2007. "The Emerging Black Middle Class: Single and Living Alone." *Social Forces* 86(2):735–62.

Martin, Joyce A., Brady E. Hamilton, Michelle J. K. Osterman, Anne K. Driscoll, and T. J. Mathews. 2017. "Births: Final Data for 2015." NVSR National Vital Statistics Reports 66(1). Hyattsville, MD: National Center for Health Statistics. Retrieved July 15, 2018 (https://www.cdc.gov/nchs/data/nvsr/nvsr66/nvsr66_01.pdf).

Martin, Joyce A., Brady E. Hamilton, Stephanie J. Ventura, Michelle J. K. Osterman, Sharon Kimeyer, T. J. Matthews, and Elizabeth C. Wilson. 2009. "Births: Final Data for 2009." NVSR National Vital Statistics Reports 60(1). Hyattsville, MD: National Center for Health Statistics.

Mathews, T. J., and Brady Hamilton. 2009. "Delayed Childbearing: More Women Are Having Their First Child Later in Life." NCHS Data Brief, No. 21. Hyattsville, MD: National Center for Health Statistics. Retrieved May 14, 2012 (http://www.cdc.gov/nchs/data/databriefs/db21.pdf).

Mathews, T. J., and Brady Hamilton. 2016. "Mean Age of Mothers Is on the Rise: United States, 2000–2014." NCHS Data Brief, No. 232. Hyattsville, MD: National Center for Health Statistics. Retrieved April 9, 2017 (https://www.cdc.gov/nchs/products/databriefs/db232.htm).

Matias, Nathan J. 2015. "Were All Those Rainbow Profiles Another Facebook Study?" *The Atlantic.* Retrieved August 28, 2015 (http://www.theatlantic.com/technology/archive/2015/06/were-all-those-rainbow-profile-photos-another-facebook-experiment/397088/).

Matthews, Karen A., Linda C. Gallo, and Shelley E. Taylor. 2010. "Are Psychosocial Factors

Mediators of Socioeconomic Status and Health Connections?" *Annals of the New York Academy of Sciences* 1186(1):146–73.

Matz-Costa, Christina, Elyssa Besen, Jacquelyn Boone James, and Marcie Pitt-Catsouphes. 2014. "Differential Impact of Multiple Levels of Productive Activity Engagement on Psychological Well-Being in Middle and Later Life." *Gerontologist* 54(2):277–89.

Maynigo, Traci P. 2017. "Intercultural Couples and Families." Pp. 309–36 in *Diversity in Couple and Family Therapy: Ethnicities, Sexualities, and Socioeconomics,* edited by S. Kelly. Santa Barbara, CA: Praeger.

McCann, Laurie A., and Cathy Ventrell-Monsees. 2010. "Age Discrimination in Employment." Pp. 356–72 in *The New Politics of Old Age Policy,* edited by R. B. Hudson. Baltimore: Johns Hopkins University Press.

McHugh, Kevin E., and Elizabeth Larson-Keagy. 2005. "These White Walls: The Dialectic of Retirement Communities." *Journal of Aging Studies* 19:241–56.

McMunn, Anne, Mel Bartley, and Diana Kuh. 2006. "Women's Health in Mid-Life: Life Course Social Roles and Agency as Quality." *Social Science and Medicine* 63(6):1561–72.

Meadow, Tey, and Judith Stacey. 2006. "Families." *Contexts* 5(4):55–57.

Menec, Verena H. 2003. "The Relation between Everyday Activities and Successful Aging: A 6-Year Longitudinal Study." *The Journals of Gerontology: Series B* 58(2):S74–S82.

Miech, Richard, Fred Pampel, Jinyoung Kim, and Richard G. Rogers. 2011. "The Enduring Association between Education and Mortality: The Role of Widening and Narrowing Disparities." *American Sociological Review* 76(6):913–34.

Miller, Dorothy A. 1981. "The 'Sandwich' Generation: Adult Children of the Aging." *Social Work* 26(5):419–23.

Minichiello, Victor, Gail Hawkes, and Marian Pitts. 2011. "HIV, Sexually Transmitted Infections, and Sexuality in Later Life." *Current Infectious Disease Reports* 13(2):182–87.

Mirowsky, John. 2005. "Age at First Birth, Health, and Mortality." *Journal of Health and Social Behavior* 46(1):32–50.

Mirowsky, John. 2010. "Cognitive Decline and the Default American Lifestyle." *The Journals of Gerontology: Series B* 66B(1):I50–I58.

Mirowsky, John. 2013. "Depression and the Sense of Control: Aging Vectors, Trajectories, and Trends." *Journal of Health and Social Behavior* 54(4):407–25.

Mirowsky, John, and Catherine E. Ross. 1992. "Age and Depression." *Journal of Health and Social Behavior* 33(3):187–205.

Mirowsky, John, and Catherine E. Ross. 1999. "Well-Being across the Life Course." Pp. 328–48 in *A Handbook for the Study of Mental Health: Social Contexts, Theories, and Systems,* edited by A.V. Horwitz and T. L. Scheid. Cambridge: Cambridge University Press.

Mirowsky, John, and Catherine E. Ross. 2002. "Parenthood and Health: The Pivotal and Optimal Age at First Birth." *Social Forces* 81:315–49.

Mirowsky, John, and Catherine E. Ross. 2003a. *Social Causes of Psychological Distress.* 2nd edition. New York: Aldine de Gruyter.

Mirowsky, John, and Catherine E. Ross. 2003b. *Education, Social Status, and Health.* New York: Aldine de Gruyter.

Mirowsky, John, and Catherine E. Ross. 2008. "Education and Self-Rated Health: Cumulative Advantage and Its Rising Importance." *Research on Aging* 30(1):93–122.

Mirowsky, John, and Catherine E. Ross. 2015. "Education, Health, and the Default American Lifestyle." *Journal of Health and Social Behavior* 56(3):297–306.

Miskelly, Frank. 2001. "Assistive Technology in Elderly Care." *Age and Ageing* 30(6):455–58.

Moen, Phyllis. 2016. *Encore Adulthood: Boomers on the Edge of Risk, Renewal, and Purpose.* New York: Oxford University Press.

Monte, Lindsay M., and Renee R. Ellis. 2014. *Fertility of Women in the United States: 2012.* Population Characteristics. Washington, DC: U.S. Census Bureau. Retrieved December 20, 2015 (https://www.census.gov/content/dam/Census/library/publications/2014/demo/p20-575.pdf).

Montgomery, Rhonda J. V., J. G. Gonyea, and N. R. Hooyman. 1985. "Caregiving and the Experience of Subjective and Objective Burden." *Family Relations* 34:19–26.

Moore, Mignon R., and Michael Stambolis-Ruhstorfer. 2013. "LGBT Sexuality and Families at the Start of the Twenty-First Century." *Annual Review of Sociology* 39(1):491–507.

Mortimer, Jeylan T., and Michael J. Shanahan. 2003. *Handbook of the Life Course.* New York: Kluwer Academic/Plenum.

Mosisa, Abraham, and Steven Hipple. 2006. "Trends in Labor Force Participation in the United States." *Monthly Labor Review* 129(10):35–57.

MSNBC. 2009. "World's Oldest New Mom Dies, Leaves Two Toddlers." Retrieved May 14, 2012 (http://www.msnbc.msn.com/id/31921390/ns/health-womens_health/t/worlds-oldest-new-mom-dies-leaves-toddlers/).

Mudrazija, Stipica, Mieke Beth Thomeer, and Jacqueline Angel. 2015. "Gender Differences in Institutional Long-Term Care Transitions." *Women's Health Issues* 25(5):441–49.

Mueller, Margaret M., B. Wilhelm, and Glen H. Elder Jr. 2002. "Variations in Grandparenting." *Research on Aging* 24(3):360–88.

Munnell, Alicia H., and Matthew S. Rutledge. 2013. "The Effects of the Great Recession on the Retirement Security of Older Workers." *Annals of the American Academy of Political and Social Science* 650(1):124–42.

Myers, Dowell. 2009. "Aging Baby Boomers and the Effect of Immigration: Rediscovering the Intergenerational Social Contract." *Generations* 32(4):18–23.

Myrskylä, Mikko, and Andrew Fenelon. 2012. "Maternal Age and Offspring Adult Health: Evidence from the Health and Retirement Study." *Demography* 49(4):1231–57.

National Alliance of Caregiving. 2015. "Caregiving in the U.S. 2015." Retrieved January 10, 2016 (http://www.aarp.org/content/dam/aarp/ppi/2015/caregiving-in-the-united-states-2015-report-revised.pdf).

National Center for Education Statistics. 2016. "Table 302.10. Recent High School Completers and Their Enrollment in 2-Year and 4-Year Colleges, by Sex: 1960 through 2014." Retrieved November 16, 2016 (https://nces.ed.gov/programs/digest/d15/tables/dt15_302.10.asp).

National Down Syndrome Society. Fact sheet. Retrieved April 15, 2015 (htttp://www.ndss.org).

National Family Caregivers Association (NFCA). 2015. "Caregiving in the United States." Retrieved April 3, 2015 (http://www.caregiving.org/wp-content/uploads/2015/05/2015_CaregivingintheUS_Final-Report-June-4_WEB.pdf).

National Family Caregivers Association (NFCA) and Family Caregiver Alliance. National Alliance for Caregiving in collaboration with AARP. 2009. "Executive Summary: Caregiving in the U.S." Retrieved March 19, 2012 (http://www.caregiving.org/pdf/research/CaregivingUSAllAgesExecSum.pdf).

Natoli, Jaime L., Deborah L. Ackerman, Suzanne McDermott, and Janice G. Edwards. 2012. "Prenatal Diagnosis of Down Syndrome: A Systematic Review of Termination Rates (1995–2011)." *Prenatal Diagnosis* 31:389–94.

Nazareth, Linda. 2007. *The Leisure Economy: How Changing Demographics, Economics, and Generational Attitudes Will Reshape Our Lives and Our Industries.* Mississauga, Ontario, Canada: John Wiley & Sons.

Nef, Tobias, Raluca L. Ganea, René M. Müri, and Urs P. Mosimann. 2013. "Social Networking Sites and Older Users—A Systematic Review." *International Psychogeriatrics* 25(07):1041–53.

Nelson, S. Katherine, Kostadin Kushlev, Tammy English, Elizabeth W. Dunn, and Sonja Lyubomirsky. 2013. "In Defense of Parenthood: Children Are Associated With More Joy Than Misery." *Psychological Sciences* 24(1):3–10.

Newman, David M. 2009. *Families: A Sociological Perspective.* Boston: McGraw Hill.

Nimrod, Galit. 2011. "The Fun Culture in Seniors' Online Communities." *Gerontologist* 51(2):226–37.

Noël-Miller. Claire. 2010. "Longitudinal Changes in Disabled Husbands' and Wives' Receipt of Care." *Gerontologist* 50(5):681–93.

OASDI Trustees Report. 2015. "The 2015 Annual Report of the Board of Trustees of the Federal Old-Age and Survivors Insurance and Federal Disability Insurance Trust Funds." Retrieved January 10, 2016 (https://www.ssa.gov/oact/TR/2015/index.html).

O'Connor, Melissa L., Jerri D. Edwards, Virginia G. Wadley, and Michael Crowe. 2010. "Changes in Mobility among Older Adults with Psychometrically Defined Mild Cognitive Impairment." *Journal of Gerontology: Psychological Sciences* 65B(3):306–16.

Oeppen, Jim, and James W. Vaupel. 2002. "Broken Limits to Life Expectancy." *Science* 296:1029–30.

Office of Minority Health. 2016. "Profile Black/African Americans." Retrieved October 6, 2016 (http://minorityhealth.hhs.gov/omh/browse.aspx?lvl=3&lvlid=61).

Olshansky, S. Jay, Toni Antonucci, Lisa Berkman, Robert H. Binstock, Axel Boersch-Supan, John T. Cacioppo, Bruce A. Carnes, Laura L. Carstensen, Linda P. Fried, Dana P. Goldman, James Jackson, Martin Kohli, John Rother, Yuhui Zheng, and John Rowe. 2012. "Differences in Life Expectancy Due to Race and Educational Differences Are Widening, and Many May Not Catch Up." *Health Affairs* 31(8):1803–13.

Olshansky, S. Jay, Bruce A. Carnes, and Douglas Grahn. 1998. "Confronting the Boundaries of Human Longevity." *American Scientist* 86(1):52–62.

Olshansky, S. Jay, Dana P. Goldman, Yuhui Zheng, and John W. Rowe. 2009. "Aging in America in the Twenty-First Century: Demographic Forecasts from the MacArthur Foundation Research Network on an Aging Society." *The Milbank Quarterly* 87(4):842–62.

Olshansky, S. Jay, Douglas J. Passaro, Ronald C. Hershow, Jennifer Layden, Bruce A. Carnes, Jacob Brody, Leonard Hayflick, Robert N. Butler, David B. Allison, and David S. Ludwig. 2005. "A Potential Decline in Life Expectancy in the United States in the 21st Century." *New England Journal of Medicine* 352(11):1138–45.

O'Rand, Angela. 2003. "Cumulative Advantage Theory in Life-Course Research." Pp. 14–30 in *Annual Review of Gerontology and Geriatrics*. Vol. 22, *Focus on Economic Outcomes in Later Life*, edited by S. Crystal and D. Shea. New York: Springer.

Ozawa, Martha N., and Hong-Sik Yoon. 2008. "How Economically Disadvantaged Are American Elderly Women? Gender Differences in Economic Well-Being in Old Age." In *Handbook of Families and Poverty*, edited by D. Russell Crane and Tim B. Heaton. Los Angeles: Sage.

Padilla-Walker, Laura, and Larry J. Nelson. 2012. "Black Hawk Down? Establishing Helicopter Parenting as a Distinct Construct from Other Forms of Parental Control during Emerging Adulthood." *Journal of Adolescence* 35(5):1177–90.

Pai, Manacy, and Anne E. Barrett. 2007. "Long-Term Payoffs of Work? Women's Past Involvement in Paid Work and Mental Health in Widowhood." *Research on Aging* 29(5):436–56.

Pai, Manacy, and Deborah Carr. 2010. "Do Personality Traits Moderate the Effects of Late-Life Spousal Loss on Psychological Adjustment?" *Journal of Health and Social Behavior* 51(2):183–99.

Palacios, Santiago, Rosario Castaño, and Alessandra Grazziotin. 2009. "Epidemiology of Female Sexual Dysfunction." *Maturitas* 63(2):119–23.

Parke, Mary. 2007. "Are Married Parents Really Better for Children? What Research Says About the Effects of Family Structure on Child Well-Being." *Couples and Marriage Research and Policy*. Washington, DC: Center for Law and Social Policy (CLASP). Retrieved May 1, 2008 (http://www.healthymarriageinfo.org/docs/May08Marriage_Brief3.pdf).

Parker, Kim. 2012. "The Boomerang Generation: Feeling OK about Living with Mom and Dad." Pew Research Center. Retrieved April 22, 2014 (http://www.socialtrends.org).

Passuth, Patricia, and Vern L. Bengtson. 1988. "Sociological Theories of Aging: Current Perspectives and Future Directions." Pp. 333–55 in *Emergent Theories of Aging*, edited by J. E. Birren and V. L. Bengtson. New York: Springer.

Patterson, Charlotte J. 2000. "Family Relationships of Lesbians and Gay Men." *Journal of Marriage and Family* 62:1052–69.

Patterson, Joan M. 2002. "Integrating Family Resilience and Family Stress Theory." *Journal of Marriage and Family* 64(2):349–60.

Pavalko, Eliza K., and Joseph D. Wolfe. 2016. "Do Women Still Care? Cohort Changes in U.S. Women's Care for the Ill or Disabled." *Social Forces* 94(3):1359–84.

Peek, Chuck, Tanya Koropeckyj-Cox, Barbara A. Zsembik, and Raymond T. Coward. 2004. "Race Comparisons of the Household Dynamics of Older Adults." *Research on Aging* 26:179–201.

Perls, Thomas. 2006. "The Different Paths to 100." *American Journal of Clinical Nutrition.* 83(2):484S–487S.

Perls, Thomas, Margery Silver, and John Lauerman. 2000. *Living to 100: Lessons in Living to Your Maximum Potential at Any Age*. New York: Basic Books.

Perrin, Andrew. 2015. "Social Media Usage: 2005–2015." Pew Research Center. Retrieved January 8, 2016 (http://www.pewinternet.org/files/2015/10/PI_2015-10-08_Social-Networking-Usage-2005-2015_FINAL.pdf).

Perry, Brea L., Kathi Harp, and Carrie B. Oser. 2013. "Racial and Gender Discrimination in the Stress Process: Implications for African American Women's Health and Well-Being." *Sociological Perspectives* 56(1):25–48.

Pew Research Center for the People and the Press. 2012. "Partisan Polarization Surges in the Bush, Obama Years: Trends in American Values from 1987–2012." Retrieved June 30, 2012 (http://www.people-press.org/2012/06/04/partisan-polarization-surges-in-bush-obama-years/).

Pew Research Center. Religion and Public Life. 2011. "The Future of the Global Muslim Population: Projections for 2010–2030." Retrieved February 8, 2013 (http://www.pewforum.org/2011/01/27/the-future-of-the-global-muslim-population/).

Pew Research Center. Religion and Public Life. 2015. "America's Changing Religious Landscape." Retrieved August 25, 2015 (http://www.pewforum.org/2015/05/12/americas-changing-religious-landscape/).

Plane, David A., and Jason R. Jurjevich. 2009. "Ties That No Longer Bind? The Patterns and Repercussions of Age-Articulated Migration Up and Down the U.S. Urban Hierarchy." *Professional Geographer* 61(1):4–20.

Plotnick, R. D. 2009. "Childlessness and the Economic Well-Being of Older Americans." *The Journals of Gerontology: Series B* 64B(6):767–76.

Popenoe, David. 1989. *Disturbing the Nest: Family Change and Decline in Modern Societies.* New York: Aldine de Gruyter.

Popenoe, David. 1993. "American Family Decline, 1960–1990: A Review and Appraisal." *Journal of Marriage and Family* 55(3):527–42.

Porter, Katherine. 2012. "Driven by Debt." Pp. 1–24 in *How Debt Bankrupts the Middle Class,* edited by Katherine Porter. Stanford, CA: Stanford University Press.

Powell, Brian, Catherine Bolzendahl, Claudia Geist, and Lala Carr Steelman. 2010. *Counted Out: Same Sex Relations and Americans' Definitions of Family.* New York: Russell Sage Foundation.

Powell, Brian, Lala Carr Steelman, and Robert Carini. 2006. "Advancing Age, Advantaged Youth: Parental Age and the Transmission of Resources to Children." *Social Forces* 84(3):1359–90.

Putnam, Michelle, Nancy Morrow-Howell, Megumi Inoue, Jennifer Greenfield, Huajuan Chen, and YungSoo Lee. 2013. "Suitability of Public Use Secondary Data Sets to Study Multiple Activities." *Gerontologist* 54(5):818–829.

Quadagno, Jill. 2005. *Aging and the Life Course: An Introduction to Social Gerontology.* 3rd edition. New York: McGraw Hill.

Quesnel-Vallée, Amélie, and Miles Taylor. 2012. "Socioeconomic Pathways to Depressive Symptoms in Adulthood: Evidence from the National Longitudinal Survey of Youth 1979." *Social Science and Medicine* 74(5):734–43.

Regnerus, Mark, David Sikkink, and Christian Smith. 1999. "Voting with the Christian Right: Contextual and Individual Patterns of Electoral Influence." *Social Forces* 77(4):1375–1401.

Raley, R. Kelly, Megan M. Sweeney, and Danielle Wondra. 2015. "The Growing Racial and Ethnic Divide in U.S. Marriage Patterns." *Future Child* 25(2): 89–109.

Reinhard, Susan, Lynn Friss Feinberg, Rita Choula, and Ari Houser. 2015. "Valuing the Invaluable: 2015 Update." AARP. Retrieved January 8, 2016 (http://www.aarp.org/content/dam/aarp/ppi/2015/valuing-the-invaluable-2015-update-new.pdf).

Reitzes, Donald C., and Elizabeth J. Mutran. 2004. "Grandparenthood: Factors Influencing Frequency of Grandparent-Grandchildren Contact and Grandparent Role Satisfaction." *Journal of Gerontology: Social Sciences* 59B(1):S9–S16.

Remle, Robert Corey. 2008. "Kinship Status and Life Course Transitions as Determinants of Financial Assistance to Adult Children." PhD dissertation, Duke University. Retrieved from ProQuest Dissertations and Theses (PQDT).

Reuters. 2008. "Japan 61-Yr-Old Surrogate Mum Gives Birth: Clinic." Retrieved May 14, 2012 (http://www.reuters.com/article/2008/08/20/us-japan-surrogate-idUST15434720080820).

Reuters. 2009. "Canadian Woman, 60, Gives Birth to Twins: Report." Retrieved May 12, 2012 (http://www.reuters.com/article/2009/02/05/us-twins-idUSTRE5145BP20090205).

Rhee, Nari. 2013. "Race and Retirement Insecurity in the United States." National Institute on Retirement Security. Retrieved February 11, 2014 (https://www.nirsonline.org/reports/race-and-retirement-insecurity-in-the-united-states/).

Ribeiro, Oscar, and Constança Paúl. 2008. "Older Male Carers and the Positive Aspects of Care." *Ageing and Society* 28(2):165–83.

Riediger, Michaela, Alexandra M. Freund, and Paul B. Baltes. 2005. "Managing Life through Personal Goals: Intergoal Facilitation and Intensity of Goal Pursuit in Younger and Older Adulthood." *The Journals of Gerontology: Series B* 60(2):P84–P91.

Riley, Matilda W. 1983. "The Family in an Aging Society: A Matrix of Latent Relationships." *Journal of Family Issues* 4:439–54.

Riley, Matilda W., and John W. Riley Jr. 1993. "Connections: Kin and Cohort." Pp. 169–89 in *The Changing Contract Across Generations,* edited by V. L. Bengtson and W. A. Achenbaum. New York: Aldine de Gruyter.

Riley, Matilda White, and John W. Riley. 1994. "Structural Lag: Past and Future." Pp. 15–36 in *Age and Structural Lag: Society's Failure to Provide Meaningful Opportunities in Work, Family, and Leisure,* edited by M. W. Riley, R. Kahn, and A. Foner. New York: John Wiley & Sons.

Riley, Matilda White, and John W. Riley. 2000. "Age Integration: Conceptual and Historical Background." *Gerontologist* 40(3):266–70.

Riley, Matilda W., Anne Foner, and John W. Riley Jr. 1999. "The Aging and Society Paradigm." Pp. 327–343 in *Handbook of Theories of Aging*, edited by V. L. Bengtson and K. W. Schaie. New York: Springer.

Riley, Matilda White, Robert Kahn, and Anne Foner. 1994. *Age and Structural Lag: Society's Failure to Provide Meaningful Opportunities in Work, Family, and Leisure.* New York: John Wiley & Sons.

Rindfuss, Ronald R. 1991. The Young Adult Years: Diversity, Structural Change, and Fertility." *Demography* 28(4):493–512.

Rix, Sara E. 2014. "The Employment Situation, January 2014, and a Look Back at 2013: Fewer Older Workers Unemployed, More Out of the Labor Force." AARP Public Policy Institute. Retrieved February 10, 2015 (http:// www.aarp.org/content/dam/aarp/research/ public_policy_institute/econ_sec/2014/the-employment-situation-january-2014-AARP-ppi-econ-sec.pdf).

Rosen, Anita L. 2014. "Where Mental Health and Elder Abuse Intersect." *Generations* 38(3):75–79.

Rosenfield, Sarah, and Dawn Mouzon. 2013. "Gender and Mental Health." Pp. 277–96 in *Handbook of the Sociology of Mental Health*, edited by C. S. Aneshensel, J. C. Phelan, and A. Bierman. Dordrecht: Springer.

Rosnick, David, and Dean Baker. 2010. "The Impact of the Housing Crash on the Wealth of the Baby Boom Cohorts." *Journal of Aging and Social Policy* 22(2):117–28.

Ross, Catherine E., and Patricia Drentea. 1998. "Consequences of Retirement Activities for Distress and the Sense of Personal Control." *The Journal of Health and Social Behavior* 39(4):317–34.

Rowe, John, and Robert Kahn. 1998. *Successful Aging.* New York: Random House

Ruggles, Steven J., Trent Alexander, Katie Genadek, Ronald Goeken, Matthew B. Schroeder, and Matthew Sobek. 2010. Integrated Public Use Microdata Series: Version 5.0 (Machine-readable database). Minneapolis: University of Minnesota.

Russell, Richard. 2007. "The Work of Elderly Men Caregivers: From Public Careers to an Unseen World." *Men and Masculinities* 9(3):298–314.

Russo, Karen. 2008. "World's Oldest Mom." ABC News. Retrieved May 14, 2012 (http:// abcnews.go.com/Health/ActiveAging/story?id=5309018&page=1).

Ryan, Camille L., and Kurt Bauman. 2016. "Educational Attainment in the United States: 2015. Population Characteristics." Current Population Reports P20-578. U.S. Census Bureau. Retrieved July 13, 2018 (https:// www.census.gov/content/dam/Census/library/ publications/2016/demo/p20-578.pdf).

Sanchez-Ayendez. M. 1998. "Middle-Aged Puerto Rican Women as Primary Caregivers to the Elderly." *Journal of Gerontological Social Work* 30(1–2):75–97.

Sandin, S., D. Schendel, P. Magnusson, C. Hultman, Pål Surén, E. Susser, T. Grønborg, et al. 2016. "Autism Risk Associated with Parental Age and with Increasing Difference in Age between the Parents." *Molecular Psychiatry* 21(5): 693–700.

Sau, Koushik, Kritika Premnath Amin, Archana Sharma, and Samuel Olusegun Fakorede. 2014. "Participation in Activities of Daily Living Can Reduce Loneliness in Older Adults." *Indian Journal of Psychiatry* 57(4):430–31.

Schnure, Calvin, and Shruthi Venkatesh. 2015. "Demographic and Financial Determinants of Housing Choice in Retirement and the Rise of Senior Living." *Social Science Research Network* online repository. Retrieved April 3, 2017 (https://ssrn.com/abstract=2588026).

Schor, Juliet. 2004. *Born to Buy: The Commercialized Child and the New Consumer Culture.* New York: Scribner.

Schor, Juliet. 2010. *Plenitude: The New Economics of True Wealth.* New York: Penguin Press.

Schumaker, John F. 2001. *The Age of Insanity: Modernity and Mental Health.* Westport, CT: Praeger.

Scommegna, Paola. 2012. "More U.S. Grandchildren Raised by Grandparents." Population Reference Bureau. Retrieved February 26, 2017 (http://www.prb.org/Publications/ Articles/2012/US-children-grandparents.aspx).

Selwyn, Neil. 2004. "The Information Aged: A Qualitative Study of Older Adults' Use of Information and Communications Technology. *Journal of Aging Studies* 18:369–84.

Shanahan. Michael J. 2000. "Pathways to Adulthood in Changing Societies: Variability and Mechanisms in Life Course Perspective." *Annual Review of Sociology* 26:667–92.

Shanas, Ethel. 1979. "The Family as a Social Support System in Old Age." *Gerontologist* 19:169–74.

Shapiro, Adam, and R. Corey Remle. 2010. "Generational Jeopardy? Parents' Marital

Transitions and the Provision of Financial Transfers to Adult Children." *The Journals of Gerontology: Series B* 66B(1):99–108.

Sheaks, Chantel. 2007. "The State of Phased Retirement: Facts, Figures, and Policies." *Generations* 31(1):57–62.

Shippee, Tetyana Pylypiv, Lindsay R. Wilkinson, and Kenneth F. Ferraro. 2012. "Accumulated Financial Strain and Women's Health Over Three Decades." *The Journals of Gerontology: Series B* 67(5):585–94.

Siegrist, Johannes, Olaf Von Dem Knesebach, and Craig Evan Pollack. 2004. "Social Productivity and Well-Being of Older People: A Sociological Exploration." *Social Theory and Health* 2(1):1–17.

Silverstein, Melvin, and A. Marenco. 2001. "How Americans Enact the Grandparent Role Across the Family Life Course." *Journal of Family Issues* 22:493–522.

Silverstein, Merril, and Roseann Giarrusso. 2010. "Aging and Family Life: A Decade Review." *Journal of Marriage and Family* 72(5):1039–58.

Skopek, Jan, Florian Schulz, and Hans-Peter Blossfeld. 2011. "Who Contacts Whom? Educational Homophily in Online Mate Selection." *European Sociological Review* 27(2):180–95.

Smith, Aaron. 2015. "Older Adults and Technology Use." Pew Research Center. Retrieved January 8, 2016 (http://www.pewinternet.org/files/2014/04/PIP_Seniors-and-Tech-Use_040314.pdf).

Smith, Gregory, and Gregory R. Hancock. 2010. "Custodial Grandmother-Grandfather Dyads: Pathways among Marital Distress, Grandparent Dysphoria, Parenting Practice, and Grandchild Adjustment." *Family Relations* 59:45–59.

Smith, James P. 2007. "The Impact of Socioeconomic Status on Health over the Life-Course." *Journal of Human Resources* 42(4):739–64.

Smith, Kirsten P., and Nicholas A. Christakis. 2008. "Social Networks and Health." *Annual Review of Sociology* 34:405–29.

Smith, Stanley K., and Mark House. 2006. "Snowbirds, Sunbirds, and Stayers: Seasonal Migration of Elderly Adults in Florida." *The Journals of Gerontology: Series B* 61(5):S232–S239.

Spence, Naomi J., Daniel E. Adkins, and Matthew E. Dupre. 2011. "Racial Differences in Depression Trajectories among Older Women: Socioeconomic, Family, and Health Influences." *Journal of Health and Social Behavior* 52(4):444–59.

Stacey, Judith. 1993. "Good Riddance to 'The Family': A Response to David Popenoe." *Journal of Marriage and Family* 55:545–47.

Stacey, Judith. 1998. *Brave New Families: Stories of Domestic Upheaval in Late-Twentieth-Century America.* Berkeley and Los Angeles: University of California Press.

Stacey, Judith. 2011. *Unhitched: Love, Marriage, and Family Values from West Hollywood to Western China.* New York: New York University Press.

Stafford, Philip B. 2009. *Elderburbia: Aging with a Sense of Place in America.* Santa Barbara: ABC-CLIO.

Steensma, Colin, Lidia Loukine, and Bernard C. K. Choi. 2017. "Evaluating Compression or Expansion of Morbidity in Canada: Trends in Life Expectancy and Health-adjusted Life Expectancy from 1994 to 2010." *Health Promotion and Chronic Disease Prevention in Canada: Research, Policy and Practice* 37(3):68–76.

Stepler, Renee. 2017. "Number of U.S. Adults Cohabiting with a Partner Continues to Rise, Especially among Those 50 and Older." Pew Research Center. Retrieved July 14, 2018 (http://www.pewresearch.org/fact-tank/2017/04/06/number-of-u-s-adults-cohabiting-with-a-partner-continues-to-rise-especially-among-those-50-and-older/).

Stern, Michael J., Shelia Cotten, and Patricia Drentea. 2012. "The Separate Spheres of Online Health Information Searching: The Influence of Gender and Parenting on Behaviors and Feelings about Searching for Health Information on the Web." *Journal of Family Issues* 33(10):1324–50.

Sterns, Harvey L., and Boin Chang. 2010. "Workforce Issues and Retirement." Pp. 81–105 in *Aging in America,* edited by J. C. Cavanaugh and C. K. Cavanaugh. Santa Barbara: Praeger.

Stewart, Susan D. 2007. *Brave New Stepfamilies: Diverse Paths Toward Stepfamily Living.* Thousand Oaks, CA: Sage.

Stotzer, Rebecca L. 2009. "Violence against Transgender People: A Review of United States Data." *Aggression and Violent Behavior* 14(3):170–79.

Streib, Gordon F. 2002. "An Introduction to Retirement Communities." *Research on Aging* 24(1):3–9.

Sutter, John D. 2009. "All in the Facebook Family: Older Generations Join Social Networks." CNN, April 13. Retrieved February 24, 2010 (http://www.cnn.com/2009/TECH/04/13/social.network.older/).

Sweeney, Megan M. 2010. "Remarriage and Stepfamilies: Strategic Sites for Family

Scholarship in the 21st Century." *Journal of Marriage and Family* 72(3):667–84.

Sweet, Stephen, and Peter Meiksins. 2013. *Changing Contours of Work*. 2nd edition. Los Angeles: Sage.

Szinovacz, Maximiliane E., Adam Davey, and Lauren Martin. 2015. "Did the Great Recession Influence Retirement Plans?" *Research on Aging* 37(3):275–305.

Taylor, Miles G. 2010. "Capturing Transitions and Trajectories: The Role of Socioeconomic Status in Later Life Disability." *The Journals of Gerontology: Series B* 65B(6):733–43.

Taylor, Paul, and Richard Morin. 2009. "Forty Years after Woodstock: A Gentler Generation Gap." Pew Research Center. Retrieved January 23, 2015 (http://www.pewsocialtrends.org/2009/08/12/forty-years-after-woodstockbra-gentler-generation-gap/).

Taylor, Paul, Jeffrey Passel, Richard Fry, Richard Morin, Wendy Wang, Gabriel Velasco, and Daniel Dockterman. 2010. "The Return of the Multi-Generational Household." Pew Research Center. Retrieved April 12, 2014 (http://www.pewsocialtrends.org/2010/03/18/the-return-of-the-multi-generational-family-household/).

Teachman, Jay, Lucky M. Tedrow, and Kyle D. Crowder. 2000. "The Changing Demography of America's Families." *Journal of Marriage and Family* 62(4):1234–46.

Thoits, Peggy A. 2011. "Mechanisms Linking Social Ties and Support to Physical and Mental Health." *Journal of Health and Social Behavior* 52(2):145–61.

Thomeer, Mieke Beth, Rachel Donnelly, Corinne Reczek, and Debra Umberson. 2017. "Planning for Future Care and the End of Life: A Qualitative Analysis of Gay, Lesbian, and Heterosexual Couples." *Journal of Health and Social Behavior* 58(4):473–87.

Townsend, Peter. 2006. "Policies for the Aged in the 21st Century: More 'Structured Dependency' or the Realisation of Human Rights?" *Ageing and Society* 26:161–79.

Traub, Amy. 2013. "In the Red: Older Americans and Credit Card Debt." Demos and AARP Public Policy Institute. Retrieved February 9, 2015 (http://www.demos.org/sites/default/files/publications/older-americans-and-credit-card-debt-AARP-ppi-sec.pdf).

Trost, Jan. 2010. "The Social Institution of Marriage." *Journal of Comparative Family Studies* 41(4):507–14.

Twigg, Julia, Carol Wolkowitz, Rachel Lara Cohen, and Sarah Nettleton. 2010. "Conceptualising Body Work in Health and Social Care." *Sociology of Health and Illness* 33(2):171–88.

Uhlenberg, Peter. 2000. "Introduction: Why Study Age Integration?" *Gerontologist* 40(3):261–66.

Uhlenberg, Peter. 2009. "Children in an Aging Society." *The Journals of Gerontology, Series B:* 64B(4):489–96.

Uhlenberg, Peter. 2013. "Demography Is Not Destiny: The Challenges and Opportunities of Global Population Aging." *Generations* 37(1):12–18.

Umberson, Debra, Mieke Beth Thomeer, and Amy C. Lodge. 2015. "Intimacy and Emotion Work in Lesbian, Gay, and Heterosexual Relationships." *Journal of Marriage and the Family* 77(2):542–56.

Umberson, Debra, Mieke Beth Thomeer, Rhiannon Kroeger, Amy Lodge, and Minle Xu. 2015. "Challenges and Opportunities for Research on Same-Sex Relationships." *Journal of Marriage and Family* 77(1):96–111.

United Nations (UN), Department of Economic and Social Affairs, Population Division. 2015. "World Population Prospects: The 2015 Revision, Key Findings and Advance Tables." Working Paper No. ESA/P/WP.241. Retrieved January 8, 2016 (http://esa.un.org/unpd/wpp/Publications/Files/Key_Findings_WPP_2015.pdf).

U.S. Bureau of Labor Statistics (BLS). 2014. "Women in the Labor Force: A Databook." Report 1049. Retrieved January 22, 2015 (http://www.bls.gov/cps/wlf-databook-2013.pdf).

U.S. Bureau of Labor Statistics (BLS). 2017. Labor Force Statistics from the Current Population Survey. Retrieved February 11, 2017 (https://www.bls.gov/web/empsit/cpsee_e16.htm).

U.S. Census Bureau. 2010. "Foreign-Born Population by Sex, Age, and World Region of Birth: 2010." Table 3.1. Current Population Survey. Retrieved February 8, 2013 (https://www2.census.gov/programs-surveys/demo/tables/foreign-born/2010/cps2010/t3.2010.pdf).

U.S. Census Bureau. 2015. "Race and Hispanic Origin of People (Both Sexes Combined) by Median and Mean Income." Table P-4. Historical Income Tables: People. Retrieved April 5, 2017 (https://www.census.gov/data/tables/time-series/demo/income-poverty/historical-income-people.html).

U.S. Census Bureau. 2016a. "Poverty Status of People, by Age, Race, and Hispanic Origin." Table 3. Historical Poverty Tables: People and Families—1959 to 2016. Retrieved April 4, 2017 (https://www.census.gov/data/tables/time-series/demo/income-poverty/historical-poverty-people.html).

U.S. Census Bureau. 2016b. "The Majority of Children Live with Two Parents, Census Bureau Reports." Retrieved July 14, 2018 (https://www.census.gov/newsroom/press-releases/2016/cb16-192.html).

U.S. Census Bureau. 2017. "Educational Attainment of the Population 18 Years and Over, by Age, Sex, Race, and Hispanic Origin: 2016." Table 1. Educational Attainment in the United States: 2016. Retrieved April 5, 2017 (https://www.census.gov/data/tables/2016/demo/education-attainment/cps-detailed-tables.html).

U.S. Department of Health and Human Services (USDHHS). 2000. "Healthy People 2010: Understanding and Improving Health." 2nd edition. Washington, DC: U.S. Government Printing Office.

U.S. Department of Health and Human Services (USDHHS). 2005–2017. Administration for Community Living, Administration on Aging (AoA). Profiles for 2005–2017. "A Profile of Older Americans." Retrieved December 20, 2014 (https://www.acl.gov/index.php/aging-and-disability-in-america/data-and-research/profile-older-americans).

U.S. Department of Health and Human Services (USDHHS). Administration for Community Living, Administration on Aging (AoA). 2014. "Projected Future Growth of the Older Population." Retrieved February 3, 2014 (https://www.acl.gov/aging-and-disability-in-america/data-and-research/projected-future-growth-older-population).

Utz, Rebecca L., Kristin L. Swenson, Michael Caserta, Dale Lund, and Brian deVries. 2014. "Feeling Lonely Versus Being Alone: Loneliness and Social Support among Recently Bereaved Persons." *The Journals of Gerontology: Series B* 69B(1):85–94.

Van Arnum, Bradford M., and Michele I. Naples. 2013. "Financialization and Income Inequality in the United States, 1967–2010." *American Journal of Economics and Sociology* 72(5):1158–82.

Verbrugge, Lois M., Anne L. Gruber-Baldini, and James L. Fozard. 1996. "Age Differences and Age Changes in Activities: Baltimore Longitudinal Study of Aging." *Journal of Gerontology: Social Sciences* 51B(1):S30–41.

Visa. 2017. "Mapping the Future of Global Travel and Tourism." Retrieved April 3, 2017 (https://usa.visa.com/dam/VCOM/global/partner-with-us/documents/global-travel-and-tourism-insights-by-visa.pdf).

Waite, Linda J., and Aniruddha Das. 2010. "Families, Social Life, and Well-Being at Older Ages." *Demography* 47:S87–S109.

Waite, Linda J., and Maggie Gallagher. 2000. *The Case for Marriage*. New York: Broadway Books.

Wang, Wendy. 2012. "The Rise of Intermarriage." Pew Research and Social and Demographic Trends. Retrieved February 3, 2014 (http://www.pewsocialtrends.org/2012/02/16/the-rise-of-intermarriage/8/).

Wang, Wendy, and Kim Parker. 2014. "Record Share of Americans Have Never Married." Retrieved November 1, 2016 (http://www.pewsocialtrends.org/2014/09/24/record-share-of-americans-have-never-married/).

Weston, Kath. 1997. *Families We Choose: Lesbians, Gays, Kinship*. New York: Columbia University Press.

Wharton, Tracy C., and Wesley T. Church II. 2009. "Consideration of One Area of Persistent Poverty in the United States." *Social Development Issues* 31(1):28–38.

White, James M., David M. Klein, and Todd F. Martin. 2015. *Family Theories: An Introduction*. Los Angeles: Sage.

WHO (World Health Organization). 2017. "About WHO." Retrieved April 7, 2017 (http://www.who.int/about/mission/en/).

Wickrama, K. A. S., Rand D. Conger, and W. Todd Abraham. 2005. "Early Adversity and Later Health: The Intergenerational Transmission of Adversity through Mental Disorder and Physical Illness." *Journal of Gerontology: Social Sciences* 60B:125–29.

Widmer, Eric D. 2016. *Family Configurations. A Structural Approach to Family Diversity*. London: Routledge.

Williams, Beverly R. 2014. "Widowhood." Pp. 2506–9 in *The Wiley Blackwell Encyclopedia of Health, Illness, Behavior, and Society*, edited by W. Cockerham, K. Dingwall, and S. Quah. Malden, MA: Blackwell.

Williams, Beverly, Lesa Woodby, and Patricia Drentea. 2010. "Ethical Capital: 'What's a Poor Man Got to Leave?'" *Sociology of Health and Illness* 32(6):880–97.

Williams, David R., Naomi Priest, and Norman B. Anderson. 2016 "Understanding Associations among Race, Socioeconomic Status, and Health: Patterns and Prospects." *Health Psychology* 35(4):407–11.

Winstead, Vicky, William A. Anderson, Elizabeth A. Yost, Shelia R. Cotten, Amanda Warr, and Ron W. Berkowsky. 2013. "You Can Teach an Old Dog New Tricks: A Qualitative Analysis of How Residents of Senior Living Communities May Use the Web to Overcome Spatial and Social Barriers." *Journal of Applied Gerontology* 32(5):540–60.

Yost, Elizabeth A., Vicki Winstead, Ronald W. Berkowsky, and Shelia R. Cotten. 2016. "Googling Grannies: How Technology Use Can Improve Health and Well-Being in Aging Populations." Pp.146–59 in *Digital Media Usage across the Life Course*, edited by Paul G. Nixon, Rajash Rawal, and Andreas Funk. New York: Routledge.

Zhang, Zhenmei, and Mark D. Hayward. 2001. "Childlessness and the Psychological Well-Being of Older Persons." *Journal of Gerontology: Social Sciences* 56B(5):S311–S320.

Zickuhr, K. 2010. Generations 2010. Pew Internet and American Life Project. Retrieved August 11, 2011 (pewInternet.org/~/media//Files/Reports/2010/PIP_Generations_and_Tech10.pdf).

Index

Page references for figures, photos, and tables are italicized.